Opposition Government in Mexico

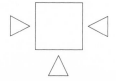

OPPOSITION GOVERNMENT IN MEXICO

Edited by

Victoria E. Rodríguez
and Peter M. Ward

University of New Mexico Press
Albuquerque

LIBRARY OF CONGRESS CATALOGING-IN-PUBLICATION DATA

Opposition government in Mexico /
edited by Victoria E. Rodríguez and Peter M. Ward. — 1st ed.
p.   cm.
Includes bibliographical references and index.
ISBN 0-8263-1577-1. — ISBN 0-8263-1578-X (pbk.)
1. Mexico—Politics and government—1988–
2. Opposition (Political science)—Mexico.
3. Political parties—Mexico.
4. Elections—Mexico.
I. Rodríguez, Victoria Elizabeth, 1954–
II. Ward, Peter M., 1951–
JL 1281.067   1995
320.972´09´048—dc20   94-36197
CIP

Designed by Stephanie Jurs
© 1995 BY THE UNIVERSITY OF NEW MEXICO PRESS
First edition

Collectively,
the editors and contributors wish
to dedicate this volume
to the memory of

Dr. Salvador Nava Martínez

A legend in his own time and
the "father" of opposition government in Mexico

Contents

Part Three
The Politics of Public Administration:
Municipal Finance and Intergovernmental Relations
Between Opposing Parties in Government

Part Four
Opposition Governments:
Perspectives for the Future

Tables

Abbreviations

AMAC	Asociación de Maquiladoras A.C.
ANCIFEM	Asociación Nacional Cívica Femenina
BANOBRAS	Banco Nacional de Obras y Servicios Públicos
CANACINTRA	Cámara Nacional de la Industria de Transformación
CANACO	Cámara Nacional de Comercio
CDP	Comité de Defensa Popular
CEESP	Centro de Estudio Económicos y Sociales del Sector Privado
CNC	Confederación Nacional Campesina
CNOP	Confederación Nacional de Organizaciones Populares
COCEI	Coalición de Obreros, Campesinos y Estudiantes del Istmo
COCOVE	Coalición de Comités de Vecinos
COPARMEX	Confederación Patronal de la República Mexicana
COPLADE	Convenio de Planeación Democrática
COPLAMAR	Coordinación General del Plan Nacional de Zonas Deprimidas y Grupos Marginados
CROM	Confederación Regional de Obreros Mexicana
CTM	Confederación de Trabajadores de Mexico
CUD	Convenio Unico de Desarrollo
DHIAC	Desarrollo Humano Integral, A.C.
FCP	Frente Cívico Potosino
FDN	Frente Democrático Nacional
FMS	Fondos Municipales de Solidaridad
FRS	Fondos Regionales de Solidaridad
INFONAVIT	Instituto Nacional del Fondo de Vivienda para los Trabajadores
ISI	Import Substitution Industrialization
JMAS	Junta Municipal de Aguas y Saneamiento
NAFINSA	Nacional Financiera, S.A.
PAN	Partido Acción Nacional

PARM	Partido Auténtico de la Revolución Mexicana
PCM	Partido Comunista Mexicano
PDM	Partido Demócrata Mexicano
PFCRN	Partido Frente Cardenista de Reconstrucción Nacional
PIDER	Programa de Impulso al Desarrollo Rural
PPS	Partido Popular Socialista
PRD	Partido de la Revolución Democrática
PRI	Partido Revolucionario Institucional
PRONAF	Programa Nacional Fronterizo
PRONASOL	Programa Nacional de Solidaridad
SAHOP	Secretaría de Asentamientos Humanos y Obras Públicas
SEDESOL	Secretaría de Desarrollo Social
SEDUE	Secretaría de Desarrollo Urbano y Ecología
SNTE	Sindicato Nacional de Trabajadores de la Educación
SPP	Secretaría de Programación y Presupuesto
UNAM	Universidad Nacional Autónoma de México

Acknowledgments

The editors wish to express their gratitude to the contributors for their forbearance and for responding so positively to numerous questions and requests for revisions. Since the originating conference at Austin in April 1992, it has been a real pleasure getting to know these Mexicanist colleagues working on democratization and "opposition" government in Mexico. Santiago Rodríguez deserves special recognition for his excellent translation into English of the chapters by Bailón, Crespo, Guillén López, and Venegas.

We are also indebted to the various politicians and government officials who were present at the Austin conference—Francisco Barrio Terrazas, Rodolfo Elizondo Torres, Imelda Flores, Samuel Maldonado, the late Dr. Salvador Nava Martínez, Sra. Conchita Calvillo de Nava, and Guillermo Pizzuto Zamanillo. Their open, frank and insightful commentaries to the academic debates enhanced our understanding of the real nature of governmental processes in Mexico.

And to all others—our students, colleagues, academics, and general public—our thanks for making it such an enjoyable conference, and for helping to generate the enthusiasm to carry this book through to completion.

Piensen por un momento, distinguidos amigos, en términos de una receta culinaria: tómese un recipiente bien grande, más o menos del tamaño de una ciudad de un millón de habitantes, de preferencia conflictiva y compleja. Vacíense en ese molde todos los escenarios maquiavélicos [...] que seguían brotando día con día de manera casi mágica. Agítese vigorosamente. Agregue un kilo de inexperiencia de todo el equipo de gobierno, y póngasele una ración generosa de los errores monumentales que cometíamos en esos primeros momentos. Revuélvase violentamente todos los días, utilizando como batidora una buena parte de los medios de comunicación, resentidos por la pérdida de sus arreglos económicos tradicionales. Espolvoréese sobre toda esta mezcla una desconección evidente con los gobiernos estatal y federal. Por último, y a manera de cereza ornativa, póngase mero encima de todo este revoltillo a un alcalde bisoño y excesivamente joven, sin la menor idea del arte de gobernar y que pasaba noches enteras despierto, asustado ante la posibilidad de que el sueño de un pueblo se desvaneciera como pompa de jabón. El resultado: a los siete días de iniciado el gobierno, en las columnas políticas de la ciudad se hacían quinielas sobre cuántos días o, en el mejor de los casos, cuántos meses, tardaríamos en caer . . .

Francisco Barrio,
describing his experience as a mayor of the opposition
Address delivered at the Headliners Club
Austin, Texas, the 2nd of April 1992

Part One

The Transition:
From Opposition Party
to a Party in Government

1

Introduction

Governments of the Opposition in Mexico

Victoria E. Rodríguez
Peter M. Ward

Political Opening and the Rise of Opposition Parties in Mexico

Until the 1980s Mexico's political system, although nominally a democracy, remained highly authoritarian. The activities of opposition political parties were closely circumscribed or outlawed altogether. The official party, the PRI (Partido Revolucionario Institucional) had governed virtually unchallenged in regular six-year cycles (*sexenios*) since its creation during the 1930s, and regularly won 85 percent of the total vote (Smith 1979:55). Until 1979 only those parties that did not question the dominance of the PRI were permitted to compete in elections, which were often rigged—not so much to prevent opposition parties from winning, but more to reduce abstentionism to a level that would not threaten the legitimacy of the regime and of the political process.

Although it kept rigidly to the constitutional principle of no reelection of legislative and executive officials, both party and governmental apparatuses were rigidly hierarchical, and orders passed from one level to the next were expected to be obeyed, without question. Most of all the national president's power was paramount, and even though the federal political structure of Mexico, on paper at least, gave considerable power to the state and municipal levels, these too, in effect, depended upon presidential and ruling-elite approval and direction (Rodríguez forthcoming). Often that power was exercised in an authoritarian manner through patronage, intimidation, and occasionally repression. Although the PRI felt increasingly uneasy with them, many rural areas were dominated by quasi-mafia leaders (*caciques*), whose informal rule was absolute and proceeded unmolested, as long as these same bosses delivered political support for the PRI when it was required (Bartra et al. 1975). This authoritarian leadership structure existed both spatially, especially in the more remote rural areas, and sectorally, in some of the coopted (*charro*) worker sindicates.

This hierarchical and authoritarian structure should not be taken to imply that the PRI was a monolithic entity, nor that there was no competition for political power. Quite the opposite. Rivalries were intense, but competition was intraparty and formed around *camarillas* (teams, or groups) led by individual political leaders and whose basis of support was tied to particular areas of interest, corporate organizations, and/or to their own political families. Ideological differences were often minor and generally did not provide the basis of allegiances. The spoils of political and governmental office were spread among these rival system-supporting groups, inevitably favoring some over others at different points in time. But part of the political bargain embodied the expectation that any imbalance in one administration would be redressed in the one that followed (Purcell and Purcell 1980).

In part it was the threat and indeed likelihood that this practice would be set aside that spawned the so-called democratic current within the PRI in 1986, which led ultimately to some former *priístas* of considerable stature and experience splitting from the party and challenging Salinas's candidacy at the polls in 1988. This timeworn practice of redressing the balance also helps to explain the sharp shifts in policy that have been observed from one sexenio to the next, which some have likened to a pendulum moving across the political spectrum from right to center to left and back again (Skidmore and Smith 1989:243). Until the 1980s these swings appeared to be both predictable and consistent, although for the first time, after President de la Madrid (1982–88), the pendulum did not swing back from the political right to the middle ground; rather, it shifted farther to the right under President Carlos Salinas de Gortari (1988–94).

The stability that this structure and process provided Mexico was widely admired. It had also provided the macroeconomic context for the country's dramatic economic growth from the 1940s onwards, built around import substituting industrialization (ISI) strategies (Hansen 1974; Teichman 1988). But by 1970 this stability began to come apart. The economy itself was becoming more unstable; structural limits within ISI were being reached; agricultural production had stagnated; and the economic miracle had not been accompanied by any significant redistribution of wealth to the working classes (Navarrete 1970; Tello 1978). Moreover, by the late 1960s, social unrest in rural and urban areas threatened to become disruptive. It was time for change, and President Echeverría (1970–76) undertook a major qualitative shift in macropolicy away from the former stabilizing development model to one referred to as shared development (Teichman 1988). This model raised the profile of state intervention in the economy, expanded the bureaucracy dramatically, and developed social welfare programs that sought to integrate the poorer classes as well as to weaken extraparliamentary opposition groups and social unrest. Most important of all, for the purposes of this book, the state began to consider the desirability of limited political reform.

A so-called *apertura política* began in 1973 and was extended in 1977. This allowed for the existence of a wider range of political parties, several of which had formerly been officially outlawed. It gave them greater electoral autonomy and, significantly, it offered them something to fight for: one hundred seats in the congress (out of four hundred) that were to be allocated exclusively to non-PRI parties on the basis of the proportion of the total vote that each party achieved in elections. In 1986 this was raised to two hundred proportional representation seats out of five hundred (Klesner 1991:167). Although their legislative power remained highly constrained, especially since the PRI never let internal divisions carry over into splits in the vote, opposition parties nevertheless now had a foot in the door. Both the activity and the quality of debate in the chamber of deputies improved, no longer blindly supportive of PRI- and executive-initiated legislation (Middlebrook 1986). But the important point to recognize is that the fundamental purpose of the reform was not to weaken the authority and role of the PRI and of the government, but rather to enhance and sustain it.

Here is not the place to provide a detailed account of the evolution of opposition parties, many of which have come and gone, split and/or merged, since the PRI was formed. Prior to the reform, they were stage-managed in order to provide a facade of democracy (González Casanova 1970; Smith 1979). The only exception was the Partido Acción Nacional (PAN), which was formed in the late 1930s in reaction to then President Lázaro Cárdenas's radical policies, in particular the expropriation of petroleum production and distribution. Since then the PAN was the only significant party to exercise a consistent voice against the PRI and its successive governments, and until the 1980s it secured around 15 percent of the vote in presidential elections; occasionally it won a deputyship outright. Prior to the 1980s, it rarely won control of a municipal presidency (that is, a city-hall administration). Ideologically the PAN stood clearly apart from the PRI. It was right-wing, eschewed social and revolutionary rhetoric, had strong clerical roots and relations with the Catholic church, and tended to attract support from small- and middle-sized businesses and from the more conservative urban middle classes (but not exclusively so). Regionally its strongholds were in the north of the country and in Yucatán, but even in these regions it never threatened the PRI in gubernatorial and senatorial elections.

The political reform of the 1970s induced a sea change in *panista* fortunes. Although the PRI continued to dominate, it no longer held such monopolistic control over national politics. Broadly speaking, the political spectrum now included certain areas where the PRI continued to exercise the same monopolistic control, while in other areas it was hegemonic. But now there were also regions and localities where genuine pluralism and intense competition between parties existed (Molinar 1989, 1991b). Prior to 1988 several opposition parties had won control of a city administration: the PDM in Guanajuato (1983); the COCEI in Juchitán (1980); the PST in Ensenada (1983); Dr. Nava's PAN/Frente Cívico in San Luis Potosí (1958 and again in 1983); and the PAN, first in Chihuahua and Ciudad Juárez (1983) and in Durango, Zamora, Hermosillo and several other important cities. However, until 1988 the PAN formed the vanguard of the opposition and therefore was the foil and the focus of the PRI's attention. Its victories in several cities in 1983 were due in large part to serious disillusionment with the performance of the López Portillo government (1976–83) and to the apparent willingness of the de la Madrid administration to conduct more open elections and to abide by the results (at least in the heady early days of his administration; see Cornelius 1986). When the opposition won or threatened to win a municipality, it was usually because a split within the PRI at the local level could not be patched up, such that there was a failure to close ranks behind a single candidate.

Opposition Governments in the 1980s

During the latter part of de la Madrid's administration there was a crackdown on political liberalism, at least as far as opposition parties were concerned. The PRI felt threatened not only by the advances of the opposition, but also because its hands were being unfairly tied by the presidency. It was expected to conduct itself more openly in elections, yet the government exercised less partisanship toward the PRI in the allocation of resources it could use to buy off the vote. In addition, certain sectors of the PRI (the CTM in particular) became less than eager to mobilize for candidates that were not of their own choosing (Rodríguez and Ward 1992). The PRI was not happy, but in exchange for its continued support for President de la Madrid's austerity and macroeconomic policy, it was allowed to assert itself in the elections of 1985 and 1986 (Bailey

1988). These elections, there is little doubt, were conducted with wide-spread electoral fraud (Aziz 1987, Chihuahua; Guadarrama 1987, So-nora; Bezdek, in this volume, San Luis Potosí). Thus, using means foul rather than fair, the PRI won back the electoral high ground, although at considerable cost to the regime's legitimacy.

It was in this context that several influential members in the PRI formed the *corriente democrática* (democratic current), out of fear that the next party nominee for the presidency was going to be a de la Madrid look-alike, who would sustain the same policies through the next sexenio, and also because their own political ambitions would be frustrated, since the rule of redressing imbalances appeared about to be set aside. A full chronology of events is beyond the scope of this introduction and has already been widely documented elsewhere.[1] In short, one of the disillusioned priístas, Cuauhtémoc Cárdenas (son of former President Lázaro Cárdenas, and himself a recent former governor of the state of Michoacán), ran against Carlos Salinas de Gortari, under the guise of a hastily formed Frente Democrático Nacional, supported by many other left-wing parties.

The rest is history. Cárdenas ran a very close race, and some analyses even insist that he won the elections (Barberán et al. 1988). Certainly it appears that the results were massaged in order to ensure an outright majority for Salinas and to stack congress with a PRI majority, given that two hundred seats were already earmarked for the opposition. But most important of all, the PRI had suffered a humiliating defeat; the government of the day and the incoming administration were discredited, and Salinas faced a major legitimacy crisis. As Salinas himself acknowledged, the day after the election, "The era of the virtual one-party system has ended, giving way to a period of intense political competition" (Cornelius and Craig 1991:1).

The mold had certainly been broken—and, significantly, by a former priísta, whose ideology and rhetoric tended to the left and was too close to that of the PRI itself. For the moment, at least, the Frente and Cárdenas's incipient party (the Partido de la Revolución Democrática, PRD) represented the unacceptable face of the opposition. The PAN did not do badly in the 1988 presidential elections (it took 17 percent of the officially declared vote), but it was temporarily eclipsed by Cárdenas's success. In elections for the lower house of congress, however, opposition parties had not supported a single candidate, and thus the left relied largely upon a significant proportion of the *plurinominal* (proportional representation) seats in order to be represented. Here the PAN did much better, gaining a combined total of 101 seats, while the Frente received 139 seats overall.

In the aftermath of 1988, the issue of opposition government has gained center stage. The PRI has been obliged to undertake internal reforms in order to become more credible during elections. Salinas himself had to act with political craft and vigor in order to assert his own authority and to stem the accusations that his administration was illegitimate. Both government and the PRI have had to revitalize their bases of support sectorally and spatially, through better and more democratic organization as well as through more appropriate social policies and new lines of funding, such as Solidaridad, to the most impoverished areas and populations (Dresser 1991; Ward 1993). Politically, too, Salinas sought to drive a wedge between the opposition parties themselves. Most of all, strong efforts were made to isolate the PRD, which has stolen much of the ideological high ground traditionally appropriated (if not adopted) by the PRI, and to discredit its leadership, which steadfastly refused to recognize Salinas as president. Part of this effort has been to reassert the nature of Mexico's democratic structure. Within an arrangement of continued PRI dominance, it suited Salinas's purposes for non-PRI parties to have effective representation in the political process, even if this meant sacrificing absolute control of some state and municipal governments. The PAN has taken (or been allowed to take) greatest advantage of this newfound political space.

The first major success was the PAN's victory in the gubernatorial elections of Baja California in 1989—the first time ever that a state government fell to a candidate not of the official party. Subsequent victories were accumulated in a variety of large cities and municipalities (Saltillo, Mérida, San Luis Potosí [twice], León [twice], Mazatlán, San Pedro Garza García [twice], Salamanca, Celaya, and many others). The 1991 congressional elections showed a major swing back to the PRI, but the PAN continued to do well. Most notably it "won" the governorship of the state of Guanajuato, after the PRI candidate's electoral conduct had been discredited and Salinas pulled him out to impose a panista in his stead. After the elections of 1992, an unprecedented three states in Mexico are led by panista governors: Baja California (Ernesto Ruffo Appel), Guanajuato (Carlos Medina Plascencia), and Chihuahua (Francisco Barrio Terrazas).

The PRD has not fared so well. It lost one of its senators in the 1991 elections (in the Federal District) and overall has confronted considerable intransigence and hostility from both Salinas and from the PRI, as became evident in the election of 1992. While the PAN's gubernatorial victory in these elections was readily recognized, the PRI maintained its claim of victory in the state of Michoacán, despite the fact that the electoral re-sults were hotly contested and the entire case widely publicized. In the end Salinas was obliged to give in, at least partially; in mid-October he forced the sworn-in governor, Eduardo Villaseñor, to take a "leave of absence" and replaced him with the secretario de gobierno, another priísta. Until the end of 1992, the PRD controlled a significant number of *municipios* (many of them important, such as Morelia), but since then its influence has been eroded, as the PRI achieved significant inroads into those urban low-income areas where Cárdenas and the left had done so well in 1988. For the remainder of the sexenio, central PRI and govern-mental responses toward the PRD and the PAN continued along the same lines—further attempts to marginalize the PRD, while conceding elec-toral victories to the PAN in order to sustain it as the official and accept-able face of opposition.

The 1994 elections became the acid test of the extent of democratiza-tion achieved in Mexico during the Salinas administration, both in the actual conduct of the elections themselves and in the outcome of a genu-inely competitive two- or three-party system. The paradox (and ultimately the fundamental contradiction) is that the democratization process is likely to proceed only to the extent that both the PRI and the government feel confident that they will not lose overall control and that opposition advances are at a level and of a nature with which the executive feels comfortable. But this takes us ahead of many of the contributions included in this volume; we will return to these points in our concluding chapter.

The Uniqueness of This Book

The process described above has been extensively analyzed and docu-mented. But while there is a voluminous literature on the nature of the Mexican political system, the PRI itself, its internal corporatist structure, issues such as centralism and *presidencialismo*, the rise of opposition par-ties, and more recently on electoral patterns and results, there has been no systematic study of opposition government experiences. No one has analyzed non-PRI municipal administrations in any depth. In part of course this is because until the early 1980s they were few and far between; their lack of replicability, as well as the monopoly held by the PRI, meant that they were perceived as isolated experiences, temporary aberrations of little wider interest and significance. However, it seems surprising that no research has given greater cognizance at least to the PAN, given the relative consistency of its support base, and especially given several of its important municipal victories prior to 1988.[2] The only exceptions were one or two isolated (and largely unpublished) studies on navismo in San Luis Potosí (Bezdek, in this volume) and an intense interest in the COCEI and in municipal politics in Juchitán, Oaxaca (see Rubin 1987). But here too the focus was upon politics per se, not upon governance. Therefore the present collection of essays is the first to systematically analyze non-PRI government experiences.[3]

In studying opposition governments there are, it appears to us, five principal issues that demand attention. First, there is the need to assess the effectiveness and capacity of opposition parties such as the PRD and the PAN to respond to the challenges of exercising power in local governments. It is one thing to be in the opposition; we imagine that exercising government must be more difficult. Second, we need to analyze the extent and ways in which partisan political rationality intervenes in the calculus of urban administration and decision making. Do opposition governments eschew partisanship in the disbursement of resources? Third, we must examine intergovernmental relations among federal, state, and municipal levels, in particular focusing upon relations between governments of different political parties (such as opposition versus PRI). In this context it is also important to shed light on the effect that the municipal reform of the mid-1980s has had upon municipal governance and on how far the respective political parties have sought to take advantage of the new provisions contained in the reformed Article 115 of the Constitution. Fourth, we need to assess the validity and viability of contemporary democratization processes in Mexico. How far are the opposition parties responding to different social bases in society and articulating new sets of interests that were effectively excluded from the political process? In short, how genuine was the political opening of the 1980s, and what factors are most likely to determine the success or failure of that process during the 1990s? Finally, it is necessary to examine the implications of political pluralism for political and administrative decentralization. The issues of deconcentration, decentralization, and devolution remain firmly on the contemporary political agenda, but the extent to which any of these options is adopted relates closely to the emergence of pluralism and to the nature of the intergovernmental relations outlined above.

Opposition Governments in Mexico: The Austin Conference

To begin to explore these issues we organized a conference at the University of Texas, Austin, in April 1992.[4] An important aim was to bring together Mexicanist academics who had worked on the opposition and a group of politicians who have held (or now hold) executive positions in a non-PRI administration. We did not ask the latter to prepare papers; rather, we invited them to listen and to comment upon the propositions, analyses, and findings of the academics. This they did openly and constructively, and many of the insights they provided have been incorporated subsequently into various essays presented in this volume. Two of the politicians who attended were Francisco Barrio and Rodolfo Elizondo, who were then campaigning for the governorships of Chihuahua and Durango, respectively. Sadly, although no one knew it at the time, this proved to be one of the last public meetings in which Dr. Salvador Nava participated, prior to his death only a few weeks later. Everyone at the conference felt honored by his presence and, collectively, it seemed appropriate to dedicate this book to his memory and to his achievements. Francisco Barrio delivered the keynote address, in which he humorously portrayed himself as being totally unprepared to govern when he assumed power as mayor of Ciudad Juárez in 1983. Given that many of the experiences he alluded to are central to the research contained in this volume, we have reproduced part of his speech as the book's epigraph. Since then, of course, Barrio has won the governorship of his state. Being one of the first governors of the opposition, he can now benefit from his past experiences and convert these lessons into future opportunities.

Organization of the Book

We have organized this book broadly to follow the program of the Austin conference. We began by looking at how opposition parties become parties in government. The second section of papers examines in greater detail the bases of support for opposition parties. The third and major section analyzes the actual experiences and practices of opposition governments, looking at the politics of public administration, municipal finances, and at intergovernmental relations between the PRI and the opposition. In the final chapter we provide a brief glimpse into the future.

Following this introduction, chapter 2, by José Antonio Crespo, looks at how the PRI and the government, as well as the media, have responded to opposition parties in their quest to become opposition governments, and then analyzes how these official responses are carried out once they are in power. His principal conclusions are that opposition governments do not receive any favorable treatment and that this hinders their ability

to govern. By analyzing in detail several instances of opposition government, both at the state and at the local level, Crespo shows how much
time is spent counteracting these "official responses" and consolidating
their own grasp on power, rather than dealing with the exigencies of
daily governance.

The central issue of Robert Bezdek's chapter is leadership, as it documents Dr. Salvador Nava's role in developing and leading the opposition
in the state of San Luis Potosí. In our dedication to this book, we have
alluded to Dr. Nava as the "father" of the opposition in Mexico; Bezdek,
informed by his intimate long-term friendship with the family, analyzes
Dr. Nava's two municipal governments (1958–61 and 1982–85) and his
two unsuccessful attempts at winning the governorship of that state. Bezdek
documents in graphic detail the authoritarian nature of the Mexican political system through three decades, and although repression of the opposition is less intense than it once was, he concludes that much remains
to be done to overcome abuses derived from an authoritarian system.

The first state in which the opposition did win a governorship was Baja
California, in 1989. Tonatiuh Guillén López analyzes the transition to
democracy in that state and the impact that the new party in government
has had on the region's power structures. Guillén looks in close detail at
the 1992 election and concludes that the responses of the electorate serve
as indicators of the performance of the Panista governments at the state
and local levels. In his view Baja California has moved rapidly toward
democracy, as a result of the possibility of genuine alternation in power
of different parties (*alternancia*).

The following four chapters explore the bases of support for opposition parties. Roderic Camp draws upon his extensive archive of political
elites and examines the social bases of the national PAN leadership. His
data do not reveal major differences between the PRI and the PAN, with
the notable exception of panista leaders' educational backgrounds and
their greater likelihood of having worked previously in the private sector.
But in class and socioeconomic terms, there are few differences. The alleged links between the PAN and the state have been overstated. Camp
concludes his analysis by looking to the future and argues that if the PAN
is to thrive, it may need to differentiate itself more clearly from the PRI.

Yemile Mizrahi's chapter develops in greater detail the backgrounds
from which panista officials are drawn. She looks specifically at the involvement of entrepreneurs in the 1983 and 1986 elections in Chihuahua. Although they were successful in that first year, they were invariably
neophytes to the party and were seen as "intruders." However, the rela-

tive weakness of the party at the time made them acceptable. Mizrahi demonstrates that these entrepreneurs did not seek sufficiently to consolidate a party political structure while in office, such that when they "lost" the election of 1986, they faded into the background. She concludes that democracy requires strong parties, not just strong campaigns.

Continuing our exploration from the general to the particular, the following chapter by Lilia Venegas examines the extent to which a political culture emerged among working-class women in Ciudad Juárez. In order to gauge their opinions about the panista municipal government of Francisco Barrio in that city (1983–86), she portrays in candid and colorful ways how these women admired the personal traits of this opposition mayor and evaluated the accomplishments and obstacles of his administration. This chapter enriches our understanding of opposition governments by incorporating a new dimension to our analysis, that of the grass roots. It also begins to redress the imbalance by looking specifically at women and at the role they play within the opposition, a theme that has remained seriously understudied.

Finally in this section, Kathleen Bruhn and Keith Yanner examine the fate of the PRD in its regional stronghold, the state of Michoacán. In 1989 the PRD won some fifty-two municipalities in that state, yet three years later this power base had been seriously eroded, more as a result of conflicts generated from above than through municipal administrative incompetence. There is little evidence that the official party withheld resources from the PRD municipalities, but the national government was successful in using Solidarity resources to win back popular support through public-works projects. Although the PRD has been able to consolidate a core of popular support, the PRI's ability to create obstacles for municipal governance and the government's control of the media and of mass organizations through the corporatist state mean that the PRD is unlikely to increase its share of the independent swing vote necessary to win future elections.

The analysis of how opposition governments fare in power is the subject of the third section. Peter Ward's chapter examines the nature of policy making and implementation for two panista city governments, those of Chihuahua and Ciudad Juárez, from 1983 to 1986. He analyzes whether there are substantive differences between PAN and PRI city administrations in terms of the recruitment of public officials and style of governance, as well as in their urban policy priorities and the extent to which they demonstrate partisanship in disbursing resources. There appear to be important differences between the two parties in many respects: panista officials came from private-sector backgrounds; they emphasized principles of efficiency and transparency in public budgeting; and their policies, while also partisan, were different, primarily because they lacked the monetary resources to carry out large-scale programs. This lack of resources, particularly in the form of intergovernmental transfers, is analyzed in the following chapter, by Victoria Rodríguez. Focusing on the same city administrations as Ward, she examines how governments seek to overcome financial shortfalls and exercise the autonomy accorded to them under the legislation of municipal reform. She demonstrates that while there is no systematic withholding of statutory state and federal transfers, the upper levels of government do resort successfully to other strategies for withholding funds. The principal conclusion is that, paradoxically, governments of the opposition appear to enjoy more autonomy from the higher levels of government than do those from the same party.

John Bailey's discussion of fiscal centralization (chapter 11) emphasizes the dominance of the center over state and local governments and discusses how this forms a critical part of President Salinas's project of economic growth and regime recomposition. According to Bailey, the opposition has found space in Nuevo León as a result of the very pragmatic idea that political opening will make economic restructuring easier; thus, in Nuevo León at least, the presence of opposition governments is far more pragmatic than principled.

Since 1989 PRONASOL funding has become a critically important mechanism for financial transfer to local communities. Jonathan Fox and Julio Moguel discuss the fortunes of leftist opposition municipal governments in securing PRONASOL funding for their local populations. They argue that many opposition mayors were frequently bypassed by Solidarity funding and that the motive was often political. However, working in two contexts (Michoacán and Oaxaca), they also found considerable variation and diversity in the patterns and extent of political discretion. In Michoacán, PRONASOL was used as a principal mechanism to undermine PRD governments. In Juchitán, which is also PRD-affiliated, significant resources were received from PRONASOL, since it served President Salinas's purpose to undertake political accommodation of the regionally important COCEI. Nor did the latter consistently reject Salinas's legitimacy as president. Thus they conclude that there is some room for maneuvering, depending upon the state electoral context and local bargaining strategies.

Finally, Moisés Jaime Bailón provides a systematic analysis of the assignment of resources to municipalities in the state of Oaxaca since the early 1980s. He shows that, within the more socially and ethnically diverse municipalities of the region, there was greater opportunity for opposition parties to emerge. He documents the growth of opposition parties within the state and demonstrates that those municipalities governed by the opposition are no different from those governed by the PRI when it comes to statutory transfers from the state, in part because such transfers have always been very low anyway. But in terms of public investment programs, opposition governments have done slightly better that have PRI governments—an outcome he attributes to the fact that they mobilize more aggressively than do official party counterparts.

In the final section, we offer an overview of the experiences related in this book and ask what they tell us about the future trend of opposition government and the democratization process in Mexico. We discuss the determinants of success in winning power and evaluate the performance of opposition governments relative to the PRI. Although in a somewhat speculatory fashion, linking as we do the past with the present, we explore the extent to which fundamental differences exist between the PAN and the PRI. How viable are non-PRI administrations in Mexico, and how viable is the political opening that offers them the opportunity of winning power? We underscore the very real advances toward genuine democratization and pluralism that have been achieved since 1988—not simply in terms of limited power sharing, but also in the improvements to the ways in which elections are conducted, the emergence of a political culture, and the appearance of change within the PRI itself. However, by 1993 it became evident that President Salinas and the PRI had gone as far as they were prepared to go, given that all eyes were beginning to focus upon the 1994 elections and the transition of power. Potentially, of course, the PRI had everything to lose. The Mexican political system has not yet evolved to the point where the PRI is willing to concede overall defeat, and thus we expect some degree of democratic retrenchment to occur during 1994–95. Finally, it must be remembered that many of the advances in Mexico's democratization have been wrought from the top down. As Dr. Nava emphasized at the Austin conference, this is a fundamental contradiction in a process that must be forged from the bottom up. Power must be mandated by popular vote, not bestowed upon a "regent" with conditions attached.

We must emphasize that the interpretations offered in the final chapter (indeed throughout the book by all of the contributors) should be viewed as a point of departure and not as a definitive statement. Only after further research has been undertaken in several regions, covering the various parties and over a longer time span, will a more authoritative account be feasible. This book is, however, one of the first serious attempts to explore the experience of opposition parties in power in Mexico. We hope that the reader will share out interest and excitement about the myriad processes currently underway and their importance in determining whether the glass of democracy is half full or half empty.

Notes

1. For a detailed account of events and the political process between 1986 and 1988, see the various papers in Cornelius, Gentleman, and Smith (1989). The most telling analysis of the 1988 presidential elections is in Barberán et al (1988). See also Molinar 1991b.

2. Several excellent analyses exist on the PAN as a political party, but none of these focuses on the PAN in municipal power.

3. Elsewhere (Rodríguez and Ward 1992) we have reported on the findings of the first phase of a major NSF-financed research project on opposition governments in Mexico, which deals with two of the earlier and most important panista administrations in two major northern cities, Chihuahua and Ciudad Juárez, for the period 1983–86. The second phase of our research analyzed the experience of the first panista state government, Baja California (Rodríguez and Ward 1994). Subsequent phases of the program will examine the contemporary experiences of state and municipal opposition governments in Guanajuato and a small selection of PRD and leftist opposition governments. Ultimately we anticipate that this will offer us an opportunity to look across multiple experiences, as we seek to make generalizations about the nature of opposition governments and about the contemporary political process in Mexico. For a detailed description of the aims and methodology adopted in this research, see Rodríguez and Ward 1991.

4. Entitled "Opposition Government in Mexico: Past Experiences and Future Opportunities." We gratefully acknowledge the financial support of the following institutions, which allowed us to mount that conference: the LBJ School of Public Affairs, the Institute of Latin American Studies, the Mexican Center of ILAS, the Ford Foundation, and the U.S.-Mexican Policy Studies Center at the LBJ School.

2

Governments of the Opposition
The Official Response
José Antonio Crespo

The extended continuity of the national Mexican political regime can be explained through several institutional characteristics that make it a highly flexible and adaptable authoritarianism, such as the principle of no re-election, the existence of a party of the masses that has managed to incorporate the majority of the politically organized popular sectors, and the legal existence of opposition parties, which have the right to compete for power in elections and to send representatives to congress. The latter makes it a hegemonic party and differentiates it from other one-party systems (Sánchez Susarrey 1991; Crespo 1982).

The legal existence of the opposition in Mexico and its formal participation in electoral assemblies is at least five decades old. This has given the Mexican party system a certain uniqueness, because unlike other similar attempts to conciliate formal competitiveness with real hegemony, it has neither resulted in a true electoral democracy nor in a one-party system.[1] However, the legal presence of the opposition in the electoral arena is not the only thing that has given the priísta regime relatively higher stability than that of one-party systems, but also the fact that under certain circumstances the priísta regime has conceded opposition victories, first at the municipal level (since 1946) and later at the gubernatorial level (since 1989).

The recognition of such opposition victories, however slow, limited, and selective, has had the effect, on one hand, of keeping the opposition at the table, even though it cannot compete on an equal level against the official party, and on the other, it has opened important escape valves for the political tension generated in different parts of the country. In addition to giving a certain democratic legitimacy to the regime, this has contributed to lessening and isolating the citizenry's pressure for democratic change.

Every time the regime has found itself obliged to make space for the opposition, several components of the official apparatus have reacted with hostility and intolerance toward the latter, whose members are normally considered to be intruders or alien and even without the right to struggle for power (by not officially being part of or originating from the revolutionary movement that gave the official party a legitimate claim to the state). In this chapter we will offer some points of reflection and analysis that should be taken into account when studying the "official response" to the attempts of the opposition to compete equitably for power, to make its legitimate victories respected, and to govern where the latter have been recognized.

The Hostility of the Local Press toward Opposition Movements

One of the essential conditions for the exercise of democracy, as has always been pointed out by theoreticians, is a relatively impartial and free mass media. In principle this would have to be translated into equitable treatment of the candidates of all parties, impartiality in judgments and comments about electoral campaigns, and free access for candidates and parties to the media as a line of communication with the electorate. In Mexico such equity generally does not exist. The most influential media, such as television, and to a less degree radio, are either subject to tight government controls or simply publicly declare themselves, by their own accord, as officialist and act accordingly, therefore justifying their open partisanship toward the government's party.[2] The majority of radio stations belong to a few families, who have a commitment to the state due to the concessions it has granted them.[3] The printed press usually has a greater margin of freedom, but it has the least influence over the broad masses.

If these restrictions and deficiencies can be observed at the national level, things are even worse in the interior of many states of the republic. The relative autonomy and impartiality of the national media seem enormous when compared with the behavior of the local media in most states of the country. Generally the media either receive direct compensation from the state authorities or are owned by people identified with the regime and its direct beneficiaries. In that way the wrongdoings that can be detected in the national media often appear magnified in the press, radio, and television at the state level. The more important cities of the interior have renowned, high-quality newspapers, such as *El Norte* and *El Porvenir* in Monterrey, but in the majority of the states the press is usually much more limited and is oriented toward covering the official interests in the state. During highly competitive campaigns, the media usually form an antiopposition block that devalues, modifies, and slants what really happened. Two examples of this can be seen in the cases of San Luis Potosí during the 1991 elections for governor and of Tabasco in the municipal elections of the same year. In both cases the officially oriented media constructed a barrier in order to disinform the people about electoral events, creating at the same time a publicity avalanche in favor of the official party and its candidates.[4] A statement made by the opposition candidate for governor, Dr. Salvador Nava Martínez, reflects the closedness of the local press: "The public square will be our newspaper."

However, the barrier put up by the local media was broken by the national media, especially by those that possessed more autonomy. In the case of San Luis Potosí, the Democratic Coalition[5] was able to get the attention of the national media by calling a meeting (the Seminar on the Democratic Transition in Mexico), to which renowned opposition politicians were invited, as well as journalists and intellectuals associated with diverse and influential elements of the national media, weeks before the elections.[6] After that, the national media paid more attention to the events in San Luis.

Among the acts of protest organized by the navista coalition after the elections, there was a boycott of the local media (Calvillo 1992). Later, the March for Dignity undertaken by Salvador Nava to Mexico City to protest the electoral results (described in more detail by Bezdek in this volume) once more forced the national media, and by then also the international media, to follow up on the electoral conflict of San Luis. A few days before the resignation of the newly invested priísta governor, Fausto Zapata, even private television stations that were clearly supportive of the regime broke the silence they had maintained about the march.

In Tabasco the influence of the national media surpassed the coverage of the local media, and the postelectoral conflict gained national importance especially after the PRD leader of the state, Manuel Andrés López Obrador, set out to duplicate the strategy followed by Nava: a march to Mexico City to demand electoral justice. Once they arrived in Mexico City, the conflict was given a partial but satisfactory solution from the point of view of those dissatisfied. The nonrecognition by the governor of Tabasco, Salvador Neme Castillo, of the agreements reached by the PRD delegates and the Ministry of the Interior in Mexico City led to his fall from power only days later. One of these agreements consisted of giving the second most important municipality of the state, Cárdenas, to the opposition.

In sum, in both San Luis Potosí and Tabasco, the barrier that the local media imposed on the opposition was broken by the national media with the support of several independent journalists and intellectuals and by taking the conflict to the national level through a march to the capital. Both outcomes, partially successful for the opposition, were a novelty in national politics. This can partially be explained by the slow disappearance of the political isolation of several states in recent years. Nowadays one can observe that the local media have an effect on the state government similar to that of the international media on the federal government; the local media (even the independent organisms, if they exist) are not given much importance, but "outside" media are.[7] The national media can in fact now exercise great political influence, which is not always favorable to the governors.[8]

The Local PRI and Defeat

We have mentioned that official recognition of some of the victories of the opposition has been beneficial for the continuity of the hegemonic party regime, and that therefore it forms part of the global strategy of the government. However, it also implies an internal cost, especially for the local PRI and the political class of the location where the opposition's victory is recognized. While most priístas are probably aware of the convenience of conceding some space to the opposition every once in a while, no one wants to be the one sacrificed.

Thus when it has been necessary to give up an important slot, the local PRI, always reluctant to accept its defeats, often reacts with resentment toward what it considers an imposition of the center. In Guanajuato, for example, an elected local deputy of the PRI made the following statement about the resignation of Ramón Aguirre to assume the governorship of the state: "First they imposed him upon us as a candidate and they made us want him. And now they force him to resign" (*Proceso*, September 16, 1991). Likewise in a priísta demonstration in León, after the appointment of panista Carlos Medina Plascencia as interim governor, the signs carried the statement, "El pueblo votó, Salinas negoció" ("The people voted, Salinas negotiated") (*Proceso*, September 9, 1991).

The level of offence, evidently, is in direct proportion to the importance of the slot lost. For that reason the reaction of the local PRI to the center is more visible where it has lost governorships, such as in Baja California in 1989 and Guanajuato in 1991. Equally so in San Luis Potosí; even though an opposition member did not get the interim governorship, the PRI felt betrayed by its national leadership and by the president himself for backing off from the legal victory (which was not necessarily legitimate) of Fausto Zapata. In Baja California the priístas did not recognize at first the verdict of its national leadership, and in Guanajuato and San Luis they took over the congress in protest to the center's decision to force the resignation of their respective gubernatorial candidates after their victory had been officially recognized.

In Guanajuato when the local congress approved the appointment of the panista Carlos Medina as interim governor, the sectional committees of the PRI took over fourteen mayorships and threatened, "We will not permit Medina to occupy Ramón's chair" (*Proceso*, September 16, 1991). When Salinas appeared in Guanajuato at the inauguration of Medina Plascencia, a priísta, referring to the president, stated "To top it off, he's come to legitimize illegitimacy" (*Proceso*, September 30, 1991). At that event, with only two exceptions, the local priísta deputies were dressed in mourning suits and ties.

Therefore the cost to the central government and to the national PRI of recognizing the victories of the opposition must be calculated and assimilated beforehand. So it appears that the government's decision first to back Fausto Zapata fully (including the presence of President Salinas at the inauguration of Zapata as governor) and then to yield to the citizen mobilization turned out to be more costly than if in the beginning, and in compliance with legislation, the election results had been declared void, due to lack of transparency. With the half solution of forcing the resignation of Zapata after legitimizing his victory, the government lost face on both sides, even if the action managed to calm the strong protest in San Luis. Had it annulled the elections (or even more, had it recognized the possible victory of Salvador Nava), the government would have had to pay almost the same cost in relation to the local PRI, but it would have won great democratic legitimacy.

In the case of Guanajuato something similar occurred, but since the PAN willingly accepted the arrangement offered by the government (the interim governorship and some key posts for panistas, the Departments of Government and of Finance for two priístas), the strategy of dialogue followed by the panista national leadership of Luis H. Alvarez was preserved. Altogether the government seems to learn from its experiences. When in July of 1992 it recognized a new panista victory in Chihuahua, the local PRI did not oppose it. Everything seems to indicate that provisions for this case had been made from the center in advance, and therefore the victory of Francisco Barrio did not seem to surprise the local priístas. In this case discipline was stronger than the discontent of defeat.

A point that must be emphasized is that the decision to recognize major victories of the opposition must come unequivocally from the center. If it does not, it constitutes an act of misconduct of the corresponding governor, which makes him liable to political sanctions including, of course, removal from office. Similarly, if a governor is not capable of retaining several slots for the PRI in his state, he can be removed as a form of punishment. Everything indicates that the official support of electoral fraud has begun to reach its limits in the last few years, but it seems possible that it will continue to be tolerated as long as the local PRI and its candidates are able to manage the situation in such a way that it does not become ungovernable. The center intervenes in the way it deems best only to resolve what local priístas cannot. The resignations of Ramón Aguirre and Fausto Zapata, even supposing that they had really won, were due more to their inability to have their victories accepted among wide sectors of the population than to the fact that they might have engaged in fraud. Of course both elements are related, but it can be said that the presidential decision responded more to the former than to the latter.

In conclusion, *presidencialismo* has been reinforced in the last few years by decisions about whether to recognize victories of the opposition in important slots. The governors and the local PRI must assume the center's line in order to avoid more opposition victories than those that may be considered convenient, to accept their victory when it has been decided by the center, and to maintain postelectoral governability.

Official Discrimination toward Opposition Municipalities

In Mexican political debate, it is common to find denouncements about how the state and/or the federal authorities treat the municipalities governed by the opposition in an inequitable and even hostile manner. Similarly, there are often boycotts against such opposition authorities by the municipal bureaucracy, which is probably associated with the PRI, by the PRI itself, and by the local media. This evidently makes the carrying out of governmental duties much more difficult. The state budget is usually negotiated with the opposition municipalities, and often the governor of the state in question manages the municipal budget directly, in order to deprive the president of the municipality of the legitimacy derived from that public expenditure. In any case, whether in municipios controlled by the PRI or by the opposition, the governor makes the ultimate decision as to the distribution of public funds in the state (Rodríguez and Ward 1991).

Such an official response to opposition governments may be due to complementary reasons: it can be a form of revenge by those sectors affected by the opposition's victory; or it can be part of a strategy to recover the lost slot on the basis that citizens will become aware of the poor management of the opposition government as compared to that of the PRI, or that they will at least realize that if the president of the municipio is a victim of official harassment even if not guilty of ineptitude or corruption, it will be the citizens who will pay the price of an opposition victory. With this it is hoped to inhibit the citizenry's enthusiasm for the opposition in the next round of elections.

It is more than likely that this strategy has been successful in several cases, as is evident in the few slots that the opposition has been able to retain consecutively. But there have also been situations in which the official harassment has been counterproductive and has ended up benefiting, rather than damaging, the besieged mayor. In this manner the resistance of Ernesto Ruffo Appel as mayor of Ensenada to the barriers that the then governor of Baja California, Xicoténcatl Leyva, tried to impose upon him, translated into a higher popularity for Ruffo, on which he capitalized during the race for the governorship in 1989. Equally the hostility of the governor of San Luis Potosí, Carlos Jonguitud Barrios, toward the opposition mayor of the city, Salvador Nava (which became evident when the governor retained the budget for the municipality), instigated a citizens' movement in support of Nava that forced Jonguitud to back off in his attempts to discredit him.[9] Far from being discredited, Nava grew in popularity as a fighter against priísta arbitrariness. The animosity of San Luis toward the PRI continued to rise and flourished openly in the struggle to keep the municipality in 1985, which prompted the fall of the entering governor, Florencio Salazar. The municipality was won again by the opposition in 1988, with Guillermo Pizzuto at its head, and once again three years later, with the victory of panista Mario Leal, shortly after the citizens' movement in support of Nava as candidate for governor for the second time induced the resignation of Fausto Zapata and the call for new elections to be held in the beginning of 1993.

Yet another example of the boomerang effect of the boycott toward opposition municipios by state authorities is that of Francisco Barrio, the panista mayor of Ciudad Juárez, in the state of Chihuahua, from 1983 to 1986. Once again the resistance of Barrio toward the governor's hostility gave him great popularity, which manifested itself in the gubernatorial elections of 1986. On that occasion the regime had to engage in fraud of enormous proportions in order to ensure the victory of its candidate, Fernando Baeza. These actions caused great public irritation throughout the country and incurred an extremely high cost in terms of legitimacy, which made the political atmosphere quite tense. Barrio ran for the governorship six years later, with a renewed popularity that made him, finally, the governor of his state.

However, it should not be taken as a rule that all municipios of the opposition, just by being such, are subject to the same discrimination on the part of higher level authorities. Many opposition mayors have commented that by being such they frequently receive more formal attention from the state authorities than their priísta counterparts, since they can create greater problems of image and governability than the latter, who are more susceptible to the PRI's hierarchical discipline and subordination. On the other hand, there is the exceptional example of the municipio of San Pedro Garza García, in the state of Nuevo León, under the municipal administration of the panista Mauricio Fernández (1989–91).[10] During his mayorship the municipality's own resources allowed it to come out of its deficit and cover its expenses with no need for the budget that came from the state. The good work that Fernández was able to carry out thanks to that, as well as his impartiality in the exercise of power, gained him the praise of many officials.[11] The same thing happened in the municipal administrations of Luis H. Alvarez and Francisco Barrio in Chihuahua and Ciudad Juárez, respectively, from 1983 to 1986 (Rodríguez and Ward, in this volume). However, as was stated earlier with respect to the disposal of the municipality's own resources, these cases are exceptions rather than the norm.

It is worth mentioning here the case of priísta municipalities whose leaders are in conflict with the state governor and are therefore subject to sanctions, boycotts, and hostilities similar to those denounced by opposition municipios. It could be argued that in such cases those municipalities turn out to be in opposition, de facto if not formally, with the disadvantage that their denouncements usually do not have the same impact as those made by the formal opposition. But beyond the controversies that may arise between municipios and governors, municipal inequality across parties seems to be the norm.[12] To avoid confusion this point should not be sidestepped when evaluating the relationship between opposition municipalities and their respective governors.

Opposition Governors

Until now, and for obvious reasons, we have usually thought of municipalities when we have spoken about governments of the opposition.

Only two governorships have been left in the hands of an opposition government in a fair manner (Baja California in 1989 and Chihuahua in 1992), with another only on an interim and shared basis (Guanajuato, 1991). Since the panista government of Ernesto Ruffo Appel in Baja California is the oldest of these, its study deserves special attention, in order to try to answer the important question asked by academics who examine opposition government in Mexico: Are the governments of the opposition significantly different from those in the hands of the priístas? And if so, how is this to be explained? (see Rodríguez and Ward 1991). At present the answer to the first question seems to be in the affirmative for the case of municipios.

This does not imply a similar response about state-level government, since the circumstances are quite different. In fact there is a qualitative difference, not only one of size, between a municipal government and a governorship. A panista municipality in a state governed by the PRI continues to be of the opposition (in the same way as the municipio of Mexicali, governed by the PRI, under the panista state government of Ruffo in Baja California), which explains the constant denouncements in the press by all opposition municipios of the discrimination their governors practice against them. But once in the state government, a party is no longer the opposition in that state, even though the federal government continues in the hands of priístas. And given the economic and institutional importance of a governorship, it is difficult to expect a reaction from the federal government toward an opposition governor similar to that of state governments toward municipalities in the hands of the opposition. Some observers did fear that the federal government would discriminate strongly against Ruffo's administration using the old strategy of boycotting opposition governments in order to recover the lost slot in the next electoral round. However, it has not been so; this is understandable, considering the risk of strong institutional tensions it would create.

At the state level, a tense and conflictive relationship is not convenient either to the governor or the federal executive. It is worth mentioning here that in his inauguration as governor, Ruffo addressed President Salinas in the following terms: "We believe you govern for all Mexicans." The solution the government found for the risk of leaving a state in the hands of the opposition was somehow to condition the recognition of the opposition's victory on a fundamentally moderate and institutional posture; in other words, the opposition-party governor should accept some of the unwritten rules of the game. Ruffo has obliged, adapting superbly to this requirement, and so has Carlos Medina Plascencia, the interim panista governor of Guanajuato.[13] On the other hand, the combative and belligerent attitude of Vicente Fox, the panista candidate for governor in that state, was sanctioned by political marginalization.[14] At least this has been the understanding in political circles.[15]

Therefore those of the opposition who now aspire to a governorship have learned that they must keep a position that is moderate, open to dialogue, and in full acknowledgment of the president. This was the result of "La Lección Fox" (the Fox lesson). In this fashion, when Francisco Barrio ran as a panista candidate for the governorship of Chihuahua in 1992, he took a very different stance from the one he had taken in 1986, and on this second occasion his victory was recognized. The message seems to have reached even the PRD. Cristóbal Arias, the PRD candidate for the governorship of Michoacán in 1992, employed a more moderate form of discourse than did many of his colleagues.[16] In this case the strategy of moderation was not successful, but that can more likely be attributed to the exclusionary policy the government has systematically followed against the PRD than to Arias's attitude. Altogether the institutional sensibility of opposition governors has been such that some of the most radical members of the opposition, as well as other dissidents, have accused them of not removing and punishing the abuses and irregularities practiced by the priísta governments that preceded them.[17]

One last item to point out is the priísta reaction in Baja California, where the PRI has turned out to be the real opposition.[18] Rodríguez and Ward (1994) have conducted a study of the concrete experience of municipalities under priísta control in Baja California. The mayors of those municipios have made some accusations similar to those of opposition municipios in other states relative to their respective state governments; the PRI of Baja California has taken positions and made demands very similar to those of other opposition parties in the rest of the country. It frequently accuses Ruffo's government of using its power, as well as its economic resources, in a skewed manner that favors the PAN. With respect to the preparation for elections for congress and the municipalities in 1992, the priístas accused Ruffo of putting into practice a process of voter registration that clearly and openly favored the PAN. Near the end of March of 1992, a denouncement signed by the PRI of Baja California appeared in the press, which could just as well have been written by the PAN in Sinaloa or the PRD in Guerrero, and Ruffo responded in terms resembling those of any priísta facing similar accusations.[19] After the elections Amador Rodríguez Lozano, the Undersecretary of Electoral Activities of the PRI at the national level, threatened to go to international

organizations and denounce the panista fraud in Baja California, a practice that is common in the opposition but condemned as antipatriotic by
the PRI.[20] The priístas of Baja California also demanded the opening of
the ballots (which electoral authorities generally refuse to do in the rest
of the country, under pressure from the PRI), and they undertook a "Dignity March" from Tecate to Mexicali, reminiscent of Salvador Nava's
celebrated march to Mexico City, to protest what they considered to be
panista government fraud.[21] Ruffo responded to the accusations of fraud
in a manner very similar to that practiced traditionally by priísta governors, pointing out that the losers always tend to reject a result that is
unfavorable to them, due to a lack of responsibility and political maturity. But he finally did agree to open the ballots, in order to dispel suspicions about the official verdict, a measure that would hardly be taken by
governments of the PRI in other states, let alone at the federal level.[22]

Ruffo has also been accused of acting within his party as priísta governors do, for example by appointing his own candidates to popularly elected
posts in the state.[23] This fact supports the hypothesis that political actors
perform according to the relative position in which they find themselves,
rather than on the basis of the qualitative differences among them. Some
of what the PRI denounces cannot be dismissed as untrue. What must be
researched is whether the PAN behaves in power in an essentially different manner from that of the PRI; whether there exist, in fact, clear lines
of differentiation in their tenure at the state level (with all of the political
strength and budgetary resources that it implies). This constitutes the basis for a closer and deeper observation of the concrete cases of the panista
state governments of Baja California, Chihuahua, and Guanajuato. Contrary to the examples listed above, which seem to indicate that panista
and priísta governors act in a very similar way, there are other examples
that point in the opposite direction. For instance, the Ruffo government
proved that it is, in fact, possible to issue voter photo-identification cards
in a short time and with few resources, which disproved the arguments
used by the federal government to slow down that process. Likewise, the
panista government of Baja California granted governmental status to the
State Commission on Human Rights and entrusted it to supervise the
electoral processes, which is something that has been denied to analogous
organizations across the country, including the National Commission on
Human Rights.

But on the other hand, it seems rather strange that the project of electoral reform presented by Ruffo, which was rejected by the priísta faction
of the local congress, did not include separating the state from the organi-

zation of elections, an issue that has always been denounced by the opposition, including, first and foremost, the PAN. When he took power, Ruffo
pledged he would push for an electoral law that would put an end to the
government's intervention in elections, but he failed to fulfill his promise.[24] There are two possible explanations for this. Either Ruffo thought it
would constitute an intolerable offence for the federal government and
chose to push the reform back on that basis, or he wanted to give the PRI
a taste of its own medicine and take advantage of holding power in the
state for the first time. The fact is Ruffo failed to seize the opportunity to
set a vanguard example of electoral legislation at the national level.[25]

Perspectives

It is not clear what the outcome of the political transition in Mexico
will be. On the one hand, democracy has strong possibilities of establishing itself in Mexico, although it is doubtful when and how this will happen. On the other hand, a different outcome cannot be overlooked, which
could be the closing in of the regime, or the indefinite prolongation of
the hegemonic party system. In any case it seems clear that democratization, if it should happen, will be slower and more gradual than in most
countries that have recently abandoned authoritarianism. In terms of the
ground yielded to the opposition, this means that if it does in fact increase, including at the governorship level, it will be in a limited and
selective way. The government, for now, will continue to appropriate the
right to decide who, when, and how those in the opposition will gain
access to power. The events of San Luis Potosí, Guanajuato, and Tabasco
indicate that the government is not yet ready to adhere to legal processes
and institutions in order to make these decisions. Probably in a gradual,
albeit diffuse manner, legality will replace both the whims and the strict
political rationale of the government's practice of dictating who occupies
what position.

As for the mass media, even though they will remain relatively closed
and critical of the opposition, a wider opening has been observed in recent years, and surely that tendency will continue, although perhaps at a
slower pace than is desirable in terms of political democratization. However, the outlook at the regional level, as stated earlier, is discouraging; it
is years behind as compared to the national media. Nonetheless, popular
movements and the wider presence of the opposition are exercising pressure in favor of a relative opening. There are also diverse initiatives emerg-

ing to create new newspapers that are more independent, impartial, and of higher quality. Such are the cases of *La Verdad del Sureste* in Tabasco and *Siglo XXI* in Guadalajara. In San Luis Potosí, a group of navistas and other citizens have made strong efforts to launch a new, independent newspaper.

"The Official Response" will probably become softer in time. The treatment by the authorities of opposition governments will become more equitable, as the latter become less exceptional. In any case vigilance among the parties, in the knowledge that victory is not certain in the next electoral round, coupled with the eventual strengthening of the other two branches, the legislative and the judicial, will translate into one of the basic objectives of democracy, public responsibility on the part of those governing toward their public. However, one of the questions that continues to be central in Mexican political debate is the degree to which the priísta government is willing to recognize and accept defeat when the opposition legitimately wins electoral positions, at what pace, and by what procedures. The relative flexibility of the Mexican political system, as well as its strong institutionalization as a hegemonic party system, enable it to press ahead with the liberalization process initiated decades ago, and it seems prepared to withstand several more years.

Notes

1. As Juan Mollinar (1991a) points out, this is the distinctive aspect of Mexican elections. Its secret is that over a long period it has made noncompetitiveness and a multiparty system compatible. Noncompetitive elections have been a very common phenomenon in the contemporary political world, but from the beginning all noncompetitive elections have been, or ended up being in a short time, elections in which only one party presents candidates.

2. For example, Emilio Azcárraga, president of Televisa, declared the following shortly before the elections of 1991: "This television consortium considers itself a part of the governmental system, and as such it supports the campaigns of the priísta candidates. I have said publicly that we are part of the system and the president of the republic is our ultimate head, and we are glad it is this way." (*Uno Más Uno*, July 30, 1991).

3. According to the magazine *Proceso* (April 29, 1991), there are fourteen families, headed by the following concessionaries: Joaquín Vargas, Francisco Ibarra, Emilio and Rogerio Azcárraga, Clemente Serna, Guillermo Salas, the Suárez family, José Luis Fernández Herrera, María Esther Gómez, Andrés García Lavín, the Arceo Corcueras, José de Jesús Partida, Francisco Antonio González, Javier Sánchez Campuzano, and the Boone Menchaca family.

4. The case of San Luis was so extreme that one newspaper, *El Heraldo de San*

Luis, published the headline "Fausto overwhelming" at 4:00 P.M., two hours before the closing of the elections, thus violating the federal electoral legislation that prohibits the publishing of propaganda on the day of elections.

5. The Democratic Coalition originated from the Frente Cívico Potosino, a navista organization; the PDM, the PRD, and finally the PAN joined in to support the candidacy of Salvador Nava.

6. Among those in the seminar were Miguel Angel Granados Chapa, José Agustín Ortiz Pinchetti, Alberto Aziz, Francisco Paoli Bolio, and Luis Javier Garrido of *La Jornada*; Lorenzo Meyer and Julio Faesler of *Excélsior*; Jorge G. Castañeda and Jorge Alcocer of *Proceso*; Adolfo Aguilar Zínzer and José Antonio Crespo of *El Financiero*; and Carlos Monsiváis, whose columns appear in several periodicals.

7. As pointed out by Castañeda and Pastor (1989:406–407), this is due to the fact that "With rare exceptions, Mexicans do not believe in the national media even if they speak the truth; however, almost all of them believe the United States media, even when they lie . . . This happens mostly because the Mexican government grants them an importance they do not have. Through concealment, indirect or indignant replies, and excess of attention, Mexican authorities have given the U.S. media a strength superior to that which they have in reality."

8. The fall of Salvador Neme Castillo had as a prelude a series of strong attacks by the national media; often the media do not act completely independently but rather under the influence of powerful politicians and power groups (Riva Palacio 1992).

9. Carlos Jonguitud was disbursing only 50 percent of the budget allocated to the city of San Luis. A collaborator of Nava at that time remembers that "during twelve days we had to work with candles, and the danger of cutting off the potable water supply lurked over the population because of debts the municipality had with the Federal Electricity Commission." Shortly before Nava's death, Jonguitud denied that such a confrontation took place: "He (Nava) did his thing and I did mine . . . I never attacked him. I was never belligerent toward him, and I never had any confrontations with him" (*Proceso*; May 8, 1992).

10. In 1988 the municipality showed an operating deficit of 5,236 million pesos. When Mauricio Fernández's term ended, Garza García had a surplus of 16,000 million pesos.

11. For example Consuelo Botello, the coordinator of the local priísta deputyship, commented on the panista mayor of Garza García: "In general, the administration of Mauricio Fernández has been very good; he has attained an infrastructure of basic services in peripheral places that had never been available in previous administrations" (*San Pedro: Tres años de resultados*; 1991:57).

12. Alvaro Arreola (1985:331) gives as an example the government of Jorge Jiménez Cantú in the state of Mexico, which in 1980 allocated 55 percent of the 2,000 million pesos of the state's municipal budget to five municipios, while the other 96 percent of the municipios received the remaining 45 percent of the budget.

13. In that sense the statements made by Medina Plascencia in his inauguration as interim governor, which was attended by President Salinas, are significant: "These are not times of opposition; they are times of coresponsibility, of

participation and joint work . . . we will maintain cordial and productive relationships with the federal entities, because we know that the strength of our federal republic is rooted in the vigor and self-sufficiency of the states."

14. Prior to forcing the resignation of Ramón Aguirre, the government had offered to annul the elections so long as neither Aguirre nor Fox presented themselves again as candidates. The PAN did not accept this proposal. Shortly after Aguirre's resignation, the local congress of Guanajuato, dominated by the PRI, approved an amendment to articles 68 and 110 of the state constitution, with the new requirement of having to be born in the state in order to become governor; an amendment clearly directed at Vicente Fox, who was born in Mexico City by chance, given that his family has lived in León, Guanajuato, since before his birth. The outgoing governor, Rafael Corrales Ayala, vetoed the amendment, not because it was intrinsically unfair or unappropriate, but because it was simply "inopportune." The congress, however, could introduce the amendment again, since the state executive only has one opportunity to veto a legislative initiative. For this reason it was considered to be a warning to the PAN to keep Vicente Fox away from a second candidacy for governor.

15. *Proceso* magazine (September 16, 1991), for example, pointed out that "Everything has been done so that Vicente Fox does not make it—either today, tomorrow, or ever—to the governorship of Guanajuato . . . Such aversion does not seem to have a reasonable explanation. Maybe Vicente Fox is considered a particularly dangerous opponent. Maybe it is all due to the retribution of a personal offence." The belligerence of Fox continued to the end; during the inauguration of Medina Plascencia, when the former panista candidate was asked if he would greet President Salinas, present there, he replied: "He can come to me if he wants to; I am in my homeland . . ." (*Proceso*, September 30, 1991).

16. He was also advised by the Michoacán intellectual Arnaldo Córdova, who has publicly expressed his disagreement with the intransigent policy of PRD leaders.

17. Vicente Fox spoke in a suspicious tone about Carlos Medina Plascencia after his first few months as interim governor, in regard to Medina's handling of the municipal elections of December of 1991 and his hesitation to square accounts with former priísta functionaries. Fox said, "I ask that those things be cleared up because only by doing so are we going to keep the support of the people. The people of Guanajuato voted for us, the panistas, so we would change and transform, not so we would administrate a state in favor of Salinas" (*Proceso*, January 13, 1992).

18. When the PAN won in Baja California, one of the questions that was immediately asked was whether the local PRI could recover without the support and funding of the state government, a privilege it had enjoyed until then, just like the priísmo of the rest of the country. Up to now the answer seems to have gone in a negative direction. The only senatorship the PRI lost in 1991 was precisely that of Baja California, where in addition three federal deputyships were lost, all in favor of the PAN. In the 1992 elections for the local congress, the PRI also ended up with a negative balance.

19. For example Ruffo pointed out in a public announcement: "It is the will of the executive of Baja California under my direction that during all stages of the

electoral process—voter registration, preparation, and the carrying out of elections—we can ALL participate with knowledge of ALL, meaning with transparency and clarity, which are the basis of confidence and credibility our electoral processes require" (*La Jornada*, March 27, 1992).

20. It must be pointed out, however, that the National Executive Committee of the PRI rushed to disqualify Rodríguez Lozano's proposal, insisting even in this case that it would be antipatriotic to go to international forums to reconcile electoral conflicts.

21. In a public denouncement, the PRI's state political council pointed out that citizens who were not on the lists had been allowed to vote, thus violating article 144 of the electoral law of the state, and that given the small difference between the votes for the PRI and those for the PAN, the panista victory seemed extremely suspicious. The difference is, in fact, minimal. In the elections for deputies, the PRI obtained 44.6 percent of the vote and the PAN 45.2 percent and in the municipal elections the percentage was 44.7 percent for the PRI and 45.4 percent for the PAN (*La Jornada*, September 17, 1992).

22. On the contrary, the ballots of the controversial election of 1988 were burned as soon as the PRI recovered the qualifying majority in the congress, after the legislative elections of 1991.

23. It was said he used his power to appoint Héctor Osuna Jaime as the panista candidate for mayor of Tijuana. Ruffo responded, "if the *dedazo* is natural in Mexicans, a *dedo azul* does not exist" (*La Jornada*, May 8, 1992). *Dedazo* refers to the practice of selecting candidates for office.

24. In fact in his State Development Plan (1990–95), Ernesto Ruffo pledged to invest the state with a new electoral legislation more in line with democratic requirements. Among them was that of creating a completely autonomous electoral organization in which the electoral processes would be "managed by the people and the political parties. The authorities will intervene only to provide the elements the processes may require and to guarantee their orderliness and security." Contrary to that, the preliminary project sent by the state executive to the state congress in September of 1991 states that "The organization of local elections are a state function carried out by the legislative and executive powers of the state with the participation of the political parties and the people."

25. Paradoxically the priísta government in Guerrero, with the approval of the local congress, priísta in its majority, placed the electoral processes under the control of the legislative branch, which is no small step in the evolution of electoral legislation in Mexico.

3

Democratic Changes
in an Authoritarian System

*Navismo and Opposition Development
in San Luis Potosí*

ROBERT R. BEZDEK

In the 1960s some scholars of the Mexican political system indicated that the regime was in transition to a more democratic polity (Scott 1965; Padgett 1966). Perhaps most thought that Mexico's transition from 1960 to 1980 would parallel that of certain Latin American nations listed as democratic: Colombia, Costa Rica, the Dominican Republic, Ecuador, and Venezuela (Dahl 1989). Furthermore, it was thought that Argentina, Bolivia, Brazil, Honduras, and Peru might reach democratic status sometime in the 1990s. Mexico was not on either list, and noted Mexican scholars such as González Casanova (1970) remained skeptical. However, since the controversial presidential elections of 1988, there have been greater hopes and expectations for democratization. Indeed some authors have proclaimed the end of the PRI's dominance (Linowitz 1988/ 89:59; Cornelius and Craig 1992). Others, such as Coleman and Davis (1988), continue to be cautious and argue that the regime will maintain its dominance. The purpose of this chapter is to show that while the electoral practices of Mexican political leaders have become more democratic over the last three decades, many of the regime's authoritarian practices persist and are likely to continue for the foreseeable future.

The evidence for these generalizations is derived from my longitudinal study in the state of San Luis Potosí of the opposition led by Dr. Salvador Nava Martínez (1914–92). His movement, *navismo*, first began in the late 1950s, ended in the early 1960s, and then reemerged in 1982. His successor as mayor in the capital city of San Luis Potosí, Guillermo Pizzuto Zamanillo, lost the 1985 contest due to fraud, but was recognized after the 1988 elections. Nava's latest efforts, in 1991, involved a campaign for governor and subsequent protests over the election, which compelled President Carlos Salinas de Gortari to force the resignation of the PRI governor. To understand these developments, it is necessary to briefly review opposition activities in San Luis Potosí from 1958 to 1990, before focusing on the 1991 gubernatorial election. First, however, I will discuss the significance today of democratic development in Mexico.

With the collapse of communism, most leaders throughout the world have emphasized democracy as a goal for their country. President Carlos Salinas de Gortari is no exception, for he stated his commitment to democracy on October 4, 1989, in an address to a joint session of the United States Congress. In part, of course, these statements were designed to deflect some of the criticism from his questionable victory (at least in terms of his "winning margin") in the controversial 1988 election.

To measure a regime's level of democratic development, Dahl (1989: 221) lists seven institutions (see Table 3.1). Free and fair elections, freedom of expression, alternative information, and associational autonomy are of greatest relevance to the Mexican polity during the present period of development. I will highlight these institutions in this chapter and then discuss how the Mexican polity measures up against these four criteria in a longitudinal analysis of its treatment of opposition in San Luis Potosí.

A second component of my conceptual framework is an attempt to delineate the cultural underpinnings of authoritarian governments struggling with the difficult steps of democratic development. Conflicts in San Luis Potosí between PRI officials and opposition leaders indicate that each of these groups is operating from different cultural norms, with the former following authoritarian modes of behavior and the latter utilizing more democratic standards. Coleman and Davis (1988) refer to these differences as the "operational" (the actual practices) and the "normative" (what should be) cultures. Briefly, members of the regime see themselves

Table 3.1: Dahl's seven institutions of democracy

1. Control over government decisions is constitutionally vested in elected officials.
2. Voters choose elective officials in impartial, regular elections.
3. All adults have the right to vote.
4. Most adults have the right to run for office.
5. Citizens have an enforced right to freedom of speech, including criticism of government leaders.
6. Citizens have an enforced right to alternate sources of information not controlled by the government.
7. Citizens have an enforced right to form and join political organizations, including parties and interest groups.

as the legitimate heirs of the revolution and the only ones capable of ruling the country and carrying out such presidential goals as economic development. They portray the opposition as somehow incapable of ruling and as not having the ties to the central government necessary to channel resources to their particular entity. Because checks and balances are virtually nonexistent, they are able to use the public treasury for enormous campaign expenditures and frequently apply the laws favorably for themselves and their friends. Moreover, many see personal enrichment as part of the rewards of years of discipline and loyalty to the system. On the other hand, opposition leaders tend to extol democratic values, especially a sense of fair play and accountability. The basis of the opposition critique has been the rapid enrichment of PRI officeholders at the expense of fulfilling some of the basic needs of the people. Moreover, an important demand of opposition policy is fighting corruption, as Ward (this volume) has outlined for Ciudad Juárez and Chihuahua.

The Origins of *Navismo*

Nava, an ophthalmologist, entered politics to challenge the stranglehold exercised over San Luis Potosí by a *cacique* or a political boss.[1] Gonzalo N. Santos ruled arbitrarily as governor during the 1940s and controlled the state's politicians afterwards. Some examples of his grip upon San Luis Potosí are his vast landholdings (many acquired illegally), a monthly "kickback" from some city budgets, the imposition of his own people as candidates, control of the press, and even assassinations. His insatiable appetite to acquire wealth and to manipulate people was reported by Mendoza Rivera (1958). Specifically, he calculated Santos's liquid assets at 40 million U.S. dollars and estimated that he was responsible for killing 250 individuals who had attempted to oppose him. In fact, in his own memoirs the cacique boasted: "I am capable of killing an enemy, burying him, and distributing death notices . . . " (Santos 1984:782). Virtually all sources report that he applied the law of the three *ierros* to his opponents: *el encierro*, *el destierro*, and *el entierro* (imprisonment, banishment, and burial). But because he was able to deliver votes for various national presidents, they generally protected him and even appointed him to national positions, when he lost his stranglehold over San Luis Potosí.

Because others refused to challenge Santos, Nava became a consensus mayoral candidate in 1958. Rejected by the PRI, he ran as an indepen-

dent, and his movement united all sectors of Potosinan society against the
regime, as evidenced by his receiving 94 percent of the vote. In late November some violence had occurred between the regime and the opposition, and emotions were running high. Nava feared more violence but
could not get the attention of the national government, until President
Adolfo López Mateos took office on December 1. A few days later some
locally garrisoned soldiers killed one youngster, and the new regime
changed military commanders. When General Alberto Zuno Hernández
arrived in the state, the day before the December 7 mayoral election, he
stated that the army should not fight the people and promised impartial
elections. He kept his promise by stationing soldiers at the polling places,
thereby allowing the *navistas* to vote. Clearly the new president decided
not to support Gonzalo Santos, allowed an impartial election to occur,
and recognized Nava as the first opposition mayor of a state capital.

The Nava administration made major changes. For example, the mayor
immediately stopped the monthly payment of 8,000 U.S. dollars to Santos
from the meager city budget. His correction of other abuses increased
funds by 49 percent during the first year without raising taxes. The new
administration soon installed drainage systems, expanded electrical services and running water, paved streets, etc. Moreover, Nava published
the city budget daily in front of city hall, so that the people could scrutinize the income and expenses. In addition he fired one of his department
heads for corruption, thereby sending a clear message to other municipal
employees.

Shortly afterward, the opposition administration received favorable
reports from national newspapers. For example, *Excélsior* (September 19,
21, and 22, 1959) reported that San Luis Potosí was the only city where
the mayor was elected and not imposed by the PRI. Furthermore, it was
reported that the administration felt an obligation to keep the citizens
informed of its activities. In just seven months the city had extended the
installation of public electric lighting, paid off much of the debt left by
previous administrations to the electric company, and had installed 6,500
meters of sewer lines. The newspaper also referred to the animosity of
PRI officials, who were trying to sabotage these efforts. After Nava's first
annual report to the people, newspapers such as *El Universal* wrote positive accounts of progress in San Luis Potosí. The title of the article gave
the flavor of the contents: "With honesty, dignity, and work, San Luis
Potosí leaves its abandoned status" (December 14, 1959).

President López Mateos visited the state in August 1960 and acknowledged the successes of the opposition administration. He had an aide

divide a list of governmental accomplishments in the state capital according to city and state sponsorship. Then when the president addressed a large gathering and gave more credit to the opposition administration by reading its longer list of accomplishments, many interpreted this presidential gesture as tacit approval for Nava's candidacy for governor. Moreover, Nava reported that the president told him that he would no longer have to deal with the state PRI under Santos but now would deal directly with the national PRI, thus implying his support for the reform mayor.

Nava resigned as mayor to run for governor in December 1960. Soon afterward he visited the national PRI president, Alfonso Corona del Rosal, in an attempt to obtain the official party's nomination. After initial assurances that he only needed to show that he had statewide support, Nava returned to Mexico City at the insistence of the PRI president. But Corona del Rosal's attitude had changed, and he explained to Nava that he simply could not become the PRI candidate. As the campaign progressed, it became clear that the central government would not permit him to become the first opposition governor. Indeed it is easier to understand the regime's behavior during this time period if one recalls Stevens's (1974:259) classic characterization: "The regime deals with bona fide groups almost as though they were enemy nations." During the campaign, for example, at least two hundred opposition supporters were injured, and Jesús Acosta, a key coordinator for the Nava campaign, was assassinated. Only one of the assassins spent time (six months) in jail, and Nava insisted that the regime had planned the killing (*Tribuna* May 25, July 21).

One development that made this campaign different from all other opposition efforts in San Luis Potosí was that the navistas had their own newspaper, *Tribuna*. Informants report that its circulation reached about fifteen thousand copies daily, while the previously dominant newspaper, *El Sol de San Luis*, declined to about five thousand copies. Remarkably, the regime allowed the opposition newspaper to publish its version of events throughout the campaign and only embarked upon massive repression of the opposition after the elections. To be sure the paper was not impartial, for the editors clearly stated their policy to reject advertisements for the official candidate (April 15, 1961), although they desperately needed the money.

As was to be expected, the regime stole the 1961 election, as Jesús Reyes Heroles told me when he was president of the PRI's Central Executive Committee (he made a similar admission to Cornelius [1987:38]). This time the soldiers had orders to reverse the roles they played in the

1958 election. As a result they prevented many navistas from voting and literally carried away some of the ballot boxes.

The opposition protests lasted for more than two months. But on the night of September 15 (independence celebrations in Mexico), the regime attacked the opposition on various fronts simultaneously. First, soldiers began shooting in the main plaza, shortly before midnight. Second, the army disarmed the municipal police (which were under the opposition administration's authority) and placed them under military custody. Third, they wrecked the offices of *Tribuna* early the next day and threatened its key personnel. Fourth, the governor dismissed the legitimate mayor and council members and replaced them with handpicked successors in less than twenty hours and without legislative approval. Fifth, the regime arrested Nava. Finally, soldiers conducted searches of numerous houses and arrested about four hundred navistas.

The regime took Nava to Mexico City, where they tried him for "sedition" and other crimes. Many feared that he would remain in prison for the remainder of President Adolfo López Mateos's term (some three years), because his crime was "political." During the trial the regime apparently realized the weakness of its case and released him after a three-week imprisonment.

Nava tried to form a political party, but the repression had succeeded in silencing his movement. In July 1962 he officially notified his followers that he was suspending political activity. However, his popularity remained high, as Potosinans would frequently shout his name when they encountered Governor Manuel López Dávila. In February 1963 he was arrested and physically beaten. Nava stated that he had a broken rib, a hemorrhage in the heart, numerous bruises over all parts of his body, and that he could not move his right arm (see also the medical report in Calvillo 1986:117). He spent ten days in the hospital recuperating (Borjas Benavente 1992:187). Meanwhile *Gobernación* sent agents to the state to investigate the state government, and shortly afterward the state attorney general and several others resigned. It is difficult to explain this attack on Nava, because he had stopped his political activities about six months previously.

One can attempt to reconstruct how federal and state officials dealt with the opposition in San Luis Potosí from 1958 to 1963. First President López Mateos allowed Nava to become the mayor in 1958 and appeared to encourage him to run for governor. Perhaps because of opposition from PRI leaders, the official party president then reversed his earlier position and insisted that Nava would regret running for governor. After the July 1961 election, the regime sent federal deputies to warn the opposition leader that continued protest of the election results would lead to violence. Apparently, after two months of protests and the jailing of some opposition leaders, the regime decided in mid-September to put an end to the protests by jailing Nava and many others. In short, there appeared to be a threshold of regime tolerance, after which the opposition suffered considerable repression. In 1962 the state government allowed the navistas to organize for a few months but then must have received orders to silence the movement. The jailing and beating of Nava in February 1963 seems to have been an initiative of the governor and brought the ire of the federal government down on his administration, because several state officials were forced to resign. In other words, during the late 1950s and early 1960s, the rules of the game suggest that the opposition could mobilize and even win the mayoral position, given the right window of opportunity—a hated cacique and a new president attempting to show that he was different from his predecessors. But the opposition's continued protests exceeded the regime's tolerance, after which the navistas were silenced.

The Return of Nava in 1982

Nava reluctantly ran for mayor again because of Potosinans' frustration with Governor Carlos Jonguitud Barrios. Frequent complaints against the governor were his tendency to hire senior staffers from outside of San Luis Potosí (the so-called "foreign legion"); that he continued to spend a considerable amount of time outside the state (he was head of the SNTE, the national teachers' union); and that he exhibited vulgarity by urinating in public when he was drunk. Moreover, they considered him pretentious, because he would travel about the city at high speed, with a police escort and bodyguards.

On this occasion Nava did not even consider seeking the PRI nomination, because he had his own independent party, the Frente Cívico Potosino (FCP). Rather than run as an independent candidate, he sought and obtained the endorsement of two established political parties: the National Action Party (PAN) and the Mexican Democratic Party (PDM). Initial returns from precincts supervised by the PRI and opposition poll watchers gave him 74 percent of the vote. He met with the incoming Minister of the Interior, Manuel Bartlett Díaz, who promised him recognition after seeing Nava's copy of the precinct results. Nevertheless, the PRI delegate to the state visited Nava to inform him that his margin of victory would have to be lowered to 60 percent.

His accomplishments the second time around did not match his previous ones, because he had to spend much of his time fighting Jonguitud, who did not want to give the city its allocation of federal funds. In addition, the deteriorating economy left his administration with few resources. The feud between Jonguitud and Nava attracted national attention, especially when the governor had the electricity shut off in city hall, thereby forcing the city administration to work with candles for about a week. In May 1983 Nava organized a protest march to demand that the city receive its fair share of federal money. The governor capitulated, but the opposition insisted that the national congress investigate Jonguitud. Such an investigation never materialized, but Nava had forced the governor to behave in a more responsible manner.

In January 1985 there were considerable rumors about the choice of a new governor. To prevent Jonguitud from handpicking his successor, Nava took a leave of absence, which led observers to believe that he would run for governor if the PRI did not find an acceptable alternative. Soon Florencio Salazar Martínez became the official candidate, and Nava returned to his position as mayor. When Salazar Martínez became governor in September, he and Nava worked together more closely than any governor and opposition mayor had in the state. That cooperation stopped abruptly with the electoral fraud in the December mayoral election.

Guillermo Pizzuto Zamanillo

At the end of Nava's term as mayor in 1985, the FCP chose Pizzuto to challenge the PRI candidate, Guillermo Medina de los Santos. Pizzuto had a positive image in the community, because he had served as the director of the Chamber of Commerce (CANACO) and had criticized some of Jonguitud's excesses. He received the endorsement from only one political party, the PAN. Like Nava he was financially independent, because he had set up a successful iron foundry in 1974. Unlike Nava, however, he was also able to raise an estimated 80,000 U.S. dollars and implemented an effective television advertisement campaign.

After the December 1 election, many people thought that Pizzuto had won. The results in opposition-supervised precincts showed 38,333 votes (64 percent) for Pizzuto, 19,471 (32 percent) for Medina de los Santos, and 2,303 for other candidates. But after the Electoral Commission met,

Table 3.2: The official PRI and PAN results of the 1985 mayoral election by percentage range

Percentage Range for PAN/Pizzuto	Num. of Pre-cincts	PAN Votes	PRI Votes	PRI % of PRI-PAN Votes	% of PRI Votes	Cumu-lative PRI %	Median Turnout
0%	19	0	4,532	100%	10%	10%	102%
0.1–9.9%	26	429	12,561	97%	29%	39%	98%
10–19.9%	5	890	4,385	83%	10%	49%	73%
20–29.9%	6	1,229	4,073	77%	9%	59%	89%
30–39.9%	1	319	671	68%	2%	60%	26%
40–49.9%	14	3,120	3,465	53%	8%	68%	35%
50–59.9%	36	4,782	3,230	40%	7%	75%	35%
60–69.9%	61	13,386	6,227	32%	14%	90%	36%
70–79.9%	56	14,207	4,458	24%	10%	100%	35%
80–89.9%	1	81	10	11%	0%		10%
90–100%	0						
Total	225	38,443	43,612				

the official results changed to 38,311 (47.5 percent) for the PAN and 42,276 (52.5 percent) for the PRI (*El Sol de San Luis*, December 9). I have organized these data by deciles (see table 3.2), which indicate that there was no attempt to conceal the blatant fraud. For example Pizzuto officially received zero votes from 19 of the 225 precincts, where the median turnout was 102 percent. Moreover, he received less than 10 percent of the votes from the next 26 precincts, where the median turn-out was 98 percent. Thus these 45 precincts account for 39 percent of the total PRI votes. Perhaps the most flagrant example of vote alterations, or of the regime's alchemy, comes from precinct 68 in District I. The vote supervised by representatives of both parties showed that he received 305 votes to his opponent's 131. The Electoral Commission members simply added one thousand votes to Medina de los Santos's 131, and thus the official result became 1,131 for the PRI to 305 for the opposition. It is important to point out that electoral fraud in San Luis Potosí during this period was not unique, and that many opposition victories throughout the country were overturned (Cornelius 1987).

Medina de los Santos took the oath of office early in the morning rather than at midday, as scheduled, on January 1, 1986. As residents gathered in the plaza in front of city hall, violence erupted, and some individuals burned the wooden doors to city hall. News reports blamed Governor

Florencio Salazar Martínez for the violence, and within a month some key officials from his administration resigned. The opposition protested the violence through a series of rallies and even held a public trial, in which they found the governor guilty of violating democratic principles. Shortly afterward Salazar's natural allies (local legislators, PRI officials, and the local press) deserted him. Finally, in May of 1987, he asked for a leave of absence.

In 1988, with FCP and PAN support, Pizzuto ran again and won, with 55 percent of the vote. He estimates that he spent half of his time and resources defending himself against harassment from PRI officials; not an atypical situation, as others in this book have described (see also Bezdek 1973; Barrio 1992). A case in point is vehicle-pollution control. On the one hand, the state constitution stipulates that the mayor must establish a procedure for determining the pollution level of vehicles, something that is already done in several major Mexican cities. On the other hand, state legislators denounced and investigated Pizzuto for the system he established. The aim appears to have been to discredit him personally as well as to discredit Nava, about one month before the 1991 gubernatorial election. Pizzuto hired a prestigious attorney from Mexico City and published his letter in press advertisements, thus forcing the PRI legislators to drop the issue.

The 1991 Gubernatorial Election

Although some democratic practices had emerged since Nava's 1961 gubernatorial campaign, many vestiges of the authoritarian system remained. Some of the infringements of democratic principles during this 1991 contest were the enormous resources (most taken from the public treasury) allocated to the PRI candidate, the support from the local press, and the regime's control over voter registration as well as over the various electoral commissions. Clearly the playing field was far from level.

Nava hoped to become the opposition candidate for governor a second time, but his age (seventy-six) and treatment for cancer appeared to exclude this possibility. After four months of chemotherapy in Mexico City, he returned home in January 1991. The local press response was favorable, which he used to his advantage in order to fashion a "democratic coalition" of the PAN, the PDM, and the PRD. But the local newspapers withdrew their positive coverage of him once the *dedazo*, or imposition of the PRI gubernatorial candidate, Fausto Zapata Loredo, was announced, on February 28.

This contest was different from previous ones. While Nava enjoyed a high level of popularity because of his accomplishments, he did not have such an obvious enemy as in the past; Zapata was no Santos, López Dávila, or Jonguitud. In short, while Zapata was identified with President Luis Echeverría (1970–76) as his press secretary during the government-staged takeover of *Excélsior* (Vargas 1977), he was able to persuade many priístas to close ranks behind him to win the governorship, even though he was attacked in the national press (Aziz Nassif 1991, 1992). Furthermore, the state's population had doubled in the past three decades, and many Potosinans appeared less interested in this race than in previous ones.

A survey of thirty-three hundred capital-city residents, commissioned by Pizzuto and conducted by a Guadalajara research firm in February 1991, showed high negative evaluations of the political process and of the official party. For example, two-thirds of the respondents felt that fraud existed in elections, a belief that fosters apathy. Moreover, the PRI's negative evaluations were more than double those of the PAN (42 percent to 16 percent), and in response to an open-ended question, over a fourth (27 percent) volunteered that the PRI was corrupt. Furthermore, by a three-to-one margin (31 percent to 11 percent), residents felt that city services under Pizzuto were better as compared to the previous PRI administration and indicated that they would vote, by a two-to-one margin (39 percent to 22 percent), for a PAN mayor again. One should note that opposition support might have been even higher than these results indicate, because polling experts argue that many Mexicans are reluctant to criticize the government and its official party (Miguel Basáñez, interview, September 24, 1992).

During the campaign the four local newspapers and all other media favored Zapata. Nava this time could rely only on the weekly *Tribuna* and a new biweekly magazine, *Expresiones de San Luis*, published by one of his supporters, Eduardo Martínez Benavente. However, one should note that the local press did not appear to be as manipulated by the government in 1991 as it was in 1961. Nevertheless favorable reporting on PRI candidates paid richer dividends that did such reporting on the opposition, which spent much less money on advertisements and did not supplement the journalists' meager income. In other words, in demonstrating partisanship, local reporters might well have been following their economic interests more than the dictates of an authoritarian regime. A case in point was the number of advertisements to welcome Zapata as the official candidate. *Expresiones de San Luis* (March 11) reported on forty

Table 3.3: Percent of column inches, black and white pictures, and color pictures for Nava in the four newspapers

	Column Inches		B & W Pictures		Color Pictures	
	Nava	Total	Nava	Total	Nava	Total
Pulso	32%	1,427	27%	117	41%	34
Momento	30%	987	20%	69	0	0
El Sol	23%	1,200	18%	91	4%	23
El Heraldo	13%	1,156	7%	74	0	10

statements of support from thirty-five (out of fifty-six) municipalities in the state filling twenty-two pages in the newspapers. The estimated cost to the taxpayers of the different cities involved was 21,666 U.S. dollars.

To present a rough idea of the coverage in the newspapers for Nava and Zapata, I used three simple, objective measures from June 17 to July 16. The first was to calculate the column inches of articles dealing with the primary campaign activities of the two candidates. Next I counted the number of black-and-white as well as color photographs. Table 3.3 shows the percentage of these three measures for the opposition candidate. The coverage given to Nava ranged from 32 percent of the column inches in *Pulso* to 13 percent in *El Heraldo*, while Zapata received 68 percent and 87 percent, respectively. The percentage of color pictures fluctuated from 41 percent in *Pulso* to 0 in *El Heraldo*, while the percent of black-and-white pictures varied from 27 percent in *Pulso* to 7 percent in *El Heraldo*.

These objective measures do not take into consideration the explicit and implicit bias of the articles on the opposition. Such bias is a standard practice of an authoritarian subculture. In fact Pizzuto argues that *Pulso* is the most biased newspaper, because it essentially gives the appearance of impartiality by covering the opposition more, but its statements are more biased. One event should illustrate the bias of all four papers. On July 24 Zapata held a rally close to Nava's house in a park called Tequisquiapan; many of his most loyal supporters live in this neighborhood. In spite of considerable advertisements and inducements (free food, soft drinks, and carnival rides), only twelve hundred supporters showed up. However, the four newspapers reported that either four or five thousand people attended the rally, and *El Heraldo* took the extreme position that the event dealt navismo a "mortal blow."

Shortly after the August 18 election, the official results showed that Zapata had won by a margin of almost two to one, or 329,292 to 170,646 (*Pulso*, August 23). The appropriate channel for protesting electoral fraud is the electoral commission, but Nava refused to use it because, he argued, these were the same individuals who had perpetrated the fraud.

Initially the regime refused to release the precinct results, but groups of national observers documented the election fraud. Even before any voting occurred, a team of researchers from the National Autonomous University of Mexico (UNAM), coordinated by Cuauhtémoc Rivera Godínez (1991:40), concluded that voter registration was "structured in a selective manner with political criteria" and that the "structure was directed by the official party to guarantee its monopoly in power." Later two other groups concluded that their 330 observers, who visited 744 precincts (out of a total of about 2,200), found serious electoral violations (*El Financiero*, September 25). In fact they found fifty different types of irregularities in 396 of the 744 precincts they studied (*La Jornada*, September 26).

Valuable support for Nava also came from about three dozen intellectuals, journalists, and leaders of different political parties. Many came to the state on July 26 for a forum on the transition to democracy and returned on September 6 for presentations on electoral fraud. Many of these individuals were critical of the government and for the first time unified around an opposition candidate. Their writings in national publications gave Nava additional credibility.

Protest after the Election

On August 21 Nava held a press conference in Mexico City to argue his case with the central government to prevent a manipulation of the election results. He had the support of the national directors of the PRD, the PAN, and the PDM, who appeared next to him in pictures in the major newspapers (*Uno Más Uno*, *El Nacional*, *El Universal*, *La Jornada*). The opposition leader also met with President Salinas (*La Jornada*, August 27) but reported that he was unresponsive to the charges of electoral fraud.

In order to hold a rally one week after the election, Nava had to sign an agreement with the federal government that no violence would occur. President Salinas sent the attorney general, Ignacio Morales Lechuga, to meet with Nava and Pizzuto at the governor's official residence (*Pulso*, August 25). The opposition leaders agreed to sign a document (although historically the regime, not the opposition, generally initiated any violence) in exchange for the government's commitment to force the local press to print paid advertisements for Nava's rally.

At the rally, with an estimated thirty thousand in attendance, Nava addressed two audiences. To the people of San Luis Potosí, he offered his apologies for believing the president's commitment to impartial elections. He also expressed gratitude and admiration for their support. Then he requested that those in attendance take out their voter-registration cards and hold them up. Nava then stated: "With this credential raised, with all due respect, Mr. President of the Republic, Lic. Carlos Salinas de Gortari, facing this injustice, hear the painful silence of the people" (*La Jornada*, August 26).

On September 28, two days after Zapata's inauguration, Nava began his protest march to Mexico City. Some eight thousand people accompanied him out of the state capital (*La Jornada*). Meanwhile, to prevent Zapata from functioning as governor, some opposition women staged a sit-in around the various entrances to the Governor's Palace. On one occasion Zapata and his supporters stepped on some of these women to enter the building, and one woman sustained injuries that required hospitalization (Granados Chapa 1992:21). The protestors also faced numerous abuses from PRI supporters (*Proceso*, October 7). These incidents, however, created greater resolve to continue the sit-in.

Many thought that Nava could not walk the 265 miles to Mexico City, but as he neared the halfway mark, Querétaro, the press reported that his "march of dignity" had gained momentum. When President Salinas realized that more than half a million people could march with Nava into Mexico City on November 1 and thus upstage his state of the union address, he agreed to the opposition demands that Zapata be forced to resign and that new elections be scheduled.

Nava's negotiations with the regime indicate that President Salinas wanted to avoid a public confrontation with the popular opposition leader, for the regime twice offered Nava the position of interim governor (*La Jornada*, May 25, 1992). On August 30 the Secretary of Gobernación, Fernando Gutiérrez Barrios, first approached the opposition leader with this idea. And during Nava's march to Mexico City, the offer was made again. On both occasions he refused immediately, for two reasons. First, the government wanted to place two high-ranking PRI officials in his administration, thereby reducing his freedom to make decisions (as had occurred in Guanajuato). Second, Mrs. Nava later pointed out to me that her husband did not want to accept a political position unless he was legitimately elected, since he felt that his fight was one for democracy, not just for power.

Nava returned to large crowds in San Luis Potosí on October 10. His national reputation soared, for he had in effect achieved a veto over the elections in San Luis Potosí with an imaginative strategy. He became the rallying symbol for the opposition, as intellectuals, journalists, and party leaders joined him in early December in order to lay the groundwork for a national citizens' movement for democracy. But once he encouraged a national strategy of abstention, the PAN leaders refused to follow suit, and in the December mayoral race for the capital city of San Luis, they ran Mario Leal Campos for the position. Nava felt he had been betrayed, but Pizzuto perceived the situation to be more complex. While there had been an agreement among the different parties to abstain if significant electoral reforms did not occur, the legislators had made some changes. Although Pizzuto sympathized with Nava, he argued that many state-capital residents would not wish to abstain, because that would mean three years of rule by a PRI mayor.

For a variety of reasons, the regime recognized the panista candidate's victory. One factor that helped Leal Campos was the disillusionment felt by PRI supporters once President Salinas had forced Zapata to resign. Many therefore did not vote. This counterbalanced the ardent Frente Cívico supporters, who also abstained (following Nava's lead). But as conflicts emerged over some precincts that would have given the advantage to the PRI, Nava placed an advertisement in *Pulso* (December 12) that indicated he would mobilize a protest if the vote were not respected. The government also recognized about eight opposition mayors out of the fifty-six cities in the state. Thus Nava's gubernatorial campaign did plant some seeds for democratic development, a phrase he frequently used in justifying his involvement.

Conclusion

Two types of observations emerge from this study. The first deal with democratic development, while the second relate to the patterns in the regime's recognition of opposition victories. Earlier I argued that four of Dahl's seven institutions of democracy are of particular relevance to the Mexican political system. These are items 2 (impartial elections), 5 (freedom of expression), 6 (alternative information), and 7 (associational autonomy).

Clearly the 1961 and the 1991 elections were not impartial (item 2), so that the regime maintained its monopoly. However, some improvements may be observed between these two time periods, although at the Austin conference Nava eloquently argued that "in the past, they used guns and jails, now they use computers" to steal elections (*Austin-American States-man*, April 3, 1992). But the regime did make an attempt to improve the voter-registration process in 1991. Furthermore, while soldiers played an important role in allowing Potosinans to vote in 1958 and prevented them from voting in 1961, no military personnel were present in 1991 to intimidate people. Perhaps the best indicator of an improved environment for freedom of expression (item 5) in 1991 is that there was no violence, and that the government did not arrest anyone. To be sure there were threats of violence, particularly in the rural areas, but these appeared to be relatively minor.

Access to alternative sources of information (item 6) also improved. On a number of occasions during the 1961–63 period, *Tribuna* personnel suffered repression as well as imprisonment, and soldiers destroyed their equipment. In 1991 these types of repressive acts did not occur with the weekly *Tribuna* or with *Expresiones de San Luis*. In fact some government officials even wrote dissenting columns in *Expresiones*, something that did not occur in the opposition daily three decades ago.

The right to form and join political organizations, including parties and interest groups (item 7), has also improved. Nava pointed out that people were not as fearful of attending his rallies in the rural areas in 1991 as they were previously. Perhaps most impressive were the gatherings of intellectuals, journalists, and leaders of political parties to criticize the regime. In addition, Potosinans freely joined other organizations that had emerged to scrutinize electoral practices.

The second set of observations deals with the regime's patterns in recognizing opposition victories; one model applies to the mayoral level and another to the gubernatorial level. The recognition of an opposition candidate for mayor in 1958, 1982, and 1988 occurred when a new president was taking office. Perhaps this recognition arose from the transition period, during which the new president wants to send a message of increasing democratization. After the first few years of the sexenio, the regime typically denies recognition of mayoral candidates, as occurred with Pizzuto in 1985. The exception here is 1991, with the recognition of the PAN candidate, Leal Campos. This recognition may simply mean that the PRI had too many divisions after Zapata's forced resignation. Or perhaps the central government feared another Nava protest.

Another generalization for San Luis Potosí is that the regime has been reluctant to recognize opposition victories for two consecutive terms, except for the case just discussed in December 1991.[2] Here one could add that Nava's march to Mexico City and his December 12 advertisement suggesting additional protests if the vote were not respected could have influenced the central government not to interfere with the results.

The pattern of recognition at the gubernatorial level is different. In fact the regime has recognized the victories of only two opposition governors since the formation of the official party: Ernesto Ruffo in Baja California Norte, in 1989, and Francisco Barrio in Chihuahua, in 1992, both from the PAN. The PAN also has a third opposition governor, in Guanajuato (Carlos Medina Plascencia), who serves in an interim position after the controversial elections of 1991. However, President Salinas did overturn the results of the gubernatorial elections in Guanajuato and San Luis Potosí (and subsequently in Michoacán, as well). Of course critics argued that the regime simply bought some time, but one should note that this did not occur prior to 1991.

Analyses in an earlier period indicated that the opposition had to win overwhelmingly (by a margin of perhaps three to one) in order to receive recognition. Indeed two decades ago, Wilkie (1971:4) suggested that the opposition had actually won a presidential election if the PRI candidate received "less that about 70 percent" of the vote. In the mayoral elections of 1958 and 1982, the regime recognized Nava's victories when he won with substantial margins (94 and 74 percent, respectively). In 1988, however, Pizzuto won with only 55 percent of the vote. In 1991 Mario Leal Campos won with just over 50 percent. Consequently the vote margin is not as critical for recognition today as it was previously.

Finally, while the regime has made some improvements in the electoral arena in the past three decades, Mexico cannot enter the ranks of Latin American democracies unless certain remaining abuses are corrected. Some of the most flagrant include the use of enormous sums of public money for official candidates, the use of *acarreados* (people forced to attend rallies), the bias in the local media, the manipulation of voter-registration procedures as well as the vote, the lopsided PRI membership on electoral commissions, and the harassment of opposition administrations. All these and others simply guarantee the hegemony of the official party and will continue until the regime's leaders accept the need for electoral openness. Ultimately, that will only happen when the regime and the official party establish the conditions that may well result in their loss of control at the federal level. Until that happens, the transition to democracy in Mexico will be fraught with difficulties.

Notes

1. For greater detail on this movement, see Bezdek (1984), A. Borjas Benavente (1992), T. Calvillo (1986), A. Estrada (1963), M. Granados Chapa (1992), E. Márquez (1987), and C. Martínez Assad (1985).

2. There are a few municipalities, in states such as Michoacán, Baja, California, and Nuevo León, where the regime has recognized consecutive opposition administrations.

4

The 1992 Elections and the
Democratic Transition in Baja California

Tonatiuh Guillén López

With the local elections of 1989 in Baja California, in which an opposition party won a governorship for the first time in Mexico's modern history, the subject of the democratic transition of the political system began to be discussed more persistently in the nation's political and intellectual circles. The victory of the Partido Acción Nacional (PAN) and its candidate for governor, Ernesto Ruffo, as well as the explicit recognition of this victory by the PRI at the national level, were an encouraging sign of the democratic opening of the political system. Without transforming it in essence, the 1989 elections in Baja California marked the beginning of a new era for the political system, or at least showed signs of change. Even though those elections have not had substantial repercussions at the national level, their consequences on the local power structure have been major.

Since 1989 electoral policy has increasingly been the truly decisive policy in the configuration of power in Baja California. Given that its immediate precedents can be found in the 1988 presidential election, the subsequent electoral contests (1991 and 1992) developed under a set of conditions and in forms that were increasingly distant from the fear of fraud or postelectoral negotiations.[1] If we add the new instruments of the electoral processes to this scenario, such as the emergence of a state voter registration (*registro ciudadano estatal*), it can be estimated that electoral policy in Baja California has acquired a sophistication that is very probably unparalleled in the country up to now. The purpose of this argument is not to identify the democratic transition with the PAN, but rather to acknowledge that the chief form of the transition initiated in 1989 was concentrated around the PAN (which does not exclude the possibility of other parallel or subsequent forms of transition). At this point the axis of the democratic transition in Baja California continues to be supported in considerable measure by the effects of alternating power between the PRI and the PAN.

The democratic transition in Baja California has accomplished significant advances within its regional limits, but it is still a transition of fragile characteristics, lacking in institutionalization and broader significance. It is not the purpose of this chapter, however, to discuss the general aspects by which the democratic transition in Baja California has manifested itself. The central objective is to present the transition's components from the perspective of the 1992 local elections and to try to systematize from them the new practices that are detectable in the power relationships of the region. The presentation that follows, therefore, has two principal elements: one that corresponds to the institutional aspect of the electoral process, especially in relation to state voter registration and the indicators of the transition derived from it; and one that is electoral, in which indicators of the transition from the perspective of the Baja Californian electorate are sought, particularly in their relationship with the new panista bureaucracy.

Electoral Processes and Democratic Transition

The 1992 elections in Baja California were carried out within a population universe different from that of preceding elections, both in the state itself and in relation to the other states of the country. Unlike other local elections that have taken place in Mexico after the 1991 federal elections, in Baja California voter registration had a state electoral register as its foundation, modeled after the federal electoral register (*padrón federal electoral*). Thus if we try to compare the 1989 elections with those of 1992, the first consideration leads us to voter registration.

The political alternation in the state government and the relative control of the PAN over the local Baja California congress led to a revision of the federal electoral register. Up to then the sovereignty of the states with respect to voter registration had remained limited, due to the permanent character of the agreements between the federal and state governments, which determined that federal voter registration was to be that of the states as well. Considering that voter registration was the subject of some of the greater doubts and demands on the part of opposition parties, it is understandable that one of the initial objectives of Ernesto Ruffo's government was to put together an electoral register that was unobjectionable from both a technical and a political perspective. This goal, however, coincided temporarily with the building of a new federal electoral register to be used in the 1991 elections, which had objectives identical to those sought by the panista government of Baja California. Ruffo's move tacitly questioned the legitimacy of the new federal electoral register, which was designed to become a new parameter that would give more credibility to national electoral processes. Finally, after multiple negotiations, the difference was resolved, through a new agreement between the federal and state governments, under which Ruffo's administration would construct its state electoral register on the basis of citizens registered in the federal electoral register.[2]

It was under these circumstances that the federal electoral register was subject to a detailed revision by the state electoral register of Baja California, which constituted a novelty in the electoral history of the country, because of its form and its political magnitude and meaning. From the perspective of the relations between the federal and state governments, the agreement can also be evaluated as a notable example of a new space created in the federalist project of the nation, which is constantly truncated by centralist administrative practices. In this respect, at least, the relationship between the federal government and the government of Baja California took a new direction, which did away with the intergovernmental vertical alignments that the federal government has constantly maintained.[3] In a parallel manner, the result was the generation of an electoral register with characteristics that gave greater credibility and which was used for the first time in 1992, during the first elections organized by a state government of the opposition.

Given that among the original elements of the Baja California state electoral register was that of issuing voters photo identification cards, together with a system for identifying citizens at the time of voting, only those citizens who were present in the state had the opportunity to be entered on the state electoral register. This is of great relevance to a state such as Baja California, given its intense migration dynamics. It is not strange, therefore, that important quantitative differences exist between the federal and state electoral registers, which have since become the subject of political dispute. During the 1992 elections, these differences were already controversial, and it is foreseeable that they will remain a source of tension between the state and federal governments at least until 1994. In 1992, contrary to custom, the PRI was the party making demands of state electoral institutions. According to the PRI, the number of citizens registered with the Federal Electoral Institute in 1992 amounted to 993,000, and they claimed that out of that total, 174,000 did not obtain their identification card and were therefore not able to vote. This argument raised suspicions about a policy of selective registration favorable to the

PAN.[4] But according to the state electoral register, it is possible that those missing voters were no longer in the state, which would explain why on the day of the election only 806,000 people were accounted for.[5]

From the perspective of the democratic transition of both Baja California and the country as a whole, the events described emphasize the complexity and the enormous difficulty of building new social and institutional practices in connection with electoral policy. As a starting point, we can observe in the Baja California experience the emergence of new instruments such as the federal voter registration and especially that of the state (which technically has no precedent and is superior to the federal one, although the latter already contained more rigorous elements of control). Notwithstanding the originality of the new processes, in a strict sense they have not replaced the internal structure of previous political organizations and institutions, but rather have added a new dimension to them. From this perspective it can be argued that the democratic transition in Baja California constitutes a process that, if it has not left the older structures intact, neither does it have the capability to replace them with radically new structures. This concept of addition rather than substitution comes from the knowledge that, like all transitions, that in Baja California arose from the structures of existing organizations and institutions, with the resources and the potential for change contained in them, in addition to finding itself confined by regional limits imposed by the national political system. As illustrated in the case of the state electoral register, the new institutional practices are in an initial phase; their consolidation depends on the potential for continuity of the elements that motivate this change, which for the time being basically means that the governorship must remain under the control of the PAN.

With the new practices, all the state's political actors (as well as all those other individuals who have something to do with the state's politics) are in the process of readjusting. Even in those cases where the structures have been most altered, due to the alternation of power in state government, such as in the case of the PRI in Baja California, we can observe that the difficulties they find in reconstituting themselves internally reflects a strong tendency to reproduce their preceding structure. The PAN itself is an analogous case; the simultaneous occurrence of previous tendencies and new social practices has translated into strong internal tensions, which in turn have extended to the relationship of the party with the municipal governments administered by the PAN as well as with the state government. In fact no actor in state politics can be found hanging back at the margin of the new elements that make up their political space, and this includes the federal government, which would normally position itself as an outside actor. Each of these organizations and institutions reflects the strong tendency to repeat their previous structure, trying at the same time to assimilate into it the new elements that generated the dramatic change of 1989. In some cases adapting to the new dynamics can be a conflict with no solution (for example when there is no possibility for reproducing the previous conditions), such as appears to be the case of the PRI; in other cases adaptation might be less conflictual.

In this manner the democratic transition in Baja California appears to be an external process. For whom is it internal, then? What structure can be claimed to be new, in a strict sense? It seems that it is the web of relationships between the actors (political institutions and organizations and the citizenry in relation to each of the previous two) that has ultimately been the object of major change. The decisive axis that used to define the regional power hierarchies was centered in the connection between the state government and the official party, the PRI. The simple arrival of Ruffo as governor of the state broke up that informal but effective relationship, and undoubtedly modified both parties. For the PRI that "external" change was, in the end, "internal," and even though one of its immediate consequences was not the disappearance of the party and its organizations, it did suddenly cast it into virtual anomie.[6] In the 1989 elections, with the defeat in the governor's race, the PRI also lost the central axis of its internal structure and, as a result, its external connections as well.

On the other hand, as this state of anomie profoundly altered the internal dynamics of the PRI, the fact that it has been an organization of organizations is precisely what has allowed it to survive under the new conditions imposed since 1989. The anomie of the party does not translate to anomie of the organizations, especially in the case of those whose existence is not strictly tied to the party (such as the workers' unions, which have remained virtually untouched). In this fashion the PRI can continue to be supported by its organizations and, at the same time, to appear to be a party similar to what it once was. The vertical and hierarchical channels by which the party dictated the positions and relationships among groups and organizations, as well as the quotas and internal disputes among them, including mutual pressures and threats, made sense for the PRI in a context within which electoral issues were of secondary importance. However, notwithstanding the weakening of the PRI as an organization since 1989, it has still managed to maintain its electoral appeal.[7]

This paradox illustrates three connected processes. First, that the PRI's organizations are enormously fragile with respect to its electoral appeal. Second, that the determinants of electoral policy, from the perspective of the voters of the state, essentially occur independently of the internal life of the political parties. Third, also from the perspective of the citizens, that the PRI has not been completely dismissed as a voting option. In this sense the democratic transition is determined by the voters themselves and does not exclude the PRI as a legitimate option. As will be described below, the relationship of the PRI with the electorate was much stronger in 1992 than in 1989.

The 1992 Elections and the Democratic Transition

In the elections of 1989, the PAN won the governorship, nine out of fifteen local deputyships, and two out of four municipalities.[8] In 1992 the deputyships and the municipalities came up for election again, offering the citizens of Baja California the opportunity to evaluate the first three years of a new governmental experience. As will be detailed later, if an evaluation of the PAN's victories in the 1992 elections is made, the result is not a negative one; it now has three municipalities and only one deputyship less. For our purposes, however, what we are interested in evaluating is the relationship of the electorate with the PAN, as it serves as an indicator of the democratic transition initiated in 1989. If the alternation in power is the cornerstone of this transition, then what must be evaluated is its capacity for reproduction in an increasingly open electoral atmosphere.

The 1992 results provided the PAN with a minimal advantage for preserving the results of 1989, especially in the municipio of Tijuana, which has the largest population in the state.[9] The state appears to be divided into areas that are supportive of the PAN and others that are supportive of the PRI, which is clearly related to the PAN's presence in the municipalities. Where there were previously panista municipal governments, the proportion of votes for the PAN decreased significantly, whereas the proportions of the PRI increased (in Tijuana and Ensenada). Where the municipal governments used to be priístas (Tecate and Mexicali), the relative position of the PAN improved. It seems, therefore, that in 1992 the social atmosphere of the democratic transition considered the state government to be of secondary importance as an electoral criteria, and consequently focused all of its attention on the muncipalities. Based on that, we can construct the following hypothetical scenario. These voters who had already experienced the alternation of power reduced its value as a political project, thereby making a much more calculated evaluation of their local bureaucracy (the PAN). On the other hand, those voters who did not yet have this alternation in their locale saw it as politically valuable, and caused the PAN to appear in a form and with a strength equivalent (though not identical) to that of 1989.

In consequence, the division of the state along partisan lines precludes arguing in favor of uniformity in the citizenry's evaluation of the PAN. It could be said that the position of the PAN is weak in strategic terms, that is, in those places where it is present in municipal governments and where it obtained the most support in 1989. The relative improvement it has shown in places like Mexicali probably reflects power alternation as a goal of certain urban sectors, rather than the effect of a direct interaction, as are the cases of Tijuana and Ensenada. Some details follow.

One issue that stands out among the new elements of the democratic transition in Baja California is the people's participation in elections. Between 1989 and 1992, the percentage of statewide participation increased from 50.1 percent to 80.0 percent, which is somewhat of a paradox, considering that social mobilization was much more evident in the first year. Most probably the people's interest in the elections did in fact increase, but it seems likely that the precision of the new voter registration, especially at the state level, was more decisive in that increase. In absolute terms the number of voters increased from 442,371 to 645,316, or by almost 50 percent.

But beyond the change in the voter universe and effective participation, the more relevant data relate to the recomposition of the electorate's preferences. In the 1989 municipal elections, the PAN defeated the PRI with a percentage of 45.2 to 31.8 in Tijuana. In 1992 the PAN won the mayorship again, but this time the difference was much narrower: 46.5 percent for the PAN, 44.1 percent for the PRI. If we observe this same result in terms of the increase in the number of voters each party shows in relation to 1989 (due to newly registered individuals), the recomposition of the electorate's preferences becomes more evident. The PAN increased its votes by 68.1 percent, while the PRI increased its share by 126.9 percent. In the elections for deputies in Tijuana, the six districts were won by the PAN, but only with minimal differences in most of them. In District VIII, for example, where the PAN had won in 1989 with a percentage of 40.8 to 28.3 for the PRI, in 1992 the proportions were 46.8 percent for the PAN and 46.1 percent for the PRI.[10] In the other districts the competition was similar, but still favoring the PAN: District IX, 47.9 percent PAN and 45.1 percent PRI; District X, 47.3 percent PAN and 46.1 percent PRI; District XI, 53.8 percent PAN and 37.8 percent PRI; District XII, 46.9 percent PAN and 45.1 percent PRI; District XIII, 43.3 percent PAN and 42.8 percent PRI.[11]

Although to a lesser degree than in Tijuana, the other complex situation for the PAN was the municipio of Ensenada, where the advantage of 1989 also declined in 1992, and where the increase in the number of voters also favored the PRI to a greater extent than the PAN.[12] With respect to the election of the two municipal deputies, the district corresponding to the rural area (XV) was kept by the PRI, while the PAN kept the urban district (XIV). The PRI improved its relative position in both districts, while the PAN gained only in District XV.

In the other two municipalities of the state, Tecate and Mexicali, the PAN increased its number of votes with respect to 1989. In the case of Tecate it was a very small increase, but still enough to gain the mayorship, whereas in Mexicali its relative position improved, while the mayorship remained in the hands of the PRI.[13] However, this last case represented the most significant percentage increase in the number of votes obtained by the PAN in the state, compared to those obtained by the PRI: 58.9 percent to 25.1 percent, respectively. Of the six possible deputyships in Mexicali, the PAN won only an urban one, District III.

The results of the 1992 election thus confirm another of the forms in which the democratic transition has expressed itself in the state—the tendency toward bipartisanship. The increase in the number of voters for the PAN and the PRI virtually absorbs all of the state's electorate, thus making the smaller parties a less likely option. Moreover, the loss of state registration by the PPS, the PFCRN, and the PARM, due to their failure to obtain the minimum percent 1.5 of the vote required, must be taken into account in evaluating the election results. With this loss of registration, the PRI lost some of its historic allies, fundamental for legitimizing decisions in the state congress and in the electoral institutions. For now the resulting scenario is very favorable to the PRD, which, with a minimum of votes (3.3 percent of the total), was awarded the four minority deputyships of the state congress. Eight majority deputyships went to the PAN and seven to the PRI, leaving the PRD in a very privileged negotiating situation, which could potentially result in more social recognition and, to that extent, could lessen the strong polarization of the electorate between the major parties.

Toward a New State of Democratic Transition

The 1992 local elections in Baja California can be characterized by the initiation in that state of a new stage of competitiveness with minimal differences, in which even minor mistakes can have major consequences. The electoral campaigns, in a strict sense, have become a struggle in which every citizen is sought after and in which the inclusion in the electoral register of each individual is of the utmost importance, as is the performance of electoral procedures. The campaigns of all parties and their articulation around the objective of constructing an attractive offer to the people constitute encouraging signs of the growing relevance of electoral policy, leaving behind a time when the internal policy of the PRI acted as the most important determinant in the balance of regional power. In this fashion political reality in Baja California has begun to demand more open electoral practices, with no restrictions of information and highly technical procedures, especially regarding vote counts at the polling places and in the municipal electoral districts and committees.

The policy of minimizing procedural differences has also been followed by candidates in the government plans of their campaign platforms. The PRD did not even attempt to individualize its political proposal, which in principle should be distant from that of the PRI and of the PAN. During the 1992 campaigns, the contenders did not put much effort into distinguishing themselves from one another; instead they all tried to present themselves as middle-of-the-road liberals. In this manner what has been presented in this chapter—the alternation in power and its relation to the democratic transition—appears to be less relevant to the voters of Baja California. The PRI can thus appear as a valid option and not as excluding a new level of democracy.

But as long as government institutions are not transformed, especially electoral insitutions, the actors in governmental positions will be able to exercise democracy more on a discretionary basis than as an inevitable result of pragmatic changes. Political alternation in Baja California has undoubtedly left its mark on political insitutions and organizations, especially the major parties, and has generated elements that will become part of future democratic structures; but it is important to point out that those elements have not yet constituted that structure. To begin with, the state institutions responsible for the electoral processes continue to be the same ones as before and maintain their policy virtually intact; establishing the state electoral register has been significant, but not sufficient. Institutional reform has only just begun.

Finally, the experience of the 1992 local elections in Baja California indicates that political alternation, considered as the principal mechanism the democratic transition has adopted, is a process questioned by the voters of the state themselves. However, this is a result that apparently connects two different levels of the regional political process. It could hardly be argued that by reproaching the panista bureaucracy through their votes, the voters intended to cancel their newfound political openness (especially in the municipio of Tijuana, which carries so much weight in the profile of the state). Nonetheless the political effect leads to that consequence, which of course does not equal the end of the democratic transition itself.

Notes

1. Cuauhtémoc Cárdenas, the candidate of the FDN, gained more votes than the PRI candidate, Carlos Salinas, or the PAN candidate, Manuel Clouthier.

2. *La Voz de la Frontera,* April 5, 1991.

3. Another delicate subject of negotiation between the federal government and the government of Baja California was the agreement concerning fiscal coordination, which determined the amounts of federal contributions to the state. Obviously the state government demanded more money from the federal government.

4. Public denouncement of the State Directive Committee of the PRI in Baja California, published in the state and national presses just days before the elections. Taken from *Diario 29,* July 27, 1992.

5. Since 1990 Mexico's voter registration has acquired a great complexity, which has had quantitative repercussions in the voter universe. With respect to the federal register, there is a first universe of citizens of eighteen years and older, commonly called catalogados ("catalogued"), which is filtered down later to those who formally request their voter identification card, called *empadronados* (those incorporated into the register), who in turn filter down again to those who actually do obtain their identification card and appear in the final voting lists. In Baja California the process of building the state electoral register begins with those incorporated into the federal electoral register, who in turn have to request their inclusion in the state registry and their photo identification card, in order to appear later in the voting lists on the day of elections. In this series of procedures, it is inevitable that important quantitative differences arise between the first and the last steps.

6. Even though the party's corporate structure and the organizations that mainly depended on their relationship with the state (especially the urban popular organizations) were dismantled, other organizations, such as those of the trade unions and peasants, were virtually unaffected, because their existence did not depend so entirely on the state government.

7. The internal weakening of the PRI in Baja California would have critical consequences for its reproduction, if it depended exclusively on local resources,

especially financial ones. The direct intervention of the National Executive Committee of the PRI and of its economic resources effectively makes up for local weaknesses brought about by the state of internal anomie.

8. Notwithstanding the results, the PAN did not gain control of the state congress, due to the presence of four minority deputies from the smaller parties, the PPS, PRD, PFCRN, and PARM.

9. According to the 1990 census data, 45 percent of the state's population of 1,660,855 resided in the municipio of Tijuana. The remaining municipalities show the following population percentages: Mexicali, 36.2 percent; Ensenada, 15.7 percent; Tecate, 3.1 percent. INEGI, 1990.

10. In real numbers, the difference was only 282 votes out of the 54,513 cast in that district.

11. The wide difference in District XI can be explained by the qualities of the PRI's candidate, an old militant with a rather negative public image.

12. The proportion of votes in 1989 for the PAN and the PRI were 51.1 percent and 35.0 percent, respectively; in 1992 they were 48.4 percent and 40.4 percent. The increase in the number of voters between 1989 and 1992 was 27.7 percent for the PAN and 55.5 percent for the PRI.

13. The proportion of its votes increased minimally, from 45.2 percent to 45.5 percent, while that of the PRI decreased from 45.4 percent to 43.1 percent. There is only one deputyship from Tecate, and it was won again by the PRI, also with only a minimal difference.

Part Two

Bases of Support for the Opposition

5

The PAN's Social Bases

Implications for Leadership

Roderic Ai Camp

The political mythology about the National Action Party (PAN), and about conservative parties generally, is that their leadership can be traced to upper-class origins. The social origins of a politician are significant, so the argument goes, because it offers some insight into their policy preferences, it links them more closely to other leadership groups, it affects their recruitment patterns, and it influences their proximity to various constituencies. This chapter examines the social origins of the PAN and explores some of the potential consequences for its leaders. Some significant linkages between social origins and other background variables are also developed. Comparisons are drawn between the National Action Party's leaders and those representing the established, government elite.

Introduction

An analysis of national panista leaders reveals many characteristics of local political leadership, more so than is the case for the PRI, because panistas have, to a greater extent than the establishment leadership, come from careers at the state and local levels. The reason for this is simple. As of 1992 only three members of the PAN had ever obtained nationally significant executive posts, as state governors (Baja California, 1989; Guanajuato, 1991; and Chihuahua in 1992).

Assuming that popular assessments of the PAN's leadership are true, several hypotheses may be offered. Some evidence exists to support the contention that a politician's social origins affect their values and beliefs and consequently would have some impact on their policy decisions. Although it has been established that this variable alone is insufficient to affect the outcome of the decision-making process, there is no question that social origins do affect the political beliefs of various groups (Searing

1969:471–500). Thus it can be hypothesized (hypothesis one) that the political platform of the PAN reflects the social origins of its leadership; given the panistas' alleged upper-class origins, their ideology should favor the wealthy classes and business groups.

Social scientists have also been intrigued with the social background of politicians because of their focus on leadership composition. The makeup of leadership groups, including social origins, sheds considerable light on the openness of the recruitment process and the fluidity of leadership channels (Meisel 1962). The higher the social origins of a party's leadership, given the fact that upper-class origins in most societies (including Mexico) account for only a small percentage of citizens, the narrower the recruitment pool.

Typically political analysts have been intrigued by this variable's potential to alter the stability of a political system by placing a lid on upward mobility in the public sector. Although the PAN is an opposition party in a system where the establishment leadership largely dominates the executive and legislative branches of government, indirectly the same question applies. In other words, to what degree does the opposition, as distinct from the government leadership, offer a channel for upward social mobility? It can be hypothesized (hypothesis two), again assuming the accuracy of the earlier assumptions about the PAN leadership's social origins, that they further restrict the pool of eligible leaders in Mexico. It could be argued, however, that if the establishment leadership ignores middle- and upper-class recruits, then the PAN actually opens up this channel to another, unrepresented group.

A third assumption about the social origins of a leadership group is that all elites (economic, social, military, religious, and political) share similar backgrounds. Individuals from shared social backgrounds develop close ties with one another, providing them with the crucial links necessary to rise up the ladder of their various professions and to collaborate in the governing process. This explanation is tied to C. Wright Mills's classic theories about the existence of a power elite, elaborated in the work of Thomas Dye and others (Dye 1990). There is a conventional wisdom in Mexico that asserts close ties between the panista leadership and the Mexican business and Catholic elite. Therefore a third hypothesis is that panista leaders are closely linked in terms of social origins and through fictive and kinship ties with prominent clergy and businessmen. Within the wider Latin American context, it would also be argued that a strong linkage might exist with the officer corps, a third pillar often tied to conservative political movements.

Finally, some analysts point to the significance of mass-elite relationships as a significant variable in political development (Putnam 1976:134 ff.). One of the potential determinants of the closeness of this relationship is the leadership's representativeness vis-à-vis society generally. The implication of this argument is that not only will a socially elite leadership ignore rural and urban working-class interests, but that these groups in turn will not identify with a party whose leaders' social origins are so different from their own.

A potential consequence of this relationship between leaders and masses, if it exists, is that it limits the growth of the party to groups who identify with their leadership's social origins. Therefore a fourth hypothesis can be offered. Since panista leaders allegedly come from upper-class backgrounds and are identified in the popular minds with upper-class interests, they will receive the support of similar groups, to the exclusion of other, larger voting constituencies.

The following analysis of the social origins of the PAN is based on an examination of collective biographical data on 2,002 Mexican politicians who have held nationally important offices in all branches of government, including as state governors, from 1934 through 1991. Of these politicians 101 are members of the National Action Party, a sample that includes more than half of all panistas reaching such high-level offices. It is important to reiterate at this point, however, that the panista leaders comprise almost exclusively those whose career tracks have been in the legislative branches of government—primarily state and federal deputies. As Rodríguez and Ward point out in their introduction to this volume, there are also an increasing number of panista leaders who have held executive positions, albeit at the municipal level. Some of these local government officials are discussed in detail in other chapters, and if Ward's description of the backgrounds from which panista municipal officers are drawn is widely replicated elsewhere, then it may mean that there are significant differences of background between the PAN's national political leadership and those who serve in municipal and state governments.

The Social and Class Backgrounds of *Panista* Leaders

How does the popular mythology about panista leaders square with the reality? The most obvious point in the data presented in table 5.1 is that the PAN's leaders do indeed overwhelmingly come from middle- and upper-class social origins. On the other hand, so do members of the

Table 5.1: Socioeconomic backgrounds of national politicians
from the PAN

	Leadership Group (%)	
Parents' Socioeconomic Status	PAN	PRI
Middle and Upper Class	85	70
Working Class	15	30
Totals	100	100

establishment party and other national politicians. The figures indicate
that 70 percent of the government and the Institutional Revolutionary
Party's (PRI) leadership share the same origins with leaders from the
PAN. Although 85 percent of the PAN's leaders come from similar
backgrounds, a figure 20 percent higher than that for the priístas, it
can be argued that the PRI sample represents a somewhat older group
of leaders, at a time when working-class backgrounds were better
represented among the political leadership. In other words, the PAN
did not obtain any number of significant offices until the 1950s, at a
time when the middle classes accounted for a larger percentage of the
total population. Also, the tripartite corporatist structure of the PRI
(consisting of the CNC, CTM, and what used to be the CNOP) has
offered a structure through which working-class leaders may rise to
prominent national and executive positions.

An additional argument exaggerating the importance of higher social
origins among panistas than among government leaders can be offered.
Remembering that more than 98 percent of the PAN's leaders have held
posts in the senate or chamber of deputies, the 85 percent figure for middle-
and upper-class backgrounds would be substantially higher than the figure
for all members of the PRI who have served only in this branch of
government. Differences are sharper when confined to the same political-
career paths, and the social origins of PRI members better represent their
legislative districts than do those of members of the PAN.

Nevertheless, there is no disputing the fact that most Mexican political
leaders are from the middle and upper classes, and that the PAN's
leadership, as an alternative to establishment politicians, offers little
variation from this norm. Indeed if one compensates for the age of the
two groups, the PAN narrows the social origins of Mexican politicians
compared to the PRI's leadership. In fact in the last two administrations,
85 percent of top politicians were from these same social origins.

As far as theories on social stability and elite leadership are concerned, the PAN is not providing an alternative to the PRI; if anything, it is contributing to the increasing distortion of Mexican political leadership's social origins compared to those of the population generally. By the 1970s a generous estimate of the middle classes put their numbers at 30 percent of the population, a figure that declined by one-quarter with the advent of the economic crises in Mexico after 1980 (Weintraub 1990:36).

It is important to point out that the social origins of both panistas and priístas are middle and upper-middle class, not upper class. Fewer than 5 percent of their parents could be characterized as upper class, suggesting the small role that group plays in producing future Mexican political leadership generally, and panista leadership specifically.

Family Backgrounds and Links With the Past

Of course social origins measured by class alone are not the only variable worth examining. Often more specific characteristics within class origins can suggest other distinctions. A characteristic related to upward social mobility obscured in social origins is father's occupation, specifically whether the father held a high-level position in politics or the military. A youngster with political ambitions whose father held such a job would be in an advantageous position to pursue such career goals, given certain features of the Mexican political process. One would expect that successful establishment politicians, having long dominated Mexican politics, would have politically active parents to a much greater degree than any opposition-party members.

Surprisingly, almost no difference exists between national-level panista politicians and establishment politicians when comparing fathers' political connections. Among both sets of politicians, only one in ten could count on a prominent political or military father to assist their careers. Even though establishment politicians have had access to such offices for longer periods of time, older panista figures have given their children similar opportunities. Between 1939 and 1992, examples of father-son (or father-daughter) political ties were typical between the founding generation and their children. Illustrative of this at the highest levels of the PAN is Manuel Gómez Morín, cofounder and president of the national executive committee of the party between 1939 and 1949, and the father of Juan Manuel Gómez Morín Torres, who joined the youth section of the PAN in 1939, at fifteen years old, undoubtedly because of his father's role in the party's organization. He eventually served as secretary general of the national executive committee.

If the scope of the panista leaders' family connections are expanded beyond that of their fathers, a substantial difference in family background compared with those of the PRI emerges. If nuclear family and fictive and kinship ties, including aunts and uncles, nieces and nephews, and in-laws are included, then family ties among establishment politicians become much more prevalent than those found among the PAN's leaders. Slightly more than one out of four (27 percent) government officials count such familial ties in their social origins, which is true for only 19 percent of panista leaders. Although future PAN members may use family ties to promote their political careers, those ties are less well developed than similar links among government officials. Also, were it possible to extend the analysis to include larger numbers of panista leaders in executive government positions, then I suspect that the significance of family connections emanating from within the PAN would be even less marked. As Mizrahi and Ward both show in their respective chapters, many of these officials have come from the private-business sector.

Political analysts interested in the social origins of politicians have also been intrigued by the ideological origins of their families, origins that may suggest long-term social influences, although not exclusively. In Mexico, which underwent a major social revolution from 1910 to 1920, the persistence of important prerevolutionary elites and revolutionary elites have been the most interesting sources of influence. Establishment leaders in Mexico claim strong ties to the revolution, identifying themselves as the "true" inheritors of revolutionary ideology. Critics of the PAN, on the other hand, allude to their leaders and their values as associated with the interests of Porfirian families, who were opposed to the revolution.

If the family ties of panista members and those of other politicians are traced to these two historic groups, the differences are intriguing. Generally speaking, neither group has significant ties to either set of families. However, a substantial difference does exist between the nature of their linkages to these two historic groups (table 5.2). Twice as many PAN politicians are tied to important Porfirian families as are establishment leaders. Although members of the postrevolutionary government might have tried to obscure or hide such ties, given the rhetoric of these administrations, it is doubtful that this alone would explain the disparity. At the same time, although politicians' ties to prominent revolutionary families are even fewer, only one-third as many panistas were found to have such ties, compared to their establishment peers.

Table 5.2: PAN leadership connections to important families

Relation to Family	Leadership Group (%)	
	PAN	PRI
Porfirian	7	3
Revolutionary	1	3
Both	1	.4
Totals	11	6.4

The implications of these findings are twofold. In the first place, the PAN does provide some representation, at least in terms of social origins, for a group of people who were temporarily disenfranchised by the 1910 revolution, thus establishing a thread from the Porfirian era to the present. In that sense panista leaders added to the diversity of social origins represented among Mexico's national leadership after 1935. On the other hand, some evidence exists to support the charges that the PAN, based on social origins alone, represents a reactionary or antirevolutionary constituency. Too much should not be made of this, however, given the fact that, as table 2 demonstrates, only a mere 7 percent of panistas had such ties and that social origins extending back two generations may have little relevance to the values or social interests of the present leadership generation.

Social, Educational, Religious, and Regional Provenance of Party Leaders

The relationship between the social origins of a political party's leaders and citizens' perceptions about the party's interest in their affairs can be linked somewhat in an analysis of voter sympathies for the various parties. The data in table 5.3 are quite revealing. In the first place, the PRI obtains most of its support from middle- and upper-class voters. On the other hand, the Democratic Revolutionary Party (PRD), which offers a populist, state-led economic platform and is identified as a left-of-center party in the Mexican arena, captures the sympathy of primarily lower- and middle-income voters. As the data in table 3 suggest, the PAN's support is weak among the working class, who give it the least support among the three parties, but strong among upper-income voters. Although these voters

Table 5.3: Mexican partisan sympathies by socioeconomic status

Sympathy for	Voter Income Level (%)			National Totals
	High	Middle	Low	
PRI	44	38	26	31.4
PAN	21	13	12	13.1
PRD	5	16	17	15.5
Other	3	3	3	3.2
None	21	23	32	28.1
Don't Know	4	5	7	6.4
No Answer	1	1	2	2.2
Totals	99	99	99	99.9

Source: Los Angeles Times poll, August 1989, courtesy of Miguel Basáñez, in Roderic Ai Camp, Politics in Mexico (New York: Oxford University Press, 1993), table 4-3.
Note: Totals do not add up to 100 percent, due to rounding.

are not as likely to vote for the PAN as the PRI, suggesting they see the latter as better able to preserve and enhance their economic interests, upper-income voters make up a larger percentage of panista supporters than they do for the other two parties. Although the PAN leadership is middle and upper-middle class, voters perceive it as representative of upper-class interests, casting their votes accordingly (see also Guillén López, 1987a).[1]

Social origins have also been used to allege class control over various sectors of a society, including linkages leading to decision making by a "power elite." In Mexico evidence of a power elite is tenuous at best. Power is exercised by a diverse and unconnected leadership. Nevertheless some leaders have more extensive ties to various elites than others. Ties among the Mexican political, intellectual, and business communities have been alleged; in fact these ties are quite minimal. Only 5 percent of top government officials have known familial ties to intellectuals and leading businessmen. Among panista leaders, however, those ties are small in number but proportionately much more extensive than among their government peers. In the case of businessmen, 7 percent of panistas have such ties and 6 percent are related to prominent intellectuals. This is nearly three times the figure for government leaders. These numbers provide some evidence to support, in the popular mind, an alleged relationship between the business community and the PAN. Once again if the overlap

Table 5.4: Urban and rural origins of national PAN leaders

Place of Birth	Leadership Group (%)	
	PAN	PRI
Urban	83.5	68.7
Rural	16.5	31.3
Totals	100.0	100.0

in social relations described by Mizrahi and Ward for panista municipal officers and the business and commercial sectors are repeated elsewhere in the country, then this relationship is likely to emerge even more significantly than it appears in my data.

The PAN's ties to business can be further tested by examining the careers of its politicians before they entered politics. Although many government officials also pursued other careers before entering politics, most did so in the professions, as practicing lawyers, economists, physicians, etc. Panistas, on the other hand, were much more likely to have worked for the private sector, especially at the management level, before embarking on public careers. For example, 14 percent of panista leaders held business-management posts prior to their first national political office, compared to only 5 percent of all establishment government officials. Thus the social origins of political leaders definitively influence many other variables, and are intertwined with place of birth, region of birth, and level, type, and place of education. These background variables in turn influence ties among politicians, career choices, and linkages to other groups.

Any study of Mexican leadership groups discovers that top Mexicans from all stripes come overwhelmingly from urban backgrounds. Politicians are no exception. Since 1935, when urban settings (at least five thousand people) accounted for nearly half of all politicians' birthplaces, that figure has risen to 94 percent of Salinas' first-time national office holders. For the entire period, as the data in table 5.4 suggest, slightly more than two-thirds of establishment politicians have come from urban backgrounds.

Among panistas the figures are even higher; in fact they correspond closely to the percentages for middle- and upper-class social backgrounds. This is not surprising, given the location of the PAN's support among the electorate. As a district-by-district analysis suggests, the PAN receives most of its support from urban centers, generally large cities—including the

Table 5.5: Origins of national PAN leadership

Region of Birth	Leadership Group (%)	
	PAN	PRI
Federal District	29	18
East Central	11	15
West	17	15
North	18	15
South	4	9
Gulf	7	13
West Central	12	13
Foreign	1	1
Totals	99	99

capital, the urban sprawl extending from Mexico City into the state of México, and many major cities in the states of Yucatán, Guanajuato, Jalisco, Nuevo León, Chihuahua, Sonora, Baja California, and Sinaloa (Camp 1991a:110–11).

These figures are perhaps more disconcerting for their implications for political-stability theory than for what they tell us about the relationship between the PAN's leadership and the average voter. Panista politicians do not alleviate the sharp trend toward eliminating rural-born politicians altogether from Mexican leadership posts. In this sense the PAN does not enhance the diversity of backgrounds among national political leaders, because they are in general overwhelmingly urban in origin.

The PAN's strength is local and regional, and therefore a regional bias exists in the composition of the national leadership. Although the Federal District has always been overly represented in the backgrounds of Mexican politicians, it is even more strongly represented among panistas, who have historically done well in Mexico City. Other PAN strongholds have been in the north and west, also indicated in the leadership's composition (table 5.5).

A strong relationship also exists among social origins, urban birthplace, and education. The increasing importance of educational credentials only ensures the spread of middle- and upper-class social origins and urban birthplaces among political figures. Those families with these origins are the ones most likely to obtain the educational credentials necessary to make them competitive with other potential politicians and with the establishment political leadership. Therefore opposition politicians from

Table 5.6: Educational levels of national PAN leaders

	Political Group (%)	
Level of Education	PAN	PRI
Primary	4	7
Secondary	6	6
Normal	3	6
Preparatory	13	6
University	55	49
Postprofessional	3	7
M.A., Ph.D., LL.D.	18	19
Totals	102	100

Note: Totals do not add up to 100 percent, due to rounding.

the PAN are no exception to the general educational trends among Mexican politicians (table 5.6). Three-quarters of them have been college educated, one-fifth beyond a bachelors or professional degree. These figures correspond quite closely to the educational levels for Mexico's establishment political leadership. The PAN's leaders are slightly better educated, reflecting their slight advantage in middle- and upper-class social origins.

As has been shown in earlier works, education plays a substantial role in the Mexican recruitment process. Those obtaining a college education make the contacts necessary to rise up the political ladder. Higher education and political recruitment have been intimately intertwined in Mexican politics. Interestingly, members of the PAN do not deviate from this norm, establishing different types of recruitment channels. They too use the university system; what is interesting about the linkage between educational backgrounds and panista channels of upward political mobility, however, is the difference in where that education occurs. The PAN's leaders, because of some differences in social origins, have attended private institutions, specifically religious-affiliated institutions, in numbers greater than their establishment peers. This pattern begins at a young age. Among those panista leaders whose early education is known, more than half (59 percent) attended private primary or secondary school. Fewer than half as many establishment leaders attended such schools. This experience distinguishes the PRI and the PAN leaders more than almost any other background variable.

As panista leaders pursue their educations, these patterns become less pronounced. Nearly the same percentage of PAN as PRI leaders (42 and

45 percent, respectively) have attended the country's largest institution, the National Autonomous University of Mexico (UNAM). Roughly the same number (25 percent) attended public, provincial universities. However, fewer than half as many establishment politicians (4 percent) graduated from private schools as did panista leaders (11 percent). Especially among younger panista graduates, the Iberoamericana and La Salle universities (both with strong religious affiliations) have been increasingly important. But recent government officials from the PRI have also attended private colleges and universities in larger numbers.

Perhaps more important to understanding their social bases and their linkage to other groups is the direction of politicians' education. What is most striking about the educational backgrounds among panistas is the omission of economists: not one PAN leader in my sample graduated with a degree in economics. Not surprisingly, three times as many panistas as PRI government officials graduated as certified public accountants, indicating a business orientation. They were most frequently educated in law (40 percent), medicine (9 percent), and engineering (8 percent), the same three traditional fields providing members of the PRI.

What explains the lack of interest among future PAN leaders for economics? And particularly at a time when the establishment leadership has been overtaken by this field, to the extent that the number of economists for the first time equals that of lawyers among younger government officials. It is explained partly by the fact that historically the most important economics department, the National School of Economics (which trained President Salinas) was for some time strongly influenced by Marxist ideology. And many panistas obtained degrees in business administration and certified public accounting, emphasizing the practical over the theoretical.

Among the variables important to a comprehensive understanding of a group's social origins is religion. In Mexico, however, it is not a question of one religion versus another, but rather of the intensity of Catholic beliefs, that distinguishes the population. Some analysts have alleged strong ties between the PAN and the Catholic church. Yet the most careful study of the party, by Donald Mabry, found no evidence of the party representing church interests, even though its platform was strongly flavored by Catholic social doctrine (Mabry 1973:110). It is true, however, that a number of prominent leaders in the early history of the party were members of Catholic lay organizations or youth groups, a feature highly atypical of PRI government leaders.

Table 5.7: Mexican partisan sympathies by religion

Sympathy for	Religion (%)			
	Catholics	Protestants	None	All Religions
None	27.5	35.1	28.2	27.9
Strong PAN	5.2	5.2	7.7	5.2
PAN	8.2	2.6	2.6	7.8
Strong PRD	6.6	10.4	12.8	7.0
PRD	8.4	9.1	7.7	8.5
Strong PRI	16.8	9.1	10.3	16.2
PRI	14.9	18.2	10.3	15.0
Other	3.2	1.3	5.1	3.2
No Answer	8.9	9.1	15.4	9.1
Totals	99.9	100.0	100.0	100.0

Source: Los Angeles Times poll, August 1989, courtesy of Miguel Basáñez, in Roderic Ai Camp, Politics in Mexico (New York: Oxford University Press, 1993), table 4–10, p. 85.

Younger panista leaders have secular career experiences, and although they are more likely to be practicing Catholics than are many of their establishment political peers, no longer are they activists in Catholic lay organizations. Despite the mythology about the linkage between the church and the panista leadership, the party's popularity is unaffected by a voter's religious background (table 5.7). These and other recent data suggest no correlation whatsoever between religious beliefs, religious intensity, and voting for the PAN. Of those Mexicans who attend church daily (in fact a very small percentage), the same percentage shows sympathy for the PAN as do Mexicans generally (Camp 1991b).

Conclusion: The PAN—Different, But Not So Different

The socioeconomic origins of panistas at the national level suggest the overwhelming domination of middle-class backgrounds. In this regard panista leaders are no different from their establishment peers, although a slightly higher proportion may be from the upper classes. Among panistas in the 1988–91 Federal District assembly, at least half had fathers who were professionals, and one out of ten grew up in a family of industrialists.

The economic ideology of the PAN largely favors middle-class interests, and in that respect it can be associated with the class backgrounds of PAN leaders and many supporters. PAN economic strategy since 1988 has been coopted by the PRI as its major economic philosophy, reflecting the shifting interests of the dominant party. The significance for the PAN is that it is more difficult to distinguish between the two economic platforms. The primary difference between the two parties in the 1990s is the political modernization issue, namely the question of democratization and fair elections. Political modernization, however, cannot be attributed specifically to the PAN leaders' social origins. The groups that could benefit most from the implementation of this philosophy make up the working classes, which are not well represented in either the PAN or the national government leadership. If social origins affect leaders' values, as is true in many countries and contexts, working-class interests will not find a ready vehicle for direct expression among the National Action Party's leaders.

The most significant finding directly connected to social origins is the influence of background variables on political leaders' upward mobility. The second hypothesis offered at the beginning of this essay, that the PAN further restricts the pool of potential leaders, is borne out by the data. Although government leadership provides little access to individuals from working-class backgrounds, the PAN's leadership does even less for this group. It can be argued that the PAN, as an alternative leadership group, expands the pool slightly by allowing different types of middle- and upper-middle-class leaders to emerge. These individuals more often have parents who were self-employed or who worked in the private sector, rather than in the professions per se. But since workers and peasants continue to account for the largest percentage of Mexicans, it is their access to upward mobility in political circles that is increasingly closed.

It was also hypothesized that the PAN's leaders had close ties to prominent businesspeople, military, and clergy. In the case of the first two groups, no such relationship exists, either with the PAN or with the PRI government leadership. But the PAN does have much stronger ties to the business community, as measured by its leaders' management careers in the private sector. Thus the PAN indeed provides a bridge to the business sector. Yet comparatively neither the PAN nor the established leaders have a strong relationship with the private sector through career experiences or familial ties. The PAN, like the PRI, recruits the majority of its future politicians from the middle classes, from the professions, and from families independent of business, the clergy, or the military.

Finally, I hypothesized that the alleged upper-class origins of panista leaders might significantly affect elite-mass linkages, demonstrated by electoral support from the middle and upper classes and a failure to receive working-class support. In reality the linkage between its supporters and its leaders, on the basis of socioeconomic status, is much more complex. Contrary to widely held beliefs, of the 13 percent of Mexicans who sympathized with the PAN nationally, working-class Mexicans were only slightly underrepresented. The PRI, not PAN politicians, proportionally received the least support from this group. The middle classes, who account overwhelmingly for the social backgrounds of panista politicians, sympathized with this party in exactly the same proportion as all other Mexicans. However, upper-income voters disproportionately sympathized with the PAN and with the PRI and gave very little support, as could be expected, to the populist PRD. The PAN, perceived to have upper-class leaders, actually has only slightly more leaders from this social category than does the PRI, but it received 62 percent more support from this group than did the government party. One aspect of the last hypothesis is true, however, insofar as the PAN appears to attract a disproportionate share of higher-income voters, although most such voters continue to sympathize with the PRI.

While it is true that the PAN has always provided an alternative source of views in the political arena, primarily in electoral campaigns and in the chamber of deputies, those views largely represent the same class. In other words, at the moment the PRI represents the dominant middle-class view, while the PAN represents another, minority sector of the middle class. Thus the PAN adds to political diversity *within* the middle classes, who control Mexican leadership, but not to any diversity *among* the classes.

This brief examination of social origins suggests that public perceptions and reality both contribute to some of the potential political linkages between leadership backgrounds and political behavior. The PAN, if it wishes to expand its electoral base, will not only have to alter its program and its ability to convey that program to the electorate, but it may also find it necessary to open up its recruitment practices to a larger social, geographic, and educational pool of Mexicans. In short, the PAN needs to maintain its distance from the PRI and to ensure that there is a clear perception in the voters' mind of those differences. At the time of writing (late 1992), despite the PAN's most recent gubernatorial success in Chihuahua, the issue of ideological purity and the extent to which the PAN leadership should compromise with or distance itself from the Salinas administration was a cause of internal splits and dissension. Some of the old guard have already withdrawn, and the current challenge for the PAN's leaders is to successfully walk the tightrope of compromise while not sacrificing the party's integrity.

Note

1. Of course such patterns may vary locally. For example, although working-class women in Chihuahua tended to vote for the PRI, the PAN under Francisco Barrio in Juárez drew away much of this support (see Venegas, this volume, and Rodríguez and Ward 1992).

6

Entrepreneurs in the Opposition
Modes of Political Participation in Chihuahua
YEMILE MIZRAHI

During the early 1980s, the Partido Acción Nacional (PAN) emerged as the most important electoral challenge to the ruling party, the Partido Revolucionario Institucional (PRI). Yet as the editors of this volume point out in their introduction, the strength of the PAN was not evenly distributed throughout the regions of the country. It was stronger in Yucatán, in Guanajuato, and in the northern states of Durango, Coahuila, Baja California, Chihuahua, Nuevo León, Sonora, and Sinaloa, where the PAN scored important electoral victories.

The novelty in these electoral contests was the unprecedented and overt participation of entrepreneurs, particularly small and medium-sized entrepreneurs, who had no previous history of participation in the electoral arena and who despite their recent incorporation into the PAN, became candidates of the party during elections. This sudden and unparalleled strength of the party in the north is puzzling, because throughout the government of Miguel de la Madrid it was the workers and the peasants who were hit particularly hard by the economic policies adopted by his administration, yet the strongest electoral challenge came from the right, not from the left. Moreover, it came from the most dynamic region of the country, not from the areas most severely hit by the economic crisis. It is clear that the strength of the opposition is not directly and automatically related to the degree of discontent nor to the degree of adverse economic impact. Rather, it is related to the capacity of those sectors of the population who are dissatisfied with the government to organize in opposition.

My purpose in this chapter is to analyze why the PAN acquired such unprecedented strength in the northern state of Chihuahua in the early 1980s, why it was weakened toward the latter part of that decade, and to identify some of the lessons of this experience for the opposition, particularly now that the opposition rules in three states. I shall argue that entrepreneurs played a leading and decisive role in the organization of the opposition against the government and that their mode of participation is critical in explaining the performance of the PAN in the electoral arena. The strength of the PAN in Chihuahua and in the north in general was in great part the result of this sector's participation in the opposition. Entrepreneurs, particularly small and medium-size entrepreneurs, overtly supported the PAN and contributed financial resources to the party. But more importantly, they accepted nominations to be candidates of the party during elections, held critical roles in the organization of the campaigns, and accepted important positions as public officials in the municipalities won by the PAN (see also some of the examples provided by Ward in this volume). Entrepreneurs infused the PAN with new leadership, tactics, financial resources, and organizational capacities. Although the electoral movement in the 1980s against the PRI incorporated a variety of social sectors, such as the middle class, women, young people, the church, and even elements of the working class, entrepreneurs became its leaders.

Prior to the involvement of entrepreneurs in the PAN, the party was electorally weak and poorly organized. The role of entrepreneurs was therefore critical in tipping the balance in favor of the party. However, I shall also argue that the mode in which entrepreneurs participated in the opposition did not lead to the strengthening of the PAN in the long run. Entrepreneurs participated mainly in the organization of the campaigns and in administrative positions in the municipalities won by the PAN, but they did not become involved in the party structure itself. As a result the party remained organizationally weak as a political institution. After the elections of 1986, when the victories of the PAN were not recognized by the government, these underlying structural weaknesses of the party became clearly evident. Coupled with the withdrawal of financial support by a significant number of entrepreneurs these structural problems intensified the electoral weaknesses of the party, which were only reversed recently with the state and municipal governments won by the PAN in 1992. The central role of entrepreneurs in strengthening the PAN was again evident in the 1992 elections, when after a period of disillusionment, entrepreneurs once more mobilized in support of the PAN. In contrast to 1986, however, this time the federal government was quick to recognize the PAN's victories at the state and municipal levels.

The following analysis addresses three questions. First, why entrepreneurs decided to organize in opposition to the government and challenge the PRI in the electoral arena; second, why they were able to become the leaders of a societywide opposition movement against the government; and third, what the consequences were of the entrepreneurs' mode of participation in the opposition.

Banks Nationalization: The Spark to the Opposition

The last year of the government of José López Portillo was a great disappointment for all, but particularly for entrepreneurs. Upon taking power, López Portillo tried to win back the confidence of industry, business, and commerce, all of which had been alienated by the populist rhetoric of the previous administration of Luis Echeverría. But if López Portillo "wooed" entrepreneurs with the wealth derived from the oil boom, he stabbed them in the back in his last year in office. The nationalization of the banks, which affected the most powerful sector of the business community, and the antibusiness rhetoric that accompanied such a measure, convinced entrepreneurs that even the most probusiness president could betray them.

Discontent within the business community was widespread, yet it did not translate into political opposition throughout the country or throughout all sectors and levels of the business community. Paradoxically the largest entrepreneurs and the bankers, who were most affected by the nationalization, adopted a more conciliatory tone. Their immediate concern was not to provoke the government with whom they were negotiating over the value of the compensation they would receive for the now nationalized banks.[1] It was the smaller and medium size entrepreneurs, those who had not really been affected by the nationalization, who adopted a more combative stance and overtly gave their support to the PAN.

In Chihuahua, as in the rest of the country, the reaction of the business community after the nationalization of banks was not homogeneous. The entrepreneurs' political behavior was to a great extent conditioned by their degree of economic ties to the government. Large entrepreneurs, who have traditionally depended more on government contracts, concessions, purchases, and credits, and who had more personalistic links to authorities, publicly gave their support to the PRI, although many also financially supported the opposition behind closed doors. They could not afford to overtly support the PAN.[2] However, they considered exerting pressure on the government in order to force the authorities to behave more "responsibly."[3] In contrast, the majority of small and medium-sized entrepreneurs gave their support to the PAN. According to the President of CANACINTRA in Chihuahua, "in 1982, about 80 percent of entrepreneurs gave their support to the PAN."[4]

What characterized these entrepreneurs was that they were economically independent from the government and had little access to the highly centralized mechanisms of decision making. Therefore they were politically marginalized from the decision-making mechanisms. Typically they were young and highly educated. Many had received their education at the Tecnológico de Monterrey, an institution regarded as one of the most important centers of "entrepreneurial culture."[5] These entrepreneurs had less to lose by overtly supporting the opposition and perceived that there was much to gain.

Ideologically the nationalization of the banks represented an attack against private property and a clear example of the "excesses" of a government that had no effective checks and balances placed upon it. The timid response of the bankers and large entrepreneurs made these smaller entrepreneurs even more conscious of their powerlessness to confront such actions. It also revealed the absence of a strong leadership within the business community, prepared to come forward in defense of private property. For them the "rules of the game" that had governed the relationship between entrepreneurs and the government had to change. As things stood the system favored the continuity of an authoritarian political system, but it also consistently discriminated against them and their interests. Being marginalized from the possibility of exerting pressure on the government from within or through the PRI, these entrepreneurs realized the need to establish alternative formal mechanisms to limit and control the highly discretionary power of the executive.

Although many of these young entrepreneurs lacked access to the central authorities and felt politically marginalized, they were able to gain leading positions within their local business organizations. By the time the banks were nationalized in 1982, the business chambers in the state of Chihuahua were led by small and medium-sized entrepreneurs. This was partly the result of their growing numerical importance, which gave them bargaining strength within their business community. Since the 1970s Chihuahua has experienced a dramatic economic growth, thanks to the *maquiladora* program. The dynamism of maquiladoras has triggered the emergence of a new generation of entrepreneurs in the industrial, commercial, and service sectors, and has also created a flow of wages that has in turn spurred the commercial and service sectors (Lau 1990; García 1988). But more importantly, the access of small and medium-sized entrepreneurs to leading positions within their local business organizations was the result of large entrepreneurs' lack of control over the rest of the business community. In contrast to Nuevo León, where large entrepreneurs have exerted hegemonic influence and have been in control of their local business organizations, in Chihuahua they have not enjoyed anything like the same capacity to generate consensus inside the business community (Salas-Porras 1991). They do not have a strong leadership role and have often remained apathetic to the affairs of their local business organizations. They have preferred to use their direct channels of communication when dealing with the authorities. But this has increased the leverage of smaller entrepreneurs and has given them more room to maneuver.

As leaders of their organizations, small and medium-sized entrepreneurs have acquired experience in talking to the local authorities and getting exposure through the press. They have become opinion leaders in their own communities. The recently elected governor, Francisco Barrio, is a good example. As he informed me (interview, July 6, 1992): "being president of COPARMEX became for me the greatest opportunity to receive a political education." Barrio only entered the PAN formally when he ran for the municipal presidency of Ciudad Juárez, in 1983. The larger entrepreneurs, in contrast, typically deal with the government behind closed doors, and they have been reluctant to speak in public or to defend their ideas and seek to persuade others. As one entrepreneur said of one of the largest Chihuahua industrialists: "Eloy Vallina does not know how to talk."[6]

When the bank nationalization was announced amid the worst economic crisis the country had confronted since 1929, small and medium-sized entrepreneurs had the organizational resources to articulate and voice their discontent. They were in fact the most organized sector of the population outside the tutelage of the PRI. However, since they were in a minority, in order to challenge the PRI in the electoral arena these entrepreneurs needed to make coalitions with other social classes. To that end it was necessary to seek the support of a political party.

Entrepreneurs in the Pan: Strong Campaigns, Weak Party

When entrepreneurs decided to organize in opposition to the PRI, they first thought to create a new political party but then decided that it would be more expedient to support an existing party, the Partido Acción Nacional, which shared many ideological principles with the entrepreneurs.[7] The PAN had limited resources, but it had the advantage of a preexisting electoral structure, a widely recognized name, and a tradition of being the foremost opposition party. Moreover, in contrast to other regions of the country, the PAN in Chihuahua welcomed entrepreneurs to its ranks and allowed them to redefine strategies and tactics and to organize campaigns. As a former Barrio campaign manager once said: "people in the PAN were wise enough to accept us and to let us lead the movement. After all, we were nothing but intruders."[8]

By the early 1980s, the PAN was weak as a political organization. It operated as a voluntary organization and had no paid professionals working for it. Its resources were meager, its cadres were mainly middle-class professionals with little administrative experience, and it did not have the capacity to maintain the consistent participation of its sympathizers between elections. In 1982 the party did not even own a building.[9] As a member of the PAN in Ciudad Juárez said: "the PAN as an organization was in shambles; it had only 22 active people, and it operated more like a Friends Club."[10]

Entrepreneurs infused the PAN with resources as well as with the organizational, administrative, and marketing experience they had acquired in their own businesses. They were able to coordinate an effective campaign throughout the state, encouraging people to vote and to organize in defense of the vote. For entrepreneurs the very weakness of the PAN was attractive, because it allowed them to have more room for maneuvering and to impose their conditions upon the party. For the PAN, on the other hand, it was an opportunity to gain strength and win elections.

As a result of the participation of entrepreneurs, the party started to acquire a local political dynamism that it had not seen since 1956—the last time the PAN had organized a strong campaign for the governorship, with the help of many entrepreneurs.[11] The party collected significant financial resources that allowed it to stage well-organized and aggressive campaigns. It also incorporated new tactics, particularly the use of civil resistance and civil disobedience, to gather support and mobilize wide sectors of the population.[12] Finally, the PAN relied on other civic organizations, as well as the business chambers, in a civic campaign for the promotion of the vote.[13] Although there was no formal contact between the business chambers and the PAN, the former took an active role in revising the electoral list (*padrón electoral*), encouraging their members and the citizenry in general to go to the polls, and demanding clean elections.

The dynamism of the campaigns and the success of the PAN in mobilizing people and encouraging them to vote was reflected in the electoral results of 1983. The PAN won the seven most important municipalities, comprising 75 percent of the total state population, and also won five of the fourteen local electoral districts.[14] That gave the PAN five deputies in the local congress.[15] In the midterm elections of 1985, the PAN won four out of the ten electoral districts, despite a massive resort to fraud. Faced with the growing strength of the PAN in the electoral arena, the government fell back upon widespread fraud in 1986, and as a result the PAN "lost" the governorship, all local deputies, and all but one municipality.[16]

Although the PAN was able to mount strong campaigns in 1983, 1985, and especially in 1986, it remained weak as an institution. Entrepreneurs confined their political participation to the electoral struggle; their direct involvement in the party structure was limited. After the elections the majority refrained from adopting an active role in the PAN on an ongoing basis.

This mode of participation weakened the strength of the PAN in the long run. Entrepreneurs participated actively in the campaign committees and assumed a critical role in the definition of goals and strategies. But the campaigns were organized outside of the party; campaign committees were run as parallel organizations, relatively independent from the PAN. They had their own building, with their own director, treasurer, administrative staff, press manager, and logistics department. The most important decisions and all initiatives were taken by the campaign committees, not by the party itself.[17] Virtually all staff members of the campaign committees were entrepreneurs, and many of them were not even members of the PAN. This form of participation, important though it was, failed to fortify the PAN as an institution and created many problems between the organizers of the campaign and the PAN's traditional cadres.[18]

Aside from participating in the campaign committees, many entrepreneurs also participated in an informal support group, giving advice to the candidates as well as providing financial assistance through the so-called "Grupo de Apoyo." This group was geared toward collecting financial resources for the PAN during elections, although it remained independent of the party. It was an informal and behind-the-scenes organization, in which many large entrepreneurs who did not want to be associated with the PAN were able to participate anonymously.[19] The resources this group collected were crucial for the electoral campaigns of the PAN, but they flowed to the campaign committees, not to the party itself. After the elections the PAN lacked both resources and a solid organization for the collection of funds.

From 1983 to 1986, entrepreneurs also participated in administrative positions in the municipalities won by the PAN, as well as in the city councils. In Ciudad Juárez and Chihuahua, most of the high-level positions in the municipality were occupied by entrepreneurs (see also Ward, in this volume). The presence of entrepreneurs in government brought about a new style of policymaking. Most of the municipalities governed by the opposition were characterized by their honesty in budgetary management and their efficiency, despite their relative lack of resources. They were also characterized by the use of public force against popular organizations like the CDP.[20] Once in power the panista government promoted the organization of many civic associations, which in 1986 provided a basis of support for the PAN (as Venegas has described so graphically in this volume). In the case of Ciudad Juárez, associations emerged such as the Coalición de Comités de Vecinos (COCOVE), Comerciantes Unidos y Democracia (CUDE), Jóvenes para la Democracia, and Acción Cívica de Empleados de Maquilas. All of these groups formed the Comité de Lucha de la Democracia (COLUDE), an organization created before the 1986 elections to encourage people to go to the polls (Lau 1989). Although these associations promoted the activities of the PAN, they were not formally linked to the party. Many of these civic organizations, which successfully mobilized people for the elections, disintegrated after 1986. The concentration on electoral matters gave the PAN strength in the short run, but after the elections were over the PAN was not strong enough to keep people mobilized or interested in the affairs of the party. As Alberto Mesta (secretary general of the PAN in 1989) said, "in 1986, the strength of the PAN was its campaign committee. The PAN's state and municipal committees were weak. Guillermo Prieto Luján [then president of the PAN in Chihuahua] was alone. When the campaigns came to an end, the party fell apart. By the end of 1988, when Raymundo Gómez became president of the party, the PAN was in shambles.[21]

As noted earlier, it was the very weakness of the PAN that fostered the entrepreneurs' participation in the campaigns. The party infrastructure had to be created anew. But equally important for the entrepreneurs, this mode of participation was a less-risky way of getting involved in politics. By restricting their participation to the campaigns, entrepreneurs had less to lose if the opposition lost and much to win if it won.[22]

Immediately after the elections of 1986, the weakness of the PAN became fully evident for all to see. It was limited in its capacity to mobilize and to articulate all the arguments against the government's fraud, and it was unable to lead to the postelectoral struggle. Indeed social mobilizations went beyond the PAN, to be led by the civic organizations, by the church, and by the business chambers.[23] COPARMEX, CANACINTRA, and CANACO in Chihuahua all worked in a coordinated fashion and adopted an active role in condemning the fraud and demanding the annulment of the elections. They organized a business strike, in which an estimated 80 percent of the businesses in Chihuahua participated.[24] The civic associations, on the other hand, formed the Movimiento Democrático Electoral (MDE), where both the left and the PAN participated in condemning the fraud that had occurred. This "movimiento" participated in the civil-disobedience campaigns launched by those who had been in charge of the campaigns. However, divisions between the PAN and this electoral movement soon began to appear. The PAN, pressed by its national leader, Pablo Emilio Madero, wanted to stop the mobilizations and to adopt a less-aggressive tone.[25] The social mobilization came to an end when governor Fernando Baeza assumed power amid a general environment of resentment and disappointment. In 1988 and 1989, the PRI was able to win overwhelmingly, with an abstention rate of 70 percent. The PAN had lost its electoral strength, its resources, and the active involvement of its most important leaders.

Legacies: Explaining Demobilization and Its Aftermath

After the electoral results became irreversible, entrepreneurs ceased criticizing the government and the PRI so vociferously. Large entrepreneurs and many small and medium-sized entrepreneurs who had not participated actively in the opposition reaffirmed their commitment to the government and openly gave their support to the PRI. In contrast to the past, the PRI now welcomed them and extended its patronage to them. In 1992 entrepreneurs participated in the PRI through the so-called Comités de Financiamiento de Campaña and as candidates of the PRI for electoral contests.[26]

The majority of entrepreneurs who actively participated in the opposition, on the other hand, withdrew from the political arena and returned to their businesses. How can we explain their behavior, after they had become so actively involved in the opposition? The demobilization of the panista entrepreneurs has been interpreted as a sign that their motive was to use the PAN instrumentally in order to press the government and to improve their terms of negotiation. Following this logic, once the government adopted favorable economic policies and a conciliatory attitude, there remained no reason to support the opposition.[27] This interpretation, although partially true, is simplistic and misses the central point of why entrepreneurs supported the opposition in the first place.

Moreover, it cannot explain why many of these entrepreneurs had remained anti-PRI, despite the PRI's efforts to win their support; and many had now returned to the fold, participating actively in the 1992 elections on the side of the opposition.

Rather, I feel that entrepreneurial support for the PAN was not linked to the promotion of particular economic policies on the part of the government. The motivation to support the PAN was to create checks and balances in the political system, which would be the most appropriate mechanism to make the government accountable for its actions and would provide the best guarantee of private property interests. Although many entrepreneurs welcome the current PRI government's economic policies, they still demand a greater political presence outside the tutelage of the official party. They consider this to be a precondition for curbing the traditional impunity of the government. As one entrepreneur stated, "Salinas and Baeza are performing well now, but there is no guarantee that the president won't go crazy during the last year of his administration."[28] These entrepreneurs remained sympathetic to the PAN, but were no longer active in the party.

Another reason for the apparent demise of the PAN after 1986 was that the incoming governor, Baeza, managed to neutralize the political situation by using a carrot-and-stick policy. Baeza's government adopted a conciliatory tone, in an effort to win the support of the entrepreneurs. This helped many entrepreneurs who participated in the PAN in the solution of labor disputes and he appeared to be open to hearing about their concerns. According to a priísta entrepreneur, "Baeza treats the panistas better than the priístas".[29] But the government also "punished" those entrepreneurs who were most critical of the government by auditing their enterprises. Furthermore, Baeza adopted an openness towards the PAN that had no precedent in Chihuahua. He met with PAN officials on a regular basis and consulted with them on most important matters. As Raymundo Gómez said, "we virtually rule in the state of Chihuahua.[30] That helped to smooth over the tense political situation between entrepreneurs and the government and gave entrepreneurs less concrete and immediate reasons to organize in opposition again. When entrepreneurs do not feel aggrieved by the government, it is more difficult to justify their active involvement in the organization of an opposition movement against the PRI. That, coupled with the perception that the chances of success in the opposition were few, contributed to the demobilization of entrepreneurs after 1986.

Nevertheless, despite the disenchantment after the elections of 1986, in 1992 entrepreneurs flocked again to the PAN and occupied leading positions in the party, both as candidates and as organizers of the campaigns. The remobilization of entrepreneurs for the 1992 campaign revealed that they remained loyal to the original cause which had led to their participation in the opposition in the first place, namely, the introduction of democratic reforms to curb the highly discretionary power of the executive, and the need to make the government accountable for its actions. But this remobilization also responded to more immediate causes: the expectation that this time the electoral results would be respected and that the opposition had a good chance of winning. Moreover, the experiences of Baja California, Guanajuato, and San Luis Potosí encouraged entrepreneurs to become involved in the opposition again, for it was now perceived that the government would not be able to resort to massive fraud. Also, Francisco Barrio's decision to run again as the PAN's candidate for governor improved the chances of a panista victory, thus encouraging other entrepreneurs to mobilize again in support of the opposition.[31]

As in 1986, the participation of entrepreneurs in support of the opposition in 1992 contributed to the strengthening of the PAN in the electoral arena. Although in contrast to 1986 this time the campaigns were not organized outside the PAN, it was still apparent that the party remained dependent on the support of these "occasional" activists.[32] As the personal secretary of the PAN's candidate for the municipal government of Ciudad Juárez said, "During electoral contests, the *perfumados,* that is, the people with education and resources, come to the party and displace the *huarachudos,* the rank and file who work in the party in between elections. The *perfumados* become candidates of the party, and bring their own people to organize the campaigns. That potentially creates a lot of resentment among the rank and file."[33]

The active engagement of entrepreneurs in the opposition during the 1992 elections demonstrates that many of those entrepreneurs who became disenchanted after 1986 were never "wooed" into the official party, despite their broad approval of the policies adopted by the PRI at the national and local levels. However, it is true that most entrepreneurs only become active in the party during electoral contests, a factor that does not lead to the strengthening of the PAN on a more permanent basis. It also potentially creates severe divisions within the party, as the "intruders" displace the rank-and-file activists who work in the PAN continuously.[34]

Conclusions

Throughout the 1980s the PAN acquired a dramatic presence in Mexico's political arena as it started to win local elections in several northern states and to mount strong post-electoral mobilizations in opposition to electoral fraud. Although the government tried to weaken the opposition by occasionally resorting to fraud, after the 1988 presidential elections it became clear that if the PRI wanted to maintain its hegemonic power at the national level, it was more expedient to loosen the political system and let the opposition win at the regional level. As a result, the PAN currently rules in three states.

What was novel in these electoral processes was the overt participation of small and medium sized entrepreneurs in support of the opposition. For years, entrepreneurs refrained from participating in the electoral arena. They accepted the tacit division of activities that existed between the government and the business community: production for entrepreneurs and politics for the government. The nationalization of the banks convinced many entrepreneurs, particularly the owners of small and medium-size businesses, that it was no longer possible to abstain from participating in politics and to uncritically trust in the government's commitment to private property. It was necessary to create *formal* mechanisms to limit the highly discretionary power of the executive and to prevent it from turning against business for political reasons. To that end, it was necessary to introduce democratic reforms to make the government more accountable for its actions.

In contrast to large entrepreneurs, who have traditionally enjoyed a privileged access to the highest level authorities and who have therefore had the informal means to mitigate and defend against government's possible anti-business actions, small and medium size entrepreneurs considered that their lack of access to the process of decision-making left them ill prepared to defend and to protect their interests. Furthermore, since small and medium-size entrepreneurs depended less than large entrepreneurs on government's contracts, concessions, credits, and other "favors" the government distributes in a highly discretionary fashion, they felt freer to express their discontent against the government and to support the opposition. They were less vulnerable to possible government's retaliatory actions. Moreover, as the new políticos of the opposition, entrepreneurs were viewed with respect by their local communities. Having an already established safe economic position, they were perceived as people who entered politics to defend democratic ideals, not just to promote personal interests or ambitions for power.

In this chapter I have argued that the performance of the PAN in the electoral arena during the 1980s was in great part conditioned by the political behavior of entrepreneurs. When entrepreneurs became actively involved in support of the party, the party was able to organize effective campaigns, mobilize wide sectors of the population in support of the PAN, and (provided the government did not resort to massive fraud) was able to win elections. Conversely, when entrepreneurs withdrew their active support, the party was not strong enough to organize effective campaigns that would ensure them success. It was the very weakness of the PAN as a political organization that allowed entrepreneurs to play such an important role in the electoral process. What are the lessons of this experience?

The electoral process in Chihuahua during the early 1980s demonstrated that a necessary prerequisite in the struggle for democracy is the existence of strong parties, not just strong campaigns, strong electoral movements, or strong governments. A strong party needs to have a presence in the political arena between elections. To that end it requires resources, access to the press, professional politicians, and an organizational structure to keep people interested in the affairs of the party on a more permanent basis. Strong parties are able to penetrate civil society and ensure the commitment of its constituency on issues that transcend the electoral arena. More importantly, they provide the institutional mechanisms to maintain a permanent check on the performance of the party in power and to make it accountable for its actions. A stronger party decreases the political importance of outsiders, including entrepreneurs, in conditioning its electoral fortunes. If the PAN is stronger today, as panistas claim, it will not need to rely on "intruders" to direct its campaigns, and between elections it will be able to maintain a vigorous presence within civil society.[35] Thus its fortunes will no longer fluctuate so sharply when it fails to win an electoral contest. The challenges during the early 1990s are for the party to grow and consolidate its organizational roots and branches and to avoid becoming overtly dependent upon sometime activists, no matter how influential these may be. The party must also accept that it should maintain a relative independence from the current panista government. Governor Barrio has learned the hard way, since he was a classic "intruder" when he entered the municipal presidency in 1983 and witnessed the erosion of the PAN's support after 1986. Now he has the opportunity to both build an efficient administrative machine to serve Chihuahua well, and also to encourage the PAN to strengthen and consolidate its organizational structure by refraining from subordinating the affairs of the party to the needs of his government.

Notes

1. The larger entrepreneurs were afraid that if they reacted vociferously, then the government could start expropriating more enterprises. Interview with Federico Muggenburg, former director of Centro de Estudios Económicos y Sociales del Sector Privado (CEESP), July 1991.

2. There are, of course, some exceptions. The most notable examples are Miguel Fernández, a large entrepreneur from Ciudad Juárez, and Enrique Terrazas, from the city of Chihuahua.

3. Large entrepreneurs adopted an "instrumentalist" position toward the PAN. They supported the PAN financially, but by 1985 they withdrew their support, after they were pressed by the government.

4. Interview with Oscar Sepúlveda, President of CANACINTRA in Chihuahua, February 11, 1992.

5. Besides receiving a technical education, at the Tecnológico entrepreneurs also learned "entrepreneurial ideology." Interview with Luis Felipe Bravo Mena, Mexico City, March 1991.

6. Interview with Francisco Villarreal, a medium-sized entrepreneur who is currently the municipal president of Ciudad Juárez, July 1, 1991.

7. Interview with Guillermo Vega, commercial entrepreneur and supporter of the PAN in 1983, February 1992. The decision of entrepreneurs to support the party has received many criticisms. According to Abraham Nuncio, entrepreneurs used the PAN as an instrument to promote their class interests, which he a priori defined as antiliberal, antidemocratic, and antipopular (Nuncio 1986). I do not share this interpretation and argue that although it is true that large entrepreneurs adopted an "instrumental" position, many small and medium-sized entrepreneurs decided to support the PAN because they were convinced of the need to change the rules of the game in a more democratic direction.

8. Interview with Raymundo Gómez, federal deputy and former director general of Barrio's campaign, February 1992. He became president of the PAN in Chihuahua in 1989.

9. Interview with Raymundo Gómez, November 1991.

10. Interview with Javier Corral, journalist and member of the PAN, November 18, 1991.

11. It can be argued that in many ways, history repeated itself in 1986. In 1956 a group of entrepreneurs organized in opposition to the governor and gave their support to the PAN. A young entrepreneur with no previous history of political participation became the candidate of PAN in 1956; his name was Luis H. Alvarez. For a brief historical review of this electoral process see Rubén Lau (1989).

12. Actions such as stamping bills, honking horns, and covering the license plates of cars with panista propaganda allowed people to get involved without being recognized and consequently "punished" by the government.

13. Examples of these organizations are Desarrollo Humano Integral, A.C. (DHIAC) and Asociación Nacional Cívica Femenina (ANCIFEM).

14. These municipalities were Ciudad Juárez, Chihuahua, Camargo, Parral, Delicias, Meoqui, and Casas Grandes.

15. One of them, however, was "frozen." The PRI claimed there had been irregularities in the electoral process and succeeded in annulling the electoral results in this district. New elections were scheduled for 1985; the PAN won again, and the PRI again succeeded in annulling the elections.

16. For a description of the electoral process and results see Alberto Aziz Nassif (1987); Rubén Lau (1989): and Silvia Gómez Tagle (1987).

17. Interview with Raymundo Gómez, March 1992.

18. Interview with Alberto Mesta, former general secretary of the PAN, February 9, 1992. These conflicts became more damaging after the elections of 1986, when the PAN lost all electoral contests.

19. Large entrepreneurs contributed with financial resources to the PAN until 1985, when the government pressed them to withdraw their support. Due to the many economic links between these entrepreneurs and the government, as well as to the conciliatory attitude of the PRI, large entrepreneurs shifted alliances and openly declared themselves priístas. The two most important were Eloy Vallina, president of the Grupo Chihuahua, who declared himself a nationalist entrepreneur and a supporter of the PRI after the indemnization for his bank (Comermex). Jaime Bermúdez, on the other hand, the largest entrepreneur in Juárez, who supported Barrio financially, was pressed by the government and the PRI to run as candidate of the PRI for municipal elections in 1986. The withdrawal of large entrepreneurs' financial support affected the party, particularly after 1986, when the momentum of the elections had passed. Although these entrepreneurs were a minority, their contributions were very important.

20. For an interesting comparative analysis of Barrio's administration with other priísta administrations, see Gerardo M. Ordóñez Barba (1990).

21. Interview with Alberto Mesta, February 1992.

22. A similar situation obtained in Sonora and Nuevo León (Guadarrama 1987).

23. The upper hierarchy of the church in Chihuahua wanted to close the churches as a protest against the fraud. But the government pressed the representative of the Vatican in Mexico, who in turn successfully lobbied to stop the political mobilization of the church (Campbell and Lau 1990).

24. Interview with Alonso Baeza, president of COPARMEX in Chihuahua in 1986, November 1991.

25. Interview with Francisco Ortíz Pinchetti, journalist, March 1992.

26. The most recent case is that of Jesus Macías, the PRI's candidate for governor in the 1992 elections. Macías was president of CANACO in Ciudad Juárez and later became mayor of that city.

27. Many writers have espoused this interpretation. For a good exposition, see Graciela Guadarrama (1987). She also assumes that there is a more coordinated strategy on the part of entrepreneurs: negotiation on the one hand and pressure on the other. Due to her failure to disaggregate the business community, she does not see the existing divisions between entrepreneurs or their different interests and ideas. I believe the different forms of political behavior reveal internal divisions, not a cohesive strategy.

28. Interview with Matías Mesta, November 1991.

29. Interview with Patricio Martínez, Director de Administración, Gobierno de Chihuahua, November 1991.

30. Interview with Raymundo Gómez, November 1991.

31. Barrio was a strong and charismatic candidate, especially when compared to his priísta rival, who was hardly known throughout the state. It is possible to theorize that had Barrio not run for the governorship, entrepreneurs would not have participated to the same degree in the opposition.

32. For a comparison of entrepreneur's patterns of political alignment and modes of political participation in the 1986 and the 1992 elections, see Mizrahi (1992).

33. Interview with José Mario Sánchez, June 1992.

34. As the victory of the PAN demonstrates, these divisions become even more important when the party indeed wins elections, for entrepreneurs also occupy important positions in government, displacing the party's traditional cadres. The conflicts over the nomination of Barrio's cabinet (many of them entrepreneurs) are just a small illustration of what the potential divisions within the PAN are. In Baja California the PAN has been plagued by internal divisions since the party won the governorship in 1989.

35. Panistas claim that since the end of 1988, when Raymundo Gómez (who had been Barrio's general campaign director in 1986) became the president of the PAN in Chihuahua, the party has undergone an internal process of reorganization which has strengthened it.

7

Political Culture and Women of the Popular Sector in Ciudad Juárez, 1983–1986

LILIA VENEGAS AGUILERA

There are many possible approaches to the study of the experiences of opposition governments in Mexico. This chapter deals with a multiform and heterogeneous group that was evident in the panista administration of 1983–86 in Ciudad Juárez: the women of the popular sector.[1] We will focus here on the perceptions and memories of these women about the three-year municipal administration of Francisco Barrio, as expressed in their own words.

This collective memory of what was significant to them, for better or worse, represents the initial access to a subtle but critical dimension, given that women are the privileged (albeit informal) transmitters of values and judgements, both inside and outside the family. Curiously, as Kathleen Staudt and Carlota Aguilar (1992) indicate in their study of women's participation in the 1992 elections in Ciudad Juárez, the impact of women on the changes that took place in the political life of their families, as well as their participation in Mexico's democratic transition, has not been the subject of academic study. Neither has the role of women in opposition governments. This chapter seeks to approach the subject, however indirectly, through the opinions of a group of women about a panista municipal government.

Access to Power and Changes in Political Culture

In 1983, when the people's vote carried the panista candidate, Francisco Barrio Terrazas, to the mayorship of Ciudad Juárez, few would have imagined that this would constitute a link in the chain of events that through the decade painted an unusual picture in the recent history of the country, a picture of transition, of ruptures, and of novelties in Mexico's apparently lethargic political arena.

The wave of advances of the opposition on both the right and the left of the Mexican political spectrum ceased to be seen as only an opportunistic response to the crisis, capitalizing on the people's ubiquitous discontent (Guillén 1987a), or as alliances constructed at the top, managing to persuade broad segments of the population (Rascón and Ruiz 1986). The citizenry's political behavior suddenly gained the attention of politicians and analysts as voter participation increased, political preferences became unpredictable, collective mobilizations and practices in defense of the vote were organized, and the active presence of various social actors such as women, the church, and entrepreneurs gained in strength. However, little attention was given specifically to women. Whenever there was a reference to them, it was only as one more element forming part of the civil society (Stevens 1987).

The concept of political culture served well those individuals seeking to understand the motivation, sense, and meaning of the people's political life. Classical texts on the subject (such as those of Almond and Verba) were dusted off, and half-forgotten authors were heard of again, such as Samuel Ramos and some of the earlier works of Octavio Paz. Soledad Loaeza, a pioneer in this field, published a chapter in 1989 (written in 1981) in which she provided her definition of political culture and speculated on the possible directions this concept would take. The list of authors writing on political culture grew notably toward the end of the decade and included Carlos Monsiváis, José Emilio Pacheco, Roger Bartra, Javier Guerrero, and Héctor Aguilar Camín, among others. At the risk of overgeneralizing, we can say that their works focused on the emergence of a *new* political culture.

While the literature on the political culture of the border is not abundant yet, some documents appeared as a result of the panista advances discussed in this chapter. For example, the Colegio de la Frontera Norte, the Universidad Nacional Autónoma de México, and the Universidad de Chihuahua undertook a research project on electoral behavior in the cities of Chihuahua, Ciudad Juárez, and Tijuana (Guilén 1987a), seeking to determine the socioeconomic characteristics (age, sex, and economic stratum) of the supporters of the main political parties in those cities. Based upon some of the preliminary results of this study, which was carried out shortly before the 1986 elections, we know that in Ciudad Juárez the PAN had similar degrees of support from men and from women (42.2 percent and 41.6 percent, respectively); that unlike the PRI, support for the PAN was stronger among the younger age groups; and that there were more female than male PAN sympathizers in the lowest economic level (43.7 percent of women and 35.5 percent of men).

In a study of nationalism on the northern border, Raúl Béjar Navarro and Héctor M. Capello (1988) concluded that there is a low level of national identity and of national character in the region. They found that border citizens, especially those of the larger cities, harbor little sense of enfranchisement toward the country's social, political, and economic institutions, and even less any sense of participation in these institutions. But if by institutions we mean those of the government (and therefore priísta), the interpretation could be different: a high level of dissidence toward the official party and its discourse. In another work on the border, Laura Baca and Isidro Cisneros (1988) indicate that in the creation of this region's political culture, the social right has participated in an effective and (until recent years) unusual manner, permeating wide sectors of the northern border population. Generally speaking they identify this "right" as the transmitter of a neoliberal, antistate discourse and as a promoter of gradual "democratic transformations toward capitalist modernity." According to these authors, the panista advance in Chihuahua was a result of this impetus to modernize, in the context of the nationalization of the banks, the worsening of the crisis, and the government's intention (only as of 1983) to renovate the political life of the country.

In dealing with the subject of neopanismo, Esperanza Palma (1988) asks why the PAN managed to rise electorally in the north of the country and says the answer rests on the rationale behind the panista vote. She does not agree with those who mechanically associate the crisis with the panista votes nor with those who suggest that such votes are simply anti-PRI. "We think that even though the panista electorate is not knowledgeable about the doctrine and statutes of Acción Nacional and its government program, it has felt an identification with some of the proposals of that party and the criticisms it has made of the government" (Palma 1988:99). The northern part of the country, in her opinion, contains certain cultural peculiarities that have favored the development of a particular antipriísmo and have allowed the PAN to be more effective politically. The peculiarities of the northern culture that are most strongly visible are an anticentralist and liberal tradition, an incongruity between socioeconomic modernization and traditional political practices (corporativism, single partisanship, clientelism, and fraud), and the influence of North American culture.

In general, the works discussed above barely touch the surface of a problematic field where much remains to be done. The complexity of the political culture of the border still requires much study, and especially the role of women within it.

The Women of the PAN

The identification as PAN women in the popular sector observed in northern Mexico in the beginning of the 1980s has appeared also in other regions of the country, where the cultural characteristics of the border do not appear (Yucatán and San Luis Potosí are recent examples). It seems that there is something that the PAN offers or projects, beyond its modernization and anticentralist stances, its rejection of clientelism and corporativism, and its advocacy for electoral fairness, that attracts this wide and diverse social group. This participation draws attention because it indicates what preoccupies these women and what motivates them politically.

To speak about a feminine political culture demands a few caveats. On the one hand, it does not refer to women exclusively as a gender, but rather as active and participating members in the political community. On the other hand, this concept allows one to think in terms of a common identity, as seems to be the case for the panista women of the northern, central, and southeastern areas of the country—women of different social strata brought together by a common political interest. This identity runs contrary to the interpretation, almost dogmatic, which states that class differences among women supersede gender identity. This is not said in order to propose another dogma, but rather to suggest the possible analytical usefulness of a concept that is helpful in explaining the how and why of identification among women of the PAN. In her study of middle-class women in Ciudad Satélite (near Mexico City), María Luisa Tarrés (1989) elaborates on the association of women with the PAN. She points out that it is from neighborhood and church associations, as well as from other activities and organizations that are not strictly political, that women converge on either the PAN (which was particularly successful at the time of the study) or the PRI. Staudt and Aguilar (1992) analyze the political participation of women of diverse social strata in the 1986 elections in Ciudad Juárez by focusing on the absence of an agenda for women in the platforms of both main parties, the PRI and the PAN, as well as on the diverse impacts that the participation of these panista women had on the gender relations within their families.

There are twenty-two northern panista women who appear in this chapter, between the ages of sixteen and forty-five. They all participated, in varying degrees, in the movement in defense of the vote, and some of them were members of organizations close to the PAN, such as the Comités de Vecinos or the Asociación Nacional Cívica Femenina (ANCIFEM). They had never participated politically prior to 1983. Their families are lower-middle class and have monthly family incomes of from one to three minimum salaries (approximately U.S. $133 to $400). They live in peripheral working class *colonias* or in housing projects for workers (INFONAVIT). Half of them were not born in Ciudad Juárez but had been living there for at least five years. Two-thirds of them are mothers, even though in one-third of the cases the husband or father was absent. Most have work experience, and those who were working at the time of the interviews (1987) worked as nurses, secretaries, teachers, switchboard operators, or in the maquiladora industry. The following section illustrates, first, some of the general characteristics of the participation of these women in the PAN, and secondly, the opinions they expressed about the 1983–86 municipal administration of Francisco Barrio.[2]

General Characteristics of the Panistas of Ciudad Juárez

In Ciudad Juárez, as in other cities of the world, women of the popular sector seem to be interested in voting, organization and mobilization only when such practices are compensated for by the efficacy of their actions.[3] The simple casting of the vote only takes place when there is a strong possibility that others will be voting for the same party, when it is likely that the votes will be accurately counted and respected, or when a realistic alternative appears on the political scene.[4]

Thus as it also happens with women elsewhere, the women of Ciudad Juárez display a certain degree of contempt toward politics and a low sense of political efficacy. When they are interested in participating, it is rarely in a leadership capacity. They can be willing to "give their life" for a cause, but they do not attempt to make a political career out of their participation (such as pursuing a post within the party), although there are undoubtedly women who have stood out as leaders. The women interviewed fondly remember Clara Torres, for instance, who made a strong impact as the PAN's legislative candidate in the 1986 elections, as well as Francisco Barrio's wife, Hortensia; but they also point out that it is men who lead the party, chair meetings, and speak out more frequently. As Julieta Kirkwood (1985) indicates, it seems that women have internalized the lesson that their place is in the home and with the family; when they venture into politics, they rarely pursue a personal objective. For most women investing time and energy in politics implies overcoming a series of obstacles, both tangible and intangible—it means taking on a third work shift, violating norms and traditions, and negotiating their own time and space with their husband or father. As Alejandra Massolo (1983) points out, the struggle to participate in public life begins with a struggle in a woman's private life.

These considerations serve to explain the rather informal relationship with the PAN of the women interviewed. None of them knew the programs, statutes, or doctrines of the party. Most did not have a *credencial de afiliación,* nor had they been in a PAN building. On the one hand, this can be seen as a reflection of the panista policy that, in the words of Adrián Vázquez, director of human development of the PAN (DHIAC-PAN), "[the PAN] is not interested in having people in the party, or even affiliated with it; the only thing that matters is that they vote, because if they do, it is most probable that they are going to vote for us."[5] On the other hand, the fact that these women called themselves panistas can also be interpreted as an affiliation with the opposition in an attempt to express their dissatisfaction with the policies of the previous municipal government, which was priísta.

In general terms it appears that the PAN is appealing to women of the popular sector in Ciudad Juárez because its discourse underscores a political openness to all sectors of the population; far from limiting its invitation to any particular category (such as "the people" or "workers"), it addresses citizens in general. While this does not erase the differences that do exist, it does dissolve an image of social segregation. Once the distinction between social classes is eliminated, women can search for other qualities of common identity. For the women we interviewed, this common identity was provided by the sympathy and support they showed for Francisco Barrio during his municipal administration.

Memories of Barrio and His Administration

The Leader Image

The panista women interviewed clearly approved of Barrio's administration. Beginning with the mobilization he set in motion in 1985 and 1986 and up to the OAS verdict of electoral fraud in June of 1988, there are multiple testimonials indicative of the support he enjoyed both in and outside of Ciudad Juárez.[6] The opinions, criteria, and attitudes behind that support are most interesting.

The testimonials this chapter is based upon were compiled during the winter of 1987.[7] Open interviews of an average length of three hours were conducted with thirty-three women of the popular sector who took part in the political events of 1985 and 1986 in Ciudad Juárez. Although all of them were PAN sympathizers (a criterion selected beforehand), the twenty-two presented here were the most active politically. The information, which was recorded on audiotape, was compiled in their homes or in the lunchrooms of the maquila plants in which some of them worked.

It should be made clear that the opinions expressed by the group of women interviewed for this study represent the best example of uncritical partiality; everything Barrio did, from their point of view, was right, certainly not because his administration may have been perceived as error-free, but rather because they seemed to value him more as a person than as a politician or administrator. They saw in him good intentions and the image of a strong, manly leader.

Luz Elena refers to Barrio as "the big chief," Cristina says the people were very happy with him as municipal president, and Hilda states that "we were very saddened when his reign was over." According to Josefina, Barrio "is a man who really knows how to wear his pants."

HILDA:

"For us, Barrio has definitely been the very best here, and not because he accomplished much, which he wanted to but couldn't, because he didn't get support from the state and federal governments, especially the latter. But we, all of the people, saw what Barrio wanted to do."

("Definitivamente para nosotros Barrio ha sido lo máximo aquí, y no porque haya logrado hacer mucho, pero no porque no quería, sino porque no tenía el apoyo del gobierno del estado y mucho menos de la federación. Pero nosotros, toda la ciudadanía, vió lo que Barrio quería hacer.")

The sympathy toward Barrio seems to have been reinforced by the obstacles his administration encountered and the attempts to discredit him.

LUZ ELENA:

"There were some improvements, but not everything was improved. That's impossible. . .some people. . .acted maliciously in trying to make the 'big chief' look bad."

("Hubo mejoras, no le voy a decir que una totalidad, ¿verdad? Porque es imposible. . .hay gente. . .que obró mal para hacer quedar mal a la cabeza principal.")

ANTONIA:

> ". . .he accomplished a lot. It was he who had the viaduct
> bridges built, and they didn't even let him inaugurate them. . .they
> didn't acknowledge his work."
>
> (". . .hizo mucho. Los puentes del viaducto los hizo él, y ya ve
> que no lo dejaron que los inaugurara. . .no le reconocieron el
> trabajo que hizo.")

HILDA:

> ". . .and Barrio, how often he was slighted, and in such
> strange ways! Things such as holding an important meeting and
> not inviting him. He is truly charismatic, and we are very
> pleased with the work he accomplished, but unfortunately he
> didn't shine in it, because they wouldn't let him, they would
> place obstacles in his way, they wouldn't give him money, they
> just wouldn't let him."
>
> (". . .y a Barrio, ¡cuántas veces le hacían desaires rarísimos! Que
> tenían una reunión muy importante y no lo invitaban. Ese sí tiene
> carisma, y nos gustó mucho la labor que desarrolló,
> desgraciadamente no lució su trabajo porque no lo dejaron, le
> ponían trabas, no le daban dinero, en fin, ¡no lo dejaron!")

The qualifiers used when referring to Barrio are generally "simple,
honest, not rich, genuine, committed, handsome." His discourse and good
manners also worked in his favor.

ANTONIA:

> ". . .no other mayor had said such nice things before. I even ran
> into him in the supermarket and he was saying hello to everyone."
>
> (". . .ningún otro presidente municipal había dicho cosas tan
> bonitas. Incluso yo me lo llegué a encontrar en Futurama y él
> saludaba a todo el mundo.")

ALEJANDRA:

> ". . .he has more dignity, more politeness, less despotism, less
> arrogance."
>
> (". . .tiene más elevada la dignidad, más trato con la gente, menos
> prepotencia.")

Barrio's image was one of closeness and friendliness and was virtually
unquestionable. When he went to live in a low-income colonia while still
mayor, the press criticized him and accused him of being a populist.

RAMONA, on the contrary, said:

> ". . .imagine how we felt! Because Mr. Barrio is genuine, not like
> López Portillo, who cried one day and then later revealed his claws."
> (". . .¡Pues bien bonito se sintió! Porque el señor Barrio es
> auténtico, no como López Portillo, que un día lloró y luego enseñó
> la garra. . .")

Even at the difficult moment when Barrio decided to stop the
mobilization against the electoral fraud of 1986, whether in search of a
negotiated solution or simply recognizing his defeat, he came out
untarnished.

According to CLARA:

> ". . .when we left the bridge, people started to say he had sold
> out. . .but, I mean. . .he has to look out for his family as well."
> (". . .cuando nos retiramos del puente la gente empezó a decir
> que se había vendido. . .digo yo. . .pues él también está viendo por
> su familia.")

Administration and Services

Ciudad Juárez is the oldest city on Mexico's northern border, as well as
the country's fourth-largest city, with a population of more than one
million. Its rapid growth has been due to both natural increase and to the
wave of immigrants from several other states. In 1982 it was estimated
that two-thirds of the city's population lived in peripheral colonias, where
40 percent of the residents had only some public services or none at all.[8]
It is not surprising, therefore, that the women interviewed gave special
importance to the provision of services during the 1983–86 panista
administration.

DORA LUZ:

> ". . .many improvements were made in those colonias that other
> administrations didn't even take into account; they did make
> improvements, but only in places where people with more re-
> sources lived. The neighborhoods farther away from downtown
> were lacking many services, but they are now being provided.
> Sewer systems, street lighting, water. . .they gave a lot of help in
> the matter of land and deeds; they helped the people who needed
> it the most."
> (". . .se hicieron muchas obras en las colonias que en otras
> administraciones no se habián tomado en cuenta; hacían muchas

obras, pero en lugares de gente de más recursos. Los barrios más
alejados del centro pues tenían muchas carencias, pero ya muchas
las quitaron; se puso drenaje, alumbrado público, agua...ayudaron
mucho en eso de la tierra y las escrituras; ayudaron mucho a la
gente que más lo necesitaba.")

In addition to experiencing most directly the lack of public services and
the problems this entails, women are usually the ones who have to go to
make the payments in person, voice complaints, or demand solutions.
Thus when speaking of a municipal administration, they are well qualified
to assess the efficiency and behavior of public employees. During the
panista administration, it was said that they were not as arrogant as they
used to be. Some of the women interviewed mentioned that there was
more communication and less corruption. They also said the administration
was "cleaner," a term that reminds one of the PAN's emphasis on the
transparency of public affairs.

The attention of these women focused on the management of municipal
finances.

Manuela:

"...the Barrio administration was very good, because everything
that came into the city's coffers was distributed very wisely among
the colonias."

("...la gestión del señor Barrio fue muy buena porque todo lo
que estuvo entrando a la caja municipal se supo distribuir por las
colonias muy bien.")

Some of them also remembered the city budgetary reports that Barrio
provided. Some said they were issued every three months, others every
six. They also commented on what he did for police officers (increased
their life insurance, according to Antonia), and on the elementary-school
scholarships he implemented for the poor.

The refurbishing of parks, paving works, and garbage collection were
among the improvements they pointed out most. When they did so, they
referred repeatedly to the accomplishments of the Comités de Vecinos
(Neighborhood Committees), which were instrumental in bringing the
municipal government and the community closer together. On the one
hand, they were seen as an effective mechanism for getting people actively
involved in resolving their common problems.

Luz Elena:

"...during that time we had Neighborhood Committees and we
got for the colonia what in many previous years we could not."

("...en esos años nosotros teníamos Comités de Vecinos de aquí y logramos para la colonia lo que en muchos años atrás, no.")

LETICIA:

"...they were pretty positive...because it could be seen that they wanted to participate, and they showed that what the people want is to be called to help, because what we want to do is help."

("...fueron bastante positivos...porque se miró que querían participar y ahí está el ejemplo de que la gente lo que quiere es que nos llamen a ayudar, porque lo que queremos es ayudar.")

On the other hand, the Comités de Vecinos were also valued as a place for social exchange.

DORA LUZ:

"I think they're good, because sometimes people who live in the same colonia don't even say hello to each other..."

("Me parecen buenos, porque la gente a veces vive en la misma colonia y ni se saluda...")

LUZ ELENA:

"We have a very nice relationship with each other, because we all pull our weight, we get involved in activities, and we get along well as a group; we participate, we cooperate, and we're happy doing so."

("Muy bonita relación que tenemos porque trabajamos parejo, hacemos actividades, nos juntamos y todas en conjunto nos llevamos bien; participamos, cooperamos, y nos sentimos contentas haciéndolo.")

The committees gained a large degree of acceptance because, according to MANUELA:

"...they don't ask constantly for contributions for this and contributions for that, like the delegates of the PRI, who live off the people who help them."

("...no están pidiendo siempre, que cooperación para esto, que cooperación para lo otro, como lo hacen por ejemplo en el PRI, que tienen sus líderes que viven de la gente que ayuda.")

Lastly, it is worthwhile mentioning that the committees attracted women who remained loyal to the PAN even during the priísta administration that followed Barrio's.

The Family

It would be difficult to rank the order of priorities the women interviewed followed in adopting their panista affiliation, but undoubtedly the party's position (and Barrio's) regarding the family as an institution was one of the most important ones. In fact the PAN is the only party in the Mexican political spectrum that offers, in its discourse and practice, any kind of policy regarding family life.[9]

The perceptions of the women interviewed regarding Barrio and the family is twofold. One aspect has to do with the discourse and the other with specific policies considered by these women to be favorable and protective of the family.

LUZ ELENA:

"He said things of great benefit to those of us who are mothers, and gave us very nice advice, just as his wife did."

("Hablaba cosas muy beneficiosas para nosotras las madres que tenemos hijos, y muy bonitos consejos, lo mismo que la señora Hortensia.")

MANUELA:

"He was always speaking about the family, that it should be cared for and nutured; and since he is such a religious person, he was always telling us, wisely, that we should care for the family in a proper manner."

("Siempre estaba él hablando sobre la familia, que se viera por la familia y que veláramos por ella, y pues como era una persona tan religiosa, siempre nos estaba hablando bien, que viéramos por la familia como debe ser.")

Even controversial subjects, such as the repression of the CDP (Comité de Defensa Popular) or the cholos organizations, appear in the testimonials as issues of concern about the young, family security, the use of drugs, and juvenile delinquency.

HILDA:

"I greatly approved of the program for the cholos. I wish they all tried to do what he did—win over the teenagers with problems by getting them to do worthwhile things. . .As soon as he took office, the first thing he did was to placate the CDP. He also placated the School of Agriculture; they criticized him to death, but they didn't mess with him again."

("Ví bien el programa de cholos. Qué bueno que todos intentaran hacer lo mismo que él hizo: Ganarse a los muchachos con problemas haciéndolos hacer cosas útiles. . .Nomás entró Barrio y fue lo primero que hizo, aplacar al CDP. También aplacó a los de agricultura; lo criticaron a morir, pero no le volvieron a hacer el panchito.")

Politics and Religion

On this subject, the first not-so-positive statement made by one of the interviewed women appears, as expressed by VICKY:

"He fulfilled all the requirements in the religious aspect and with his family. But it was not a good thing for him to speak of religion, because the great Benito Juárez separated the church from the state. . .It was not good because many people are not of the same religion, even though they may share the same ideology. Politics is one thing and religion another."

("Llenó todos los requisitos, en el aspecto religioso, en su familia. Pero no fue muy bueno que hablara de religión, porque nuestro señor Benito Juárez hizo que eso se apartara. . .No fue muy bueno porque hay muchas personas que no son de la misma religión, pero sí de la misma ideología. Una cosa es la religión y otra la política.")

However, the prevailing opinion among the other women interviewed was different. Most of them expressed a view of politics in which religion is considered as a dimension that should be part of the decision-making process in governing.

GENOVEVA:

"Barrio seems very human to me; he thought of things other politicians did not."

("Barrio me parece como muy humano, pensaba en cosas que los otros [políticos] no.")

IMELDA:

"His openly expressing his religious ideology was clearly fair, because he kept everything in its place. He never denied his religion, and always referred to it as a personal thing and without being two-faced about it."

("El presentar abiertamente su ideología religiosa, claramente, era justo. Porque ponía cada cosa en su lugar, sin negar su religión, pero siempre como una cosa personal, sin tener doble cara.")

These ideas take us to a particular perception, gender-specific perhaps, of the boundary between what is public and what is private. It seems that the separation between politics and religion pointed out by Vicky is somewhat superficial to the others; to most of them the city is like a house, the government and the party like a family, and the leader like a father.

Conclusion

The examination of this experience of opposition government from the point of view of the women of the popular sector of Ciudad Juárez provides new elements for insight and analysis. The fragments of the interviews presented in this chapter delineate a landscape in which the components of traditional political culture mix with new and fresh approaches, some of which, hovering between modernity and tradition, seem to respond to the specificities of gender, geography, and sociocultural reality.

Among the traditional features, those that stand out the most are the sense of political efficacy that seems to apply especially to women, the greater obstacles they face in trying to participate politically, their political participation taking place mostly from behind the scenes, their uncritical loyalty to the leader, and the degree of importance they give to the resolution of problems related to their family's daily life. The most notable of the newer elements is an attitude that is participative and civic; a coming of age of the people within a framework of political participation that is informal and not corporatist or clientelist. Work and responsibilities are expected, but honesty and efficiency are demanded of the authorities. As for what is different, the political culture of the panista women of Ciudad Juárez goes further than the norms associated with the political cultures of the border and of Mexico in general. The political participation of these women, as well as their memories, judgments, and opinions of Francisco Barrio, indicate the perception that public affairs are also personal; politics are their preserve just as much as their homes are.

In that sense the women who appear in this chapter contribute to a delineation of the opinion of a gender and a social class about an opposition government. In every phrase we can find features of the municipal government of Francisco Barrio that enrich our understanding of a new system and style of governing. In warm and incisive comments, and taking the first steps onto traditionally nonfeminine ground, these women give us a vision that informs our analysis more fully than any set of electoral results and statistical data.

Notes

1. This essay is part of a research project supported and financed by Mexico's National Institute of Anthropology and History and the Interdisciplinary Program on Women's Studies. The interviews were carried out by the author, with the collaboration of Dalia Barrera Bassols.

2. The results reported in this chapter form part of a research project that covers a wider universe; in addition to the panistas, the women included in that study are priístas, nonpartisan, or apathetic.

3. Some of the most useful sources analyzing the political roles played by women in Latin America and other parts of the world include Jaquette (1984) Iglitzin and Ross (1986) and Stoner (1988).

4. There is a character in the folklore of Ciudad Juárez who for several years represented the image of popular discontent and the desire for change: El Burro Chón. According to some of the women interviewed, El Burro Chón used to roam the city during election periods as if it were another candidate campaigning. They interpreted the joke as, "quería decir que más valía un burro para presidente, que un presidente burro" ("better to have a jackass for mayor than a mayor who is a jackass").

5. Interview with Esperanza Tuñón Pablos, 1991.

6. The OAS report was made on May 17, 1990, by the OAS's Interamerican Commission on Human Rights.

7. Translator's note: In translating the women's statements, I have taken a certain degree of liberty in order to provide a better sense of the true meaning of the slang, colloquialisms, and inverted meanings that are particular to the speech of the region.

8. According to the newspaper *El Fronterizo* (April 27, 1982), only 60 percent of Ciudad Juárez had public services, 20 percent of the colonias had at least one but not all services, and 20 percent had no services at all.

9. It should be pointed out, however, that according to panista philosophy, the role of women within the family is very limited; the father is the breadwinner and head of the family, and the mother's responsibilities are the home and the children.

8

Governing Under the Enemy

The PRD in Michoacán

KATHLEEN BRUHN AND KEITH YANNER

Between 1988 and 1991, the Partido de la Revolución Democrática (PRD) won control of more municipal governments than any other opposition party in Mexico: 89 governments to 31 for the PAN (Ureña 1991). Nearly 60 percent of those PRD governments are located in Michoacán. In the December 1989 elections in Michoacán the PRD won an unprecedented 52 of 113 *municipio* presidencies and, in July of the same year, one-half of the contested seats in the state legislature. However, in the August 1991 midterm congressional elections, the PRD failed to win a single district seat in the national chamber of deputies. While municipal boundaries do not coincide precisely with congressional districts, one can break down the August 1991 congressional vote by municipal district. In the 52 municipios governed by the PRD, PRD candidates for the national legislature "won" in only 27. Moreover, the vote for the PRD was lower in 25 of the 27 districts in the 1991 congressional election than it was in the 1989 municipal elections (Tablas Comparativas 1992). In the December 1993 Michoacán municipal elections, according to the official State Electoral Court results, the PRD won 39 municipios overall, but lost control of most of the major cities it had governed since 1989, including Morelia, Pátzcuaro, and Lázaro Cárdenas (Avalos and Alfaro, 1993:11).

The PRD's electoral failures after 1989 probably stem from a combination of factors, including the mixed record of local PRD governments, which failed to convince enough voters to give the party a majority in any of the state's thirteen legislative districts in 1991; the government and the PRI's strategic use of the Solidarity program, which allowed the official party to increase its support base through local public works projects; and the government-PRI's control over the media, which limited the PRD's ability to shape public opinion and allowed the official party to define the PRD before the electorate. The political struggle in Michoacán from 1989 to the present provides an excellent opportunity to study the experiences of local opposition governments to the left of the government-PRI, as well as the possible reasons for the failure of local PRD governments to convert independent voters by their performance in office.

To analyze the experience of the PRD in Michoacán, we first consider state and national survey data that helps to identify the bases of support for the PRD in the 1989 Michoacán election. The analysis of public opinion will establish a broad sociopolitical context in which PRD leaders governed at the local level and tried to consolidate their party, which had just received its official registry in May of 1989. We then consider the experiences of several PRD municipal presidents as they administered their offices during the 1989–1992 period, while depending on authoritarian federal and state governments for resources.

Bases of Support for the PRD

The analysis of popular support for the PRD is based on two public opinion polls taken by Miguel Basáñez at the Centro de Estudios de Opinión Pública in Mexico City.[1] The first is a November, 1989, survey of 1,079 Michoacán residents that reveals local political preferences and factors that increased the odds that a Michoacán resident would vote for the PRD or the PRI. The second is an August, 1989, national survey of 1,495 Mexicans that gives national political preferences and provides a basis for comparing state and national patterns of support for the PRD. Although limited in scope, a comparison between these two surveys (along with some political history) will help explain the PRD's success in Michoacán in 1989. The analysis will also help explain why the PRD lost to the PRI in subsequent Michoacán elections.

The PRD in Michoacán: Historical Context

The PRD's success in the 1989 Michoacán election probably stemmed in part from the state's history of opposition to the centralized national government in Mexico City. Michoacán is one of the states where the Cristero rebellion (1926–29) was most violent, and it is one of eight states where support for the opposition was strongest during the relatively competitive presidential elections of 1946, 1952, and, to a lesser extent, 1982 (Camp 1991b).

In addition, the PRD had its strongest organization in Michoacán for historical reasons. Michoacán is the home of Cuauhtémoc Cárdenas, who was state governor from 1980 to 1986, while still a member of the PRI. During that time Cárdenas built a political network in Michoacán that remained loyal to him even after he left the PRI and ran for president in 1988 as the leader of a coalition of minor parties (the Frente Democrático Nacional, or FDN). Cárdenas won 64 percent of the Michoacán vote for president in 1988, and the FDN won both federal senate seats and eleven of thirteen single-member-district seats in the national congress. The political connections that served Cárdenas well in Michoacán in 1988 provided the foundation for the state branch of his new party, the PRD, in 1989. By contrast, most PRD organizations in other parts of the country were built around local leaders with less experience in electoral politics and public administration (although Mexico City and some urban areas of the state of Mexico may be exceptions).[2]

Given those factors it is not surprising that the PRD won half of the contested state legislative seats in July of 1989 (in an election marred by extensive and well-documented charges of fraud) and fifty-two municipal presidencies in the December 1989 Michoacán elections.[3] The new opposition was led by a man whose father (Lázaro Cárdenas, also born in Michoacán) is arguably the most revered president in Mexican history. And Cuauhtémoc Cárdenas had governed the state and developed a cadre of loyal, experienced politicians and public administrators.

Predictors of Voter Support for the PRD in Michoacán

Within that historical context, the PRD enjoyed considerable support in Michoacán in 1989. Still, the following analysis of public opinion shows that the ties between a significant percentage of the voters and the PRD were very fragile. Although the PRD had been founded in May of 1989, just a few months before the December election, some 29 percent of respondents to the Michoacán poll identified themselves with the new party (35 and 12 percent identified respectively with the PRI and the PAN, and 21 percent claimed independent status). By contrast, only 15.4 percent of respondents nationwide identified with the PRD, with 31 and 14 percent identifying respectively with the PRI and the PAN, and 28 percent claiming no partisan affiliation. With the level of PRD partisans twice as high in Michoacán as in the whole of Mexico, a firm basis existed for two-party competition in the 1989 Michoacán election.

As suggested above the social bases of this competition were tenuous, and PRD strength proved ephemeral in state elections after 1989. We approach this issue through a statistical analysis of public opinion data, using a modeling strategy that has been applied to Mexican survey data by Domínguez and McCann (1991). Following their work, the research question is framed in terms of what factors influence the probability that one would vote for a given party. Then variables that theoretically should predict support for that party are tested for statistical significance.

The explanatory variables were split into three categories: partisanship, socioeconomic status, and perceptions about salient issues and political actors. The relationship between partisanship and vote choice is self-evident and well established empirically. Three measures of partisanship were included among explanatory variables: party identification; leader identification, which indicates whether respondents most identify with Salinas or Cárdenas; and respondent vote choice in the 1988 presidential election.

The relationship between socioeconomic status and political preference is more difficult to establish, especially in the Mexican context. From a classic modernization perspective, one might argue that within a traditionally authoritarian political system, high levels of income, education, job status, and urban residence should be positively related to support for the political opposition. However, classic empirical studies of Mexican political attitudes and behavior show that those with high socioeconomic status often have the biggest stake in and strongest ties to the system (see Fagen and Tuohy 1972). Moreover, Ames (1970) has shown that during the 1950s and 1960s, socioeconomic trends that theoretically should have favored the development of an opposition were accompanied by increasing popular support for Mexico's semiauthoritarian regime. He speculated that a prolonged economic decline might be required to persuade Mexico's increasingly urban, literate, and affluent society to vote for the opposition—which is what seems to have happened in the 1988 election. Finally, one might expect socioeconomic status to predict support for Mexican parties if they were organized along class lines (Przeworski and Sprague 1986). However, the corporatist organization of the PRI has reduced social class as a salient factor in Mexican politics (Malloy 1977, Escobar and Roberts 1991). As a result, it would be surprising if socioeconomic status strongly predicted popular support for either the PRD or the PRI.

The relationship between voter preference and popular perceptions about salient issues and important political actors is more straightforward. Politicians often have coattails. It would not be surprising if party preferences in the Michoacán election were shaped by how respondents felt about Salinas and Cárdenas. An approval rating for each leader was, therefore, included among the explanatory variables. In addition, party

Table 8.1: Logit estimates and (standard errors) of popular preferences in the 1989 Michoacán election

Variable	Estimate PRD		Estimate PRI	
Socioeconimic status				
Urban residence	−.34	(.14)*	.26	(.14)*
Gender	.17	(.13)	.03	(.13)
Age	−.10	(.10)	−.17	(.10)
Education	−.10	(.13)	.14	(.12)
Income	.01	(.13)	−.10	(.11)
Partisanship				
Party identification	1.97	(.14)**	2.09	(.15)**
Leader identification	.53	(.18)**	.39	(.16)**
1988 presidential vote	.43	(.14)**	.89	(.15)**
Performance measures				
Salinas approval	−.37	(.21)	−.02	(.22)
Cárdenas approval	.09	(.22)	−.02	(.19)
Service delivery	−.05	(.08)	−.01	(.08)
Personal situation	.10	(.17)	.19	(.16)
State situation	−.12	(.16)	.30	(.16)*

N = 1,079
* = p < .05; ** = p < .001
Percent of correctly predicted response: 91% for the PRD, 92% for the PRI.

preferences may be influenced by the extent to which voting-age Michoacán residents were satisfied with the delivery of public services. An index measuring respondent satisfaction with local public schools and health clinics was also included in the list of perception variables. Finally, it seems reasonable to assume that party preferences might be determined in part by whether respondents believed their personal situations and the state economy had improved or deteriorated over the previous year, with gainers favoring the PRI and losers supporting the PRD. Accordingly, measures of respondent evaluations of their personal situations and the state economy were included.

Table 8.1 shows that partisanship was the only factor to strongly predict party preferences among Michoacán residents. PRD membership, personal identification with Cuauhtémoc Cárdenas, and a vote for him in the 1988 presidential election all strongly predicted a vote for the PRD in the 1989 Michoacán election. Similarly PRI membership, personal identification with Carlos Salinas, and a vote for him in the 1988 presidential election strongly predicted a PRI vote among Michoacán residents.

By contrast, only one of the socioeconomic status variables had a statistically significant, independent effect on party preference—that of urban residence. City dwellers were more likely to vote for the PRI, and rural residents were more likely to vote for the PRD. This is an interesting result, because it differs from the effects of urban residence at the national level, where the PRI is stronger in the countryside and people in cities are more likely than their rural counterparts to vote for the PRD (Yanner 1992). However, none of the other socioeconomic status variables proved to be a statistically significant predictor of party preference, which may be explained by the fact that Mexican elites traditionally have not used pure class-based strategies to mobilize popular support (see Malloy 1977; Przeworski and Sprague 1986).

It is surprising that only one of the perception variables predicted support for either party. Respondents who thought the state economy had improved over the previous year were more likely to vote for the PRI. However, respondent perceptions about how their personal situations had changed, about the delivery of local public services, and about the leaders of the PRD and the PRI had no statistically significant effect on party preferences in the 1989 Michoacán election. Before concluding anything from these results about the political context in which PRD leaders governed after 1989, a comparison between the Michoacán and national surveys will be useful.

Taken alone the Michoacán results suggest that partisanship is the only important predictor of mass political preferences. However, the Michoacán poll did not include some variables that strongly predicted voter preferences at the national level in 1989. Although partisanship was also the strongest predictor of support for Salinas or Cárdenas in the 1989 national data, two other factors had strong, independent effects as well: perceptions about the future strength and viability of the opposition, and expectations (Domínguez and McCann 1991, Yanner 1992). Respondents who believed the opposition would gain strength in the future were more likely to support Cárdenas and the PRD at the national level; those who were pessimistic about the opposition's viability were more likely to support the PRI.

The relation between expectations and political preference was fairly straightforward at the national level. Some Mexican intellectuals, such as Luis Rubio, argue that Mexicans' expectations about whether they will be better off in any given year strongly determine voter choice.[4] The 1989 national poll supports Rubio's argument. When other factors (such as partisanship and socioeconomic status) were controlled, expectations moderately predicted respondents' candidate preferences. Optimists were more likely to pick Salinas; pessimists were more likely to choose Cárdenas (Yanner 1992).

It seems reasonable, therefore, to assume that both expectations and perceptions about the viability of the new opposition shaped voter preferences in Michoacán as well, even though these particular hypotheses cannot be tested using the Michoacán data. The point seems especially relevant in the context of independent voters, who were crucial given the structure of partisanship in Michoacán: PRD 29 percent, PRI 35 percent, independents 21 percent. Under those conditions independents would decide any election, either through abstention or participation.

Implications

Therefore we need to know what drove independent preferences. The present data suggest that it was expectations and perceptions about the viability of the new opposition. In that context those with access to the media have a decided advantage over the long run, because it is through mass media that perceptions and expectations are shaped. A chronic complaint among opposition leaders in Mexico is that the PRI dominates mass media, especially television and radio.[5] This means that opposition leaders and parties have little opportunity to define themselves before the Mexican electorate, which may not be a problem with strong partisans, but could be absolutely devastating with the independent swing vote. In addition, opposition leaders elected to state and local office cannot develop a resource base independent of the federal government, because their ability to levy taxes may be severely limited (see chapters by Bailey and Rodríguez, in this volume). By manipulating public resources from Mexico City, the PRI has the opportunity to undermine opposition governments at the state and local level. All of this puts opposition leaders elected to local office in a double bind. The resources they need to do their jobs are controlled in part by their political enemy, who also controls the access to mass media that opposition leaders need to define themselves and their party (see Crespo, this volume). It is within that hostile political environment that the fifty-two PRD municipio presidents took office after the 1989 Michoacán election. Their experiences are now considered in more detail.

PRD Municipal Governments in Michoacán

The story of the PRD's failure to convert voters after 1989 suggests the existence of inherent limitations on the ability of opposition parties to extend their influence solely through control of local governments. The principal advantage of such victories is that they establish a party as a credible threat to the PRI; the party may therefore become the beneficiary of anti-PRI protest votes and convince sympathizers that their vote will not be wasted, reducing abstention. However, these victories also expose the winning party to intense PRI efforts to "recover" the municipio. In the case of the PRD, an unusually deep antagonism between the PRI and its competitor on the left makes these efforts especially determined.[6] Above all, the PRI attempts to ensure that large and important municipalities do not remain long in opposition hands. As part of its campaign, the PRI often uses its control of the media and its affiliated popular organizations to undermine the public image of the opposition government; in this case, to shape the PRD's reputation as the party of conflict and violence. Perhaps even more fundamentally, the subordinate position of the municipio in the Mexican political system makes it difficult (though not impossible) for any municipal government to dramatically improve performance or effect significant change against determined resistance from the state. Municipal governments depend on higher levels of government (all PRI-dominated) for approval of many local regulations and function with budgets inadequate to meet extensive direct responsibilities for providing local services. If the PRD governments cannot demonstrate a substantial improvement in terms of performance over those of the PRI, voters who are not fully committed to the PRD are unlikely to convert. While such voters do not necessarily become convinced priístas either, they appear vulnerable to PRI electoral manipulation. The PRD's recent electoral setbacks probably reflect the magnitude of the PRI's electoral efforts, as much as they do any real or imagined failures on the part of PRD municipal governments.

Municipal Finance: Where It Comes From, Where It Goes

A fundamental constraint on municipal governments is the size and source of their income. The municipal government itself usually raises less than half of its overall budget. It depends for the rest on federal contributions, a small proportion of federal taxes raised in the entity and adjusted by population. PRD governments often question the honesty of state officials responsible for apportioning funds.[7] One PRD official even suggested that the state "fixed" the 1990 census to give PRD municipios fewer inhabitants, so they would receive smaller contributions.[8] To test these claims, it was necessary to rely on a small sample of eight municipios,

Table 8.2: Municipal income, 1991

	Small Municipios (population 1–15,000)		Medium-sized Municipios (population 15,001–30,000)	
	PRI	PRD	PRI	PRD
Per capita income (pesos)	89,319	141,629	61,156	41,787
Federal funds budget share	77 percent	81 percent	61 percent	76 percent
Federal funds per capita	68,416	115,140	37,255	31,766
Predial tax budget share	3 percent	2 percent	3 percent	5 percent

	Large Municipios (population 30,001–100,000)		Super Municipios (population over 100,000)	
	PRI	PRD	PRI	PRD
Per capita income (pesos)	45,830*	51,578	66,635	66,263
Federal funds budget share	64 percent	61 percent	42 percent	41 percent
Federal funds per capita	29,326*	31,317	28,026	26,947
Predial tax budget share	8 percent	8 percent	5 percent	4 percent

*The month of November does not appear to be included in raw figures. Hence absolute per capita figures are a bit low for this case.
Sources: Annual reports (*Informes de Gobierno*) or municipal treasure books. Size information from INEGI, 1990a census.

because a complete set of municipal budgets for PRI and PRD governments was not available. In each of four size categories, a PRD and PRI government were paired and interview and budget information was obtained. Although the sample is not statistically valid, it provides a rough check.

The comparisons in table 8.2 suggest that variations in the size of federal contributions and in the dependency level of the municipios relate more to the size of the municipio than to the party affiliation of its mayor: smaller municipios receive relatively more federal contributions. In two categories the PRI municipio had the advantage, while in two others the PRD had the advantage. The smallest municipios also tend to depend more heavily on federal funds. According to 1990 census data, these (under

15,000 inhabitants) make up 40 percent of all Michoacán municipios (INEGI 1990a). Interviews suggest that a major reason for this dependency is the insignificant income from *predial* taxes, those imposed on land and real estate. Small municipios are mostly rural, where land is either improperly assessed, *ejido* property (and thus exempt from transfer taxes, since it could not be sold, until recently), or inadequately documented. In addition, small and medium-sized municipios do not collect predial taxes themselves. Rather, the state of Michoacán sends representatives to collect the tax, and retains an often large portion to cover administrative costs; then it returns the rest to the municipio, thus increasing its dependence (Rodríguez 1992). Although PRD officials insist that they could collect this tax at less cost than the state, the large PRD municipio (which collected its own taxes) derived the same percentage of its budget from predial taxes as the corresponding PRI municipio (which did not collect its own taxes). Only in the case of the largest municipios does a significant difference appear, and in this case both PRI and PRD governments collected the tax themselves. The key difference between these two municipios may lie more in the quality and accuracy of the *catastro* record than in the efficiency of collection. The PRD municipio put considerable effort into increasing its predial income, but at an unknown cost in popularity among those taxed.

This dilemma reflects a more general problem for municipios trying to free themselves from dependence on federal and state money. If they try to raise money by collecting taxes efficiently or by increasing fees, they are not likely to endear themselves to the population, no matter how they spend the money. For example, the PRD government in Morelia responded to a heavy inherited debt problem in its water district by raising fees by between 100 and 300 percent, to cover a greater portion of real costs (Avila G. 1991:253). The decision created great popular dissatisfaction, particularly since the quality of the service did not improve significantly. The PRI exploited this dissatisfaction by organizing popular protests and publicizing the PRD's "anti-popular" behavior. Federal and constitutional law restrict other alternatives for raising money. Hence the real signifi-cance of dependence on federal money is not that the federal government withdraws support on a whim (although the state can create problems for a municipio by simply delaying the disbursement of funds), but that it can effectively place a cap on total municipal budgets.

An important source of additional municipal funds is the controversial social development program Solidarity. In theory each Solidarity project begins with the formation of a local Solidarity committee, which petitions the government for funds to carry out a specific idea, then receives and administers those funds with the involvement and help of the appropriate local authorities. State and federal agencies contribute money and expertise. In practice the federal government chooses which projects to fund and apparently often instigates the formation of Solidarity committees, when it wants to fund projects in a particular area. Because Solidarity funding is discretional, it is much more subject to political favoritism. PRD governments constantly complain that they are left out of Solidarity projects. Unfortunately it was not possible to directly compare Solidarity funding in each municipio; both PRD and PRI governments claimed they did not know how much Solidarity money was spent in their municipio.[9] The principal programs that both parties claimed operated in their municipios were Escuela Digna (repair and maintenance of schools), Niños de Solidaridad (scholarships and food baskets for needy children), and Apoyo a la Producción (production credits to farmers with marginal land). The two largest PRD municipios reported that they did not participate in selecting beneficiaries; they simply received a list of names. Officials from the two smaller PRD municipios and all PRI municipios said they participated in selection, but closer questioning revealed that they participated mainly on ratification committees to confirm lists drawn up by others. Municipal governments reported the most input into the Escuela Digna selection process, although only one of the PRD governments said it prioritized schools to be fixed first. In any case these programs all came painted with Solidarity colors (which are the same as the PRI's), leading one PRD official to complain that, "they stick us with the cost of distribution but we don't get the credit."[10]

The big money comes by way of federal construction projects, but these, too, are identified with Solidarity, even in the case of the tripartite works, to which the municipal government must contribute its own resources. For the most part, municipal governments (including one PRI government, which said its tripartite works were a showcase for Solidarity) reported acting mostly in a supervisory role, checking up on Solidarity committees but not participating directly in the administration of these funds. Interestingly, three of the four PRD governments claimed they had some influence over the selection of particular projects. In fact they seemed especially indignant about Solidarity's tendency to rob them of the credit for their ideas by "baptizing" everything "Solidarity."[11]

Federal influence over municipal budgets does not necessarily end with income. All PRD governments reported attempts to manipulate municipal expenditures in different ways. One common complaint was that the Federal Electricity Commission charged PRD governments extra on their

Table 8.3: Municipal expenditures, 1991

	Small Municipios (population 1–15,000)		Medium-sized Municipios (population 15,001–30,000)	
	PRI	PRD	PRI	PRD
Per capita spending (pesos)	78,698	140,056	57,960	40,356
Personal services budget share	NA	32 percent	26 percent	NA**
Public works budget share	20 percent	10 percent	25 percent	NA**
Lighting-electricity budget share	10 percent	11 percent	8 percent	15 percent
Public-debt budget share	none	none	7 percent	NA**

	Large Municipios (population 30,001–100,000)		Super Municipios (population over 100,000)	
	PRI	PRD	PRI	PRD
Per capita spending (pesos)	44,887*	51,578	68,967	69,755
Personal services budget share	30 percent	39 percent	50 percent	30 percent
Public works budget share	19 percent	9 percent	11 percent	17 percent
Lighting-electricity budget share	NA	NA	14***	14***
Public-debt budget share	3 percent	17 percent	6 percent	10 percent

*November appears missing from this account; per capita figures are thus a bit low.
**This budget was too disaggregated to place accurately in comparable categories.
***This figure for both cities represents general services—lighting plus garbage service, etc.
Source: Annual reports (Informes de Gobierno) or municipal treasury books. Size information from INEGI, 1990a census.

light bills. Another complaint accused the state of holding them responsible for debts they inherited and which, the PRD claimed, were scheduled to be written off until the PRD won the municipio. Comparisons of this sort are harder to make, because budget reports are not completely standardized across municipios, especially with regard to the classification of some expenditures. Nevertheless the comparisons available in table 8.3 do not suggest extraordinary manipulation, although the debt-service bills of PRD municipios do seem slightly higher than those of corresponding PRI municipios. As in the case of municipal financing, this contradicts frequent claims by opposition parties. Government favoritism and manipulation of municipal budgets appear to operate more often through special-project funds than through funds for general services.

The data in table 8.3 also show few consistent differences between PRI and PRD budgets. The daily administration of essential services eats up much of a municipal budget. Expenditures for personal services (mostly salaries and benefits) average about a third of the budget. Expenditures for basic municipal services (not shown) take up another 15–25 percent. This leaves little room for municipal governments to create budgets that reflect their own ideological priorities. Still, perhaps the most tantalizing figure in table 8.3 is the percentage spent on public works, which shows the PRI outspending the "popularly oriented" PRD by two to one in two of the three pairs available. This may be an indirect measure of Solidarity at work, since many Solidarity projects require municipal contributions. Whatever the reasons, in at least these few cases the PRD governments have not devoted as much to the highly visible category of public works as their PRI counterparts.

The Public Image of PRD Governments

In terms of political dialogue, the PRI has gone to considerable lengths to identify the PRD with social conflict, division, and violence. In the latest example of this effort, during the 1992 campaign for governor in Michoacán, the PRI candidate adopted "Peace and Progress" as his slogan. He urged *michoacanos* to vote against violence by voting against the PRD. Local newspapers predicted electoral violence and riots; the army was even called in to protect public order from expected PRD provocations. Actions taken by the PRD to defend its electoral victories, such as marches and demonstrations, are portrayed as disruptions by a coarse, uncivilized band of malcontents. The PRD's national stance of combative rejection of negotiations with the Salinas administration tends to reinforce this local image.

Local governments, although they do negotiate with the PRI government as part of their function, also experience attempts to portray them as conflictive, especially in the larger PRD cities, which the PRI is most anxious to recover. Any error on the part of the PRD municipio is magnified by the media; and some errors are fabricated. In Morelia, for example, the PRI-affiliated garbage workers' union struck shortly after the PRD took over. As the garbage piled up, local and even national newspapers proclaimed Morelia a dirty city and called the PRD incompetent to solve problems of social conflict. Perhaps more importantly from the local PRD government's perspective, garbage quickly affects and annoys residents. The message, even for some PRD sympathizers, is that there are costs (or punishments) associated with voting for the opposition.

While PRI governments report a low level of conflict with popular organizations, PRD governments in cities over medium size report frequent public clashes. Again Morelia stands out. Morelia depends particularly heavily on the state police to maintain order; the state capital has no municipal force. According to the PRD, the state police have permitted actions against the public interest to make the PRD look bad. For example, PRD officials claim they found out that vandals associated with the PRI planned to dump garbage in the downtown area. But after being informed, the police did nothing. Over a ton of garbage ended up in the public square. Likewise, the police did not dislodge protesters from a PRI-affiliated union of street vendors who occupied Morelia's city hall twice, most recently in July of 1992. On the second occasion, after two weeks of fruitless negotiation with the municipal government, the PRI governor resolved the conflict one day before the 1992 gubernatorial election. The message, publicized on election day in a local newspaper, was that only a PRI government could maintain social peace.

However, not all of the complaints against the PRD municipal governments are fabricated by the PRI. One common complaint, heard as often from *perredistas* as priístas, is that some PRD official, usually the municipal president himself, is authoritarian and/or arrogant. Among PRD activists this charge often reflects some deeper disappointment with the rewards of victory. Any opposition triumph is a product of the work and sacrifice of many people. When "their" candidate takes power, they expect to share somehow in that power. To call a president "authoritarian" indicates that one feels shut out from a rightful share in power. It is difficult for a municipal government to offer people a real sense of direct participation in decision making. Two larger PRD municipal governments created special participation mechanisms in the form of urban councils, through which citizens could propose solutions to urban problems. In one case, lack of participation made the council ineffective; in the other case the municipal government dissolved the council because PRD officials claimed that priístas on the council tried to usurp government functions.[12] In these same two cases, there were common complaints about the mayor's authoritarianism. The key to satisfaction seems to be access to the mayor rather than such citizen councils.

Another issue underlying complaints of authoritarianism appears to be municipal employment. Only one of the four PRD municipal governments reported replacing all of its priísta employees with PRD activists. This same municipio also reported the best relations with the public and, curiously, was the only municipio of the four that the PRD won again in 1991. The other PRD governments reported (some without being asked) that they had had problems with PRD people who wanted them to fire priísta employees and hire perredistas, or who expected special treatment because of their PRD affiliation. Yet it would be difficult for municipal governments to honor such requests, even if they wanted to do so. Most employees, especially in larger cities, belong to unions and, therefore, are difficult to dismiss. Furthermore, PRD governments are under constant state scrutiny. Some have been audited more than once. Special treatment for perredistas might be detected and certainly would be used to discredit the party.

Implications

All municipal governments face limits on their power. As one former PRI mayor put it, "the municipal government receives the pressure of social demand . . . but doesn't have the wherewithal . . . so [it] can only do 1 percent of what they are demanding, and that only with help."[13] Opposition municipal governments generally do not get this help from higher levels of government, or are excluded from credit for projects carried out with federal money. Furthermore, there is probably some truth in the perception of one PRD official that opposition governments often face more mobilized populations, and hence higher demands and expectations, either because it takes such mobilization to get an opposition victory, or because the PRI mobilizes to create these demands.[14] Opposition governments are expected to do more with less. Finally, a controlled media often portrays local PRD governments in as bad a light as possible, to discourage voters from supporting the opposition.

Nevertheless the story is more complicated. Despite such problems, the PRD vote has remained remarkably constant in absolute terms, even growing modestly since 1989. By contrast, the PRI vote has been very volatile. The data in table 8.4 and elsewhere in this chapter portray a core of PRD faithful, whose votes are not based primarily on the performance of the municipal government but on their party identification. In

Table 8.4: Vote swing in Michoacán

| Party | Year | |
	1989–91	1991–92
PRD	+63,700	–2,587
PRI	+271,832	–88,561

Sources: Partido de la Revolucion Democrática, *Tablas Comparativas* (1992), Alemán and Cuéllar (1992:14). Data for 1989 are from municipal elections; 1991 data are from federal congressional elections; 1992 data are from gubernatorial and local congressional elections.

communities where this core is smaller and the PRD must attract independent voters to form a majority, a poor performance by a PRD government can cost the party its majority.

However, the massive changes in the PRI vote can only be explained with additional reference to the PRI's electoral spending and impressive organization of "vote promoters." While not the primary theme of this chapter, these efforts contributed significantly to the PRI's recent electoral recovery in Michoacán. In 1991 the PRI introduced vote promoters in crucial states, such as Michoacán, and in Mexico City. Beginning several months before the election, the promoters identified possible PRI voters and tried to elicit a commitment to the PRI. On election day the promoters followed through by escorting these voters to the polls. Approximately forty-eight thousand promoters covered Michoacán block by block.[15] The program was so successful in mobilizing the vote that the PRI used it again in 1992. As for the PRI's campaign costs, recent estimates indicate that the party spent almost 100 billion pesos, for a cost of 239,188 pesos per vote in the 1992 Michoacán governor's race (Chávez 1992:32). The PRD spent 2 billion pesos in the same election campaign, or 6,916 pesos per vote (Chávez 1992:32). This difference must be considered as a significant factor when analyzing the role of opposition municipal governments in consolidating opposition party support.

Conclusion

The experience of governing under the enemy in semiauthoritarian Mexico has been even more difficult for the PRD than for the PAN. As mentioned above, the PRI perceives the left-wing opposition as a greater threat, because it attracted roughly two times more popular support in the 1988 national elections than the PAN, and because the PRD directly opposes the new PRI's ideological program and competes directly with the PRI for its traditional mass base. In 1989 the PRD made unprecedented gains by winning fifty-two municipal presidencies in Michoacán, which provoked a determined response by the PRI to win back lost ground. The analysis here suggests that even though the PRD was able to maintain the support of its hard-core partisans, the PRI won the battle for the independent swing vote after 1989. The official party made solid gains among swing voters by using its control over the media and popular mass organizations to create problems for local PRD governments and to shape public opinion about the PRD as the party of violence and incompetence. There is very little evidence suggesting that the official party withheld resources from PRD municipios, which contradicts a common opposition complaint; however, the PRI seems to have been successful at using the Solidarity program to attract popular support through public works projects. Although local PRD governments have had input into Solidarity projects in their municipios, the lion's share of the credit has gone to the PRI. All of this suggests that the ability of the PRD to use its control over local government as a way of increasing its mass base is extremely limited. The PRD has consolidated a hard core of popular support which, at least in Michoacán, seems immune to manipulation by the PRI. However, unless the Salinas administration ends the PRI's media monopoly and control over mass organizations through a reform of the corporatist state, the PRD is unlikely to increase its share of the independent swing vote or to win future elections.

Nevertheless, the PRD has consolidated a hard core of popular support, which at least in Michoacán seems immune to manipulation by the PRI. While not in itself enough to win elections against the resistance of the PRI-government, the PRD faithful core *is* big enough to ensure close races and even victories in many Michoacán communities—39 out of 113 in the December 1992 municipal elections, according to the State Electoral court. Perhaps more importantly, PRD militants have shown dramatically that the PRI cannot govern Michoacán without their consent. Twice in four years, PRD protests forced "elected" PRI governors to resign—once in the heady aftermath of the 1988 election, and again, with grim determination, in the fall of 1992. President Salinas himself backed the official victory of Eduardo Villaseñor in July 1992, and personally attended Villaseñor's inauguration. However, occupation of the statehouse by PRD activists—plus demonstrations and protests at Villaseñor's public appearances—prevented him from conducting normal government activities and gave him the look of a fugitive on the run. Villaseñor left office just three weeks after his inauguration, without ever setting foot in the statehouse as Michoacán's elected governor. The PRD's triumph was not unmixed. The interim governor named by Salinas had a history of anti-perredista activity and much better connections than Villaseñor within the state PRI, but the PRD halted demonstrations anyway, agreeing to suspend judgment on new governor Ausencio Chávez. As PRD gubernatorial candidate Cristóbal Arias remarked, "[Chávez] knows he is standing on a barrel of gunpowder, and I don't think it is in his interests to make it explode" (Beltrán del Río and Castellanos, 10/12/92: 21).

Yet after the municipal elections in early December 1992, PRD activists did explode in protest, alleging fraud and manipulation. In the ensuing two months, at least five people died and over a hundred were wounded in political confrontations (Beltrán del Río 1993a: 14). A month after the election, PRD protesters still occupied eighteen city halls and PRI protesters held seven (Beltrán del Río 1993b: 29).[16] Thus, whether or not the PRD can win its battles on the streets with civil disobedience, it has at least turned the PRI's electoral wins into pyrrhic victories—though possibly for itself as well as the PRI. As of this writing, while Cárdenas and the PRI gear up for the 1994 presidential elections, these electoral conflicts in the cradle of cardenismo remain unresolved, and the challenges of governing under the enemy have become more difficult than ever.

Notes

1. Our thanks to Miguel Basáñez, who generously supported this project by granting unlimited access to his data.

2. Assertions as to the PRD's relative organizational strength in Michoacán are based on more than thirty interviews with PRD leaders and Mexican intellectuals by one of us (Yanner), from October of 1989 to May of 1990. The most relevant interviews in this context were with Cuauhtémoc Cárdenas, Leonel Godoy (PRD deputy in the national congress, 1988–91, and former member of Cárdenas's gubernatorial staff), Oscar Rosas López (PRD organizer in Cuernavaca, Morelos), and Pedro Peñaloza (PRD organizer in Mexico City).

3. In July of 1989, the PRD claimed victory in all districts, and an independent tribunal of citizens found that the PRD won fourteen districts and that the remaining four should have been annulled because of excessive irregularities, which prevented the tribunal from identifying a winner (Tribunal Independiente de Ciudadanos 1989).

4. Interview by Keith Yanner, April 6, 1990.

5. The problem of media access came up frequently in interviews with PRD leaders and at the Conference on Opposition Governments in Mexico at the University of Texas at Austin in April 1992. For the 1991 midterm congressional elections, the Centro de Estudios de Opinión Pública monitored prime time Televisa news broadcasts and found that the PRI received 77 percent of the coverage given to political parties, with the PAN and the PRD getting only 12 and 9 percent, respectively. In a three-month survey of local Michoacán newspapers before the 1992 governor's race, Alemán and Cuéllar (1992) found that the PRI and PRD candidates appeared on front pages 180 and 37 times, respectively. As a political party, the PRI made 419 front-page appearances to the PRD's 150.

6. The PRI fears the PRD because it demonstrated a potential national threat in 1988 (unlike the PAN), because its ideological program conflicts with the policy goals of the new PRI under Salinas (also unlike the PAN), and because it competes directly with the PRI for its traditional mass base (unlike the PAN). The PRD fears and distrusts the PRI because it believes the PRI robbed Cárdenas of his rightful place as president in 1988 and because it believes the PRI is selling out the country to the U.S. Electoral fraud and dozens of political murders of PRD activists have aggravated the PRD's hostility.

7. Interviews by Kathleen Bruhn, July 1991 and July 1992.

8. Interview by Kathleen Bruhn, July 1992.

9. Interviews by Kathleen Bruhn, July 1991 and July 1992.

10. Interview by Kathleen Bruhn, July 1992.

11. Interview by Kathleen Bruhn, July 1992.

12. Interview by Kathleen Bruhn, July 1992.

13. Interview by Kathleen Bruhn, April 1991.

14. Interview by Kathleen Bruhn, July 1992.

15. Interviews by Kathleen Bruhn, August and September 1991. See also Castañeda (1991).

16. In one case, the PRD occupied the building in conjunction with the PRI and the PAN to protest a decision in favor of the PFCRN (Avalos and Alfaro, 1993: 11).

Part Three

The Politics of Public Administration:
Municipal Finance and Intergovernmental Relations
Between Opposing Parties in Government

9

Policy Making and Policy Implementation Among Non-PRI Governments

The PAN in Ciudad Juárez and in Chihuahua

Peter M. Ward

In this chapter my aim is to evaluate the extent to which the PAN was successful in exercising government from 1983 to 1986 in two important urban areas in the north of the country—Ciudad Juárez and Chihuahua. Specifically, I will explore how the two municipal presidents, Francisco Barrio and Luis H. Alvarez, respectively, formed their teams; how and why they developed their urban policy agendas as they did; and the extent to which their governments represented a sea change in public administration, or whether, when compared with the PRI, they constituted little more than 'new wine in old bottles.' Several of the points I describe will overlap and reinforce those made by others in this book; I hope that this chapter will be read alongside the chapters by Mizrahi and Venegas, both of which deal with Chihuahua and with the same principal protagonists. In addition, mine is the stage setting for the following chapter by Victoria Rodríguez, which focuses upon intergovernmental relations and municipal government finances in these two cities. Although individually authored, the work discussed below forms part of a joint research project with Rodríguez, the full details of which are available elsewhere (Rodríguez and Ward 1991). Before proceeding I will briefly outline the methodology that Rodríguez and I have adopted in conducting our research on opposition governments.

The Chihuahua study was carried out with graduate student assistance and participation from the LBJ School of Public Affairs and from the Institute of Latin American Studies at The University of Texas at Austin.[1] Much of the success of the Chihuahua portion of the project derived from the enthusiastic participation and commitment of our students during the course of the 1991–92 academic session.[2] The research began by drawing up a context for the two administrations, identifying the principal issues of conflict, the names of key actors and groups involved, etc. The basic framework was provided by a systematic archival analysis of two magazines: *Proceso*, which covers national politics in a fairly objective manner, and *La Nación*, the official publication of the PAN. Based upon this contextual analysis, conducted for 1980–90, we drew up a broad "Who's Who" to serve as a basis for the analysis of newspapers in each city. Three daily newspapers were examined for the full period of each municipal administration, as well as for the period leading up to the succession of power: *El Heraldo de Chihuahua* in Chihuahua, and *El Fronterizo* and *El Diario de Juárez*, in Ciudad Juárez. In summary form this provided a detailed contextual analysis and chronology covering the principal actors and issues engaged in urban politics and administration in each city, as well as a preliminary indication of the bases of support that existed for each party.

At the same time, data were collected about each city and about the state in general, in order to provide an overview of the cities' principal economic activities, rates of urbanization, spatial growth, development of infrastructure, and so on, and to assess how these had changed over the past two to three decades. With these two sets of contextual documents in mind, students developed individual research agendas and formed two teams (one for each city), undertaking fieldwork and interviews in early February 1992. These research agendas covered themes such as finances and intergovernmental relations, municipal governmental structures, and local government priorities; implementation of programs and public works and the rationality of decision making; government-neighborhood relations and political and electoral mobilization. Numerous functionaries were interviewed across a wide range of departments both from past panista administrations and from the current city governments.

Subsequently these data, interview findings, and archival materials were analyzed in depth and written up for each city, according to common guidelines which provided the basis for a synthesis looking across the two city experiences. This synthesis provided the core materials that Rodríguez and I used to write a monograph that was published late in 1992. Some of that material is also discussed in this chapter and in her chapter, which follows.

Winning Power, Forming Teams, and Setting Up Shop

Winning Power

The state of Chihuahua contains sixty-seven municipalities, each of which is governed by an *ayuntamiento*, or city council. In the election for municipal government, citizens are invited to vote for a municipal president (mayor) of a particular party and a *planilla* (slate) of *regidores*, or aldermen. Thus although they are only voting for the mayor, at the same time they are in effect voting in a team of councilors, the actual composition of which is determined under provisions contained in the local municipal code. Sometimes seats in the council chamber are allocated in proportion to the votes each party received (as in Guanajuato, for example); elsewhere the whole slate of the winning mayor is adopted, with some nominal attempt to create a pluralist council by ensuring that the principal opposition party (or parties) are also allocated one or two regidores (as in Baja California Norte and in most border states). These elected officials constitute the *cabildo*; regidores have a watching brief on the policies and actions of the executive officers appointed directly by the mayor (such as the treasurer, head of public works, and police chief). The cabildo must also approve the budgets and the level of any taxes and other income the municpality proposes to utilize. Thus the composition of the council and the extent to which the mayor can guarantee a majority for his policies is extremely important. Often, too, intraparty divisions can generate intense conflict and tension between regidores and the appointed executive officers in the ayuntamiento (Tijuana providing a classic case; see Rodríguez and Ward 1994). Significantly, however, neither Barrio nor Alvarez experienced any major difficulties in managing their respective cabildos. Indeed Barrio made it a condition of his candidacy that he not only be allowed to manage his own campaign, but that he be left to choose his planilla, thereby ensuring that, if elected, the cabildo would be stacked with his people (see Mizrahi, this volume).[3]

In the 1983 elections, the PAN won seven municipalities in the state.[4] Here is not the place to analyze the PAN's electoral fortunes, which are discussed in detail elsewhere (Aziz 1987; Guillén López 1987; Rodríguez and Ward 1992). Suffice it to note, however, that in both Chihuahua and Juárez there was a dramatic increase in the percentage of votes won by the PAN between 1980 and 1983. In Chihuahua the PAN vote increased from 29 percent in 1980 to 67 percent in 1983. In Ciudad Juárez the percentage of PAN votes jumped from 24 percent to 61 percent. Equally significant was the dramatic rise in the absolute number of votes cast, which was considerably larger in 1983 than in 1980, and particularly so in Chihuahua, where the number of voters more than doubled. It seems probable that this absolute increase was unanticipated by the PRI, such that no amount of electoral alchemy could alter the result once people started voting in droves for the PAN in the 1983 elections. There are

several reasons that help to explain the dramatic increase in the vote registered for the PAN in 1983. First, the economic crisis of 1982 encouraged increased participation at the polls by voters who were determined
to effect a change of direction in economic and city management. Also,
voters probably wanted to register their discontent with the national
government's performance, particularly in economic management. The
growth of the *maquila* industry meant that the state of Chihuahua was
less severely affected than other parts of Mexico, and this too may have
emboldened business leaders to take a stand against the official party.
Second, as Mizrahi (this volume) argues, the participation of entrepreneurs in unprecedented numbers at that moment was a turning point for
the PAN. And third, it seems clear that the incoming administration of
Miguel de la Madrid was willing to experiment with political opening, in
order to test the water of both the strength of the opposition and that of the
PRI. In Alvarez's own words, this was "an experiment" to which Chihuahua
responded in such a way that, in the following elections (1985 and 1986),
the PRI was not disposed to experiment again.[5] Nor was the PRI willing to
allow Barrio to win the gubernatorial election, which he first contested for
the PAN in 1986, and which, it is widely believed, was "stolen" from him.

The Recruitment of Senior Administrative Personnel

The normal practice in Mexico is for incoming governments to fill key
(and not so key) positions with their own people. Individual political
leaders form part of a much wider team, or *camarilla*, a sort of nested
series of hierarchical groups under the aegis of a national or regional
political leader (Cornelius and Craig 1991; Grindle 1977; Smith 1979).
Once in power leaders accommodate their most trusted followers below
them, and sometimes they also have to accommodate others foisted upon
them by a leader higher up upon whom they, themselves, depend. Thus
positions are filled on the basis of a range of criteria, including nepotism,
trusted friends and former collaborators, and intracamarilla negotiations.
Until relatively recently, talent and proven ability rarely played a part (see
Ward 1986).

For the PAN, however, putting together a government team was a totally new experience. They were unproven in government; teams were, at
best, incipient; and by and large their arrival to power had come as an
unexpected surprise. Both Barrio and Alvarez came without ready-made
teams, and thus their first major problem centered around filling the va-
cant posts with reliable and competent people. This meant that they often

had to expend considerable energy persuading people whom they knew (largely outside the party) to accept official positions within municipal government. In both cases the usual practice was to recruit from the private sector and from business, in particular. These people filled the senior positions, while most lower-echelon officials (many of them priístas), were retained. Alvarez chose as his treasurer an accountant not well known to him personally ("people said he was good"), and he retained the private secretary who had served former priísta mayors. In another case they hired a militant priísta, simply because he was far and away the best man for the particular job—in this case the director responsible for public (street) lighting. Other things being equal, Alvarez said, he would choose a panista, but it was far from a sine-qua-non, and he appears to have gone out of his way to demonstrate that the ayuntamiento was not a partisan preserve. Nor did either mayor seek to accommodate party activists and long-serving militants into their administrations. They claimed that they made a conscious decision and effort to recruit people with proven administrative experience, albeit in the private sector.

There were three major differences we observed in these two experiences compared with former priísta governments. First, these administrations recruited professionals form the private sphere, especially from business and commerce. Second, unlike PRI administrators, most of these people were not politicians, nor had they had previous experience as government officials. One might also speculate they were reasonably well off and that in most cases their municipal government salaries were unlikely to be higher than their previous incomes.[6] They were not like some PRI public officials, whom one PAN official disparagingly referred to as *buscachambas*. Indeed, on the basis of our research to date, the following three-fold typology of panista city officials emerges. First, there was a very small number of true political careerists who had, often over many years, worked in the PAN and had perhaps held political positions (such as federal deputy). Good examples are Luis H. Alvarez himself and the late Guillermo Prieto Luján, a former deputy and head of the party in the state. Second, another relatively small group was seeking to develop a political career; these were relative newcomers committed to forging a political trajectory in the party. Francisco Barrio fits this type.[7] And third, a large group comprised those officials appointed from the private sector, who at first sight appears to have had no major ambitions to use the position as a political springboard. (However, given the fact that they were obliged to return to the private sector when the PAN failed to win a second term, one cannot determine the actual number who might actually have used their positions as a stepping-stone, had the opportunity presented itself.) These last two categories constitute the "intruders" that Mizrahi described earlier.

The failure to incorporate party militants and political activists into these municipal administrations is of great interest. After the euphoria of electoral victory had died down, one would have expected some backlash from within the party political apparatus, as it became clear that the top jobs would not be shared among those who had campaigned over the years. Certainly it appears that in Baja California considerable acrimony and party infighting occurred, apparently based upon a particular group loyal to a party "hack" (Salvador Rosas Magallón), who feels that he has been passed over by the newcomers of Ruffo's government (see for example *Proceso*, February 17 and June 8, 1992). In Chihuahua this appears not to have been the case, partly because the local party was quite weak anyway (see Mizrahi, this volume), and partly because the links between the two mayors and the party political apparatus were not threatening; quite dissimilar to the pattern often found between PRI local apparatchiks and mayoral candidates, who are often foisted upon them by the governor and by other higher-ups. Another factor was that the Alvarez and Barrio administrations lasted only three years, and perhaps this is not long enough for latent disappointments to become really obvious (in Baja California, of course, the stakes are higher, since Ruffo's term lasts six years and therefore leaves more time for disillusionments to surface; see Rodríguez and Ward 1994). Neither Alvarez nor Barrio showed particular sympathy to their cause, and to the extent that there was pressure, both appear to have held their ground. Barrio confided that it had been a minor problem, as certain individuals and the party faithful had unrealistic ideas about their abilities to fill the top jobs. Interestingly, too, he acknowledged that in the future the party probably needs to find a means to cater to these people, perhaps at the second and third levels. A safety valve for the PAN is offered to long-term party activists who pursue alternative routes towards political careers as federal and state deputies. In addition, they may be pulled into local government as regidores.

Exercising Power: Administrative Goals and Urban Policy

Administrative Style and Rationality

Neither candidate, upon taking up office as mayor, sought to make any dramatic changes in the overall administrative structure of the ayuntamiento. In the case of Ciudad Juárez, Francisco Barrio made some minor modifications to that of his predecessor, Reyes Estrada. These included expanding the former functions of the General Directorate for Socioeconomic Development (renaming it the General Directorate of Community Promotion) and creating a new (but very small) General Directorate of Information and Social Communications (in essence a press office). Neither the municipal reform (which allowed for changes in administrative structure) nor the specificity of the PAN's political project generated any radical transformation in the structure of these two municipal governments (Ordóñez Barba 1990:40). However, the mode of operation within these structures did change considerably, and it is important to analyze the different administrative styles that the PAN adopted in order to effect the change.

The sharp break in operating style between the PRI governments before 1983 and the PAN governments of 1983–86 reflects the different backgrounds of the personnel coming in to occupy administrative positions. Former priísta municipal governments of Chihuahua and Ciudad Juárez resembled a microcosm of the Mexican political system. Decision making and administrative behavior followed the well-established channels of interest promotion through the PRI party organization, so that "decisions are made and resources . . . are allocated more as political and personal forces dictate than as developmental or social criteria would demand" (Fagen and Tuohy 1972:26). Seemingly little emphasis was placed on fiscal responsibility, as witnessed by the presence of substantial budget deficits under the PRI. The exercise of municipal government followed the rationale and orthodoxy of its role as a cog in the Mexican political (that is, PRI) machine. The municipal administration was, in the words of the municipal treasurer in the Alvarez administration, a "casa política."

The panista administrations of 1983–86 were characterized by operations that resembled businesses as much as public bureaucracies. They sought to emphasize fiscal responsibility and avoided debt financing of public works, which was a feature of both their predecessors and especially of the governments that followed.[8] There was greater transparency in municipal financing; budgets and expenditures were posted and published regularly (an innovation that the PRI subsequently maintained). Moreover, when Alvarez took office, the municipality was in effect bankrupt, since the outgoing administration had left insufficient funds to cover wages for the remaining two months of the year or for the traditional Christmas aguinaldo (an additional check given as a bonus). This contrasts with his departure from office three years later, when both he and

Barrio left a working surplus in the treasury. This shift in operating methods can be traced primarily to the overwhelming presence of entrepreneurs within the PAN administrations.

Several conclusions may be drawn concerning the adoption of a different management style by the PAN administrations in Chihuahua and Ciudad Juárez, which derive from the backgrounds of their administrative personnel. First, the managerial experience of virtually all those in administrative positions under Alvarez and Barrio was in the private sector rather than in government. Thus the operating logic of these individuals largely emphasized the profit goals of a private enterprise, especially through efficiency and effectiveness and nondeficit financing. During the period of transition into government in 1983, the Alvarez administration analyzed operations in order to determine areas of municipal activity that contributed to waste and ineffectiveness. While such an analysis would be expected in most transitional phases, this particular one resulted in a significant streamlining of operations, through the targeted removal of excess personnel. For example, in the Department of Public Services, lower-level managers were given the responsibility for handing out paychecks to employees. In order to receive their pay, workers had to sign a roll in front of the manager. This process revealed a substantial number of individuals who were previously receiving salaries from the municipal government without actually working there. The discovery of these so-called *aviadores* (people who simply "fly in" to pick up their paycheck) led to an effective and symbolic streamlining of operations. Also, municipal offices and telephone facilities were no longer used for PRI party purposes (nor for any other type of partisan services, according to Alvarez). This, and the savings in aviador salaries, allowed the PAN to do more with less.

A second conclusion about management style relates to the panista administrators' lack of desire and, probably, inability to work within the traditional Mexican political machine. Prior to 1983, the political system of the two cities involved a rather complex corporatist system of personal and organizational networks within government operations. In this system demands on the government usually tended to be aggregated and presented through organized groups, often incorporated into the PRI through one of its three major sectors. These include the official unions, such as the Confederación Regional de Obreros Mexicanos (CROM) and the Confederación de Trabajadores Mexicanos (CTM), but also consist of groups organized by the PRI for mass mobilization, most importantly the many associations formed to attract the support of people in the *colonias* (usually poor peripheral urban neighborhoods) through the former

CNOP, or Confederación Nacional de Organizaciones Populares. Demands on the municipal government were usually channeled through these groups to the administration, either through direct contact or, just as commonly, through the PRI organs in the city. The government would often respond through these same channels by providing the necessary service or materials to the groups demanding them. The PAN, in contrast, did not have this access to the corporate sectors of the official party nor to organized labor. Also, given that many low-income residential groups were organized through the CNOP, the PAN did not have established links to the colonias. In short, panista governments had to establish a whole new set of relations to civil society (see Guillén López, this volume).

The circumstances of the PAN's election to office in Chihuahua and Ciudad Juárez, as well as the experiences of PAN administrators within the traditional system, led to a rejection of this mode of operation. The PAN's victories were seen as a sign of a mandate by the public against these age-old methods of administration. In the aftermath of the López Portillo administration, the political climate of the early 1980s was one of disenchantment, brought about by the wastage of resources and corruption within the traditional channels of power. The PAN, therefore, was seen as a vehicle for gaveling a new form of government. Not only was the public in general disenchanted with the traditional system, but panista officials, because of their former experience in the private sector, were often unsympathetic to the corporatist labor sector. The private sector traditionally was largely excluded from the benefits of a governmental system of patronage mainly targeted at agriculture and labor. It is hardly surprising, therefore, that panista officials wanted to shift the style of government away from the traditionally incorporated systems. Furthermore, the PAN as a party did not have the organizational resources to act in the same aggregative and responsive role that the PRI was able to utilize in previous administrations. This system depended both upon a strong party, which could act as an intermediary between the grass roots and the administration, and upon attaining support from higher levels of government. Given that the state and federal governments continued to be controlled by the PRI, the panista governments could not expect a great deal of assistance in the allocation of resources to meet demands. Therefore the administrators in the Barrio and Alvarez governments were forced to operate with a rationale based more on effectiveness than upon patronage. It also meant that they had to find ways of doing more with less, since they could not expect to enjoy the same level of direct support for urban projects from the state and federal governments.

Some of those involved in the Barrio and Alvarez administrations stated that the lack of political experience and background did not affect their ability to act. For example Jorge Manzanera, state president of the PAN in 1991–92, stated that there were no adverse effects upon the fortunes of the PAN administrations brought about by their lack of political expertise. Others, however, offered the view that the inability of these governments to utilize the existing structures did hurt the PAN both politically and electorally; as the PAN's former municipal treasurer in Chihuahua stated, there were "muchas fallas por desconocer la política" during the Alvarez administration.

Although the reasons for a shift in administrative style can be debated, it appears that the PAN was successful in transforming the operational methods of public administration in the two cities, particularly insofar as these governments were based more upon principles of efficiency and effectiveness. Many panista administrators claimed that this resulted not only in a more cost-effective government, but also in a better all-around municipal administration. In fact, even the PRI's director of technical services in Chihuahua stated in 1992 that the primary legacy of the Alvarez administration was that successive administrations paid more attention to efficiency.

How far this new style of administration and the paramountcy accorded to efficiency and technical rationality over political criteria are likely to serve the PAN in the long term is a moot point. As I have argued, decision making at the municipal level traditionally has been based on partisan political criteria, not on technical ones. Some have suggested that the PAN may need to wisen up politically and sacrifice some of its ideological purity if it wants to "win friends and influence people." Now that the PAN has the experience of power and subsequent defeat in municipal government in the state of Chihuahua, the party may have learned that it needs to play the system a little more if it is to benefit in the longer term, a conclusion echoed by Mizrahi in her chapter on entrepreneurs and their ambivalent incorporation into the PAN.

Urban Policy Goals and Their Implementation

Another area in which important qualitative shifts may be observed is in the field of urban administration and financing. The 1983 municipal reform presented ayuntamientos with a whole raft of new potential responsibilities and opportunities for financing. The following chapters by Rodríguez and Bailey explore these issues in considerable depth, and therefore I will not discuss them here. Suffice it to say that the panista administrations took the initiative to insist that they be allowed to revise the cadastral register and levy land and property taxes, which would lead to a major turnaround in the basis of municipal financing.

When the panista administrations of Luis H. Alvarez and Francisco Barrio took office in 1983, they targeted several broad policy areas for immediate action. The policies and issues they addressed inevitably reflected those most salient at that time and which they could tackle within the budgetary, constitutional, and political realities of the day. In this respect they were obliged to focus upon those areas of policy that fell unequivocally within their domain and that did not depend upon strong collaboration and support from the state and federal levels of government, both of which remained in the control of the PRI and whose support they were unlikely to receive. The new policy areas also reflected the ideological bases and sectoral backgrounds of the panista administrators.

As already outlined, the principal policy goal was to improve efficiency in the provision of government services. In part at least it was hoped that this would be achieved by running the government more like a business, thereby increasing efficiency and decreasing waste. By tackling corruption, inefficiency could also be reduced and more resources could be allocated for the public good. Indeed one of the PAN's most successful contemporary slogans, "honestidad y eficiencia," was coined at that time.

A second goal was to open up the process of municipal government to public scrutiny, debate and, above all, to public participation. Both Francisco Barrio and Luis Alvarez realized the importance of involving their urban populations actively in the process of municipal governance, which was likely to have several positive outcomes: it would allow them to target funds most efficiently; it would reduce the overall costs of urban projects by incorporating community participation; it would encourage citizen responsibility in paying taxes; and, of course, it would begin to create new channels of municipal-neighborhood and municipal-sectoral relations, especially with those that had largely been left out of the system of political incorporation by the PRI. Key among these sectors were small and medium-sized businesses and entrepreneurial organizations. In both cities weekly "open-door" sessions with the public and more formal meetings with groups such as COPARMEX (a syndicate of employers) were conducted soon after the assumption of power.

In addition to these broad policy aims, a third goal of both administrations centered around improving certain specific areas of municipal service. How these were prioritized is interesting. The top item appears to have been an improvement in the provision of security; in both cities greater resources were allocated to the municipal police force. In addition, reforms were implemented within the police forces to eliminate corruption, which had become a severe problem. Police agents were fired, a police training academy was established, and major improvements were undertaken in police hardware, patrol cars, and so on, in order to improve both the effectiveness of the force and the morale of those within it. A second priority area was that of solid-waste collection (mostly garbage collection) and street and other cleaning services. In both cities the level of coverage was extended greatly, although many peripheral colonias continued to be poorly served, especially in Juárez. This expanded service was achieved through improved efficiencies; in Chihuahua, for example, the number of new garbage collection routes was increased by one-third (raising the population covered between 1983 and 1986 from 60 percent to 95 percent), while the actual labor force was reduced by some 27 percent (Rodríguez and Ward 1992).

If these were high-priority areas in both cities, it is also important to note that the Alvarez and Barrio administrations gave lower priority to those projects that were long-term, or capital-intensive, or depended upon large-scale state and/or federal support. Thus the urban programs normally emphasized by priísta governments (such as housing, plot-title regularization, street paving, water and drainage projects) were given less prominence. By focusing services on such areas as security, trash collection, and street cleaning, the PAN hoped to achieve visible results without requiring extensive resources. Moreover, responsibility for these services rested primarily with the municipality, which precluded a dependence on the higher (priísta) levels of government for the effective provision of services. Both Alvarez and Barrio were reasonably successful in their efforts to draw the line between local and state responsibilities.

It is clear that in many ways the PAN administrations in Ciudad Juárez and Chihuahua were restricted in the extent to which they could implement significant administrative changes. They were constrained principally by regulations in the municipal code, by limited resources, and by limited access to an experienced cadre of functionaries, due to their relative inexperience in government. However, the panista officials were able to translate their electoral mandate for change into a substantial shift in managerial style, particularly in the greater level of efficiency they exercised in implementing and organizing their urban program.

Partisanship: Winning Friends and Influencing People

This final section is an assessment of whether these opposition govern-ments sought to shape their policies and priorities to meet the demands and wishes of certain groups over others. How far did they target urban resources spatially or sectorally in order to "nurse" certain communities or strategic groups into compliance and political support? Classically in the United States such practices tend to be described as pork-barrel poli-tics—using city resources and handouts in order to "win friends and in-fluence people." Sometimes, too, political machines have emerged in the United States, led by a politician who directly or indirectly uses city hall and its department heads (most or all of whom owe their positions and allegiance to him) in order to extend, consolidate, and maintain his elec-toral power base. City hall, in effect, becomes part of the political machine that keeps the politician "strongman" in power and through which his influ-ence is articulated (Johnston 1979; Scott 1969). In this context decision-making processes are carried out according to personal or partisan-political considerations rather than according to technical criteria.

In Mexico, however, this sort of arrangement is exceedingly rare, at least in its full-blown form. This is because power and resources tend to be heavily centralized and weighted to higher levels of governmental au-thority. Also, political powerholders are constitutionally limited in their terms of office (usually to three years), and the principle of no relection is firmly adhered to. It was precisely in order to prevent politicians from developing a spatial or constituent power base that the constitution was so drafted (Camp 1980).[9] Only in certain remote rural regions are ca-ciques (bosses) likely to exercise authority over local officials whose posi-tions they, rather than the party, control (Cornelius 1973; Montaño 1976).

In Mexico the practice whereby priísta municipal governments have responded to popular demands and local servicing needs has evolved over many years. In essence the system had a threefold purpose in serving the needs of both the party and the administration. First, it aimed at increas-ing the popular support of the PRI as a party, since it was explicitly in-volved in delivering resources in exchange for political support mediated through colonia leaders. Second, it allowed the PRI to provide a buffer for the government "by assuming organizational and control duties that would . . . perhaps jeopardize the government's reputation" (Fagen and Tuohy 1972:32). Also, through this pattern of cooptation and incorpora-tion, the administrative system was able to reduce the level of demands from the *colonias* to a level it felt it could handle (Cornelius 1975; Ward

1986). Third, by directing resources through its sectors, as well as spatially through local communities, the municipal government could assist the PRI in its tactics of "divide and rule," whereby some groups were supported while others were frozen out. These classic tactics have been widely described elsewhere and were especially important up until the 1980s, when although opposition parties were relatively weak, local leadership factions and colonia mobilizations were strong (Montaño 1977; Cornelius 1975; Ward 1986). The 1980s saw not only a rise of non-PRI governments, but also a greater sophistication of urban social movements, some of which (such as the CONAMUP) embraced a wide range of organizations and colonias (Ramírez Saiz 1986; Foweraker and Craig 1990). There are two points to underscore here: that the PAN did not share these traditions of colonia liaison, and that the times were changing anyway, and a new form of state-community interaction and behavior was in the process of being forged.

The rise of non-PRI governments, therefore, offered a new opportunity to develop policy according to different criteria. It also provides us with an opportunity to compare the extent of partisanship and resource allocation between PRI and PAN municipal governments. In short, my concern is to form a judgment about the rationality adopted by Mayors Barrio and Alvarez. Specifically, did the panistas set their urban agenda according primarily to technical considerations or political ones?

Policies of the PAN in Contrast to those of the PRI

Perhaps the answer to this question is both; moveover, the PAN governments undertook both similar and contrasting policy priorities with respect to earlier PRI administrations. The panistas mirrored the official party in two ways: they rewarded their electorate through the provision of certain services, and they developed some showy projects (*plazismos*) to enhance the party's image in the public's eye. Like PRI administrations before them, those of Alvarez and Barrio tended to focus on the delivery of municipal services to their constituents. In both cities the PAN aimed municipal works (street paving, garbage collection, urban renewal, and police security) at downtown urban areas and suburban colonias where the middle class resides. In addition, public utilities directed to popular neighborhoods in the peripheral zones were spatially targeted toward "pockets" of party sympathizers. With regard to showy projects, the PAN carried out a number of small-scale but very visible urban programs, such as erecting historic monuments, building basketball and soccer courts, beautifying parks and cemeteries, and installing street signs. In previous administrations the PRI had exercised a similar strategy by publicizing housing and public utility projects.

This notwithstanding, the differences between PAN and PRI policy priorities appear to be greater than their similarities. Whereas the PRI functioned under more flexible rationality, greater inefficiency, and heavy reliance on the state, the PAN seemed to labor under a more rigid regime, which emphasized adherence to the law, no corruption, technical efficiency, popular participation, and the expansion of municipal autonomy. Prior to 1983 the state heavily influenced the management of local urban development, particularly in the area of water, paving, and housing. Alvarez and Barrio, however, eschewed reliance on the state and played down the significance of large public-utility projects. Instead, they focused their attention on short-term municipal services. Both panista governments prioritized services over public works for two reasons: first, because public works, by nature, are expensive, intricate, and would require working with state and federal bureaucracies such as BANOBRAS and SEDUE; and second, (and conversely) public services tend to be low-cost and comprise clearly defined local duties (unlike public works, which remain a gray area in terms of municipal authority). True, the panistas were able to continue with the extension of water and drainage services, but this was in collaboration with state and federal authorities and in the colonias often relied heavily upon local participation, through the Comités de Vecinos. But works could not be showcased, since neither Alvarez nor Barrio could claim full credit for any significant increases in service, due largely to the state's continued funding of projects and their ability to circumvent the municipality.[10]

Thus the priorities of the PAN demonstrated the combination of partisan-political and technical rationality. It focused upon providing those services it could most readily implement, given its relative autonomy from the state bureaucracy, but which, perhaps coincidentally, were most likely to appeal to the middle-class constituency from which it primarily drew its voters. Although implementation was largely addressed in a technical manner, the actual priorities seem to have been as partisan as those of the PRI administrations before and after them.

During the panista administrations obvious advances were made in security and garbage collection, as well as in a number of other small-scale local projects not mentioned here. Earlier governments had underprioritized the above responsibilities, which allowed Alvarez and Barrio the opportunity to make reforms that they could justify in technical terms

(*El Fronterizo*, October 4, 1983). In response to questions on these urban responsibilities, the panista treasurer in Chihuahua stated: "we [the PAN] do not offer what we are unable to provide." The fact that they selected municipal security and garbage collection as their priorities indicated a strong partisan-political rationality. In the context of being new to power and unfamiliar with the traditional workings of state-municipio relations, and having only three years to produce results, the panistas had to be strategic in their choices of urban policies and implementation. Therefore they centered their efforts on those areas of development where intergovernmental relations and costs were minimal, where the PAN had freedom to reorganize departments, and where results would be most immediate. In addition, these services seemed to be particularly enjoyed by the middle class and businesses located in the downtown area.

The PAN method of governing worked essentially for two reasons. First, they maintained the provision of public works but did so by keeping a low profile and allowing the state and the PRI to supply those utilities. Second, the panistas made widespread advances in municipal services, which satisfied traditional constituents and broadened their overall support among local citizens. This success did much to explain why the PAN almost certainly won the vote but lost the elections of 1986. It also helps to explain why the PAN was able to do so well in 1992. Above all, the PAN demonstrated that honest, open, and efficient government is as good as any other way of winning votes and influencing people.

Notes

1. We are extremely grateful to the LBJ School and to the Institute of Latin American Studies for generous financial support at various stages of the research program. In particular we would like to acknowledge the warm personal support afforded to us by their respective heads (Dean Max Sherman at the School, and Professor Peter Cleaves at ILAS).

2. The following students participated: Norma Alvarado, Adrianna Cuéllar, Carlos Hernández, Christopher Kennedy, René Lara, Elisa Long, Cristopher McElvein, Eric Nichols, and Daniel Sisbarro.

3. This was quite unusual. Although the mayor has considerable freedom to appoint his executive officers (subject only to appointments imposed upon him by the governor), nominations for regidores are more likely to be the preserve of party apparatchiks and of the local party chief in particular. Aldermen tend to be drawn from the more militant partisans, and this is one way in which party activists are rewarded. They receive a salary for their part-time endeavors. In 1992 for a middle-sized city, the stipend for a regidor was around $1000 a month.

4. According to Luis Alvarez (personal interview), the PAN actually won eleven municipalities, although only seven were officially recognized. However, these seven included those considered to be most important.

5. In 1986 the official recorded number of votes increased substantially in both municipalities (see Rodríguez and Ward 1992: tables 3:2 and 3:3). In Chihuahua the number of voters increased more than 100 percent, from approximately 74,000 to almost 150,000, while in Juárez the number of voters increased by approximately 40 percent. Although the percentage vote accorded the PAN decreased from 67 percent to 41 percent in Chihuahua, some 11,000 more voters favored the PAN in 1986 than in 1983. In Juárez the trend is similar, but less dramatic; the percentage of PAN votes decreased from 61 percent to 40 percent, while the number of votes declined by around 5,000. Put another way, the PRI's success in 1986 was the result of a massive increase of voting on its behalf, rather than of a dramatic decline in votes for the PAN. Whether this increase was due to its supporters having abstained in protest in 1983 or to the result of an inflated electoral roll in 1986, we are unable to say definitively, although we strongly suspect the latter. These data suggest major manipulation of the vote in the two cities (especially in Chihuahua), certainly in 1986 and probably also in 1980. Of course Chihuahua was not the only state to suffer in this way (see Bezdek, this volume, for an account of the blatant fraud that occurred in San Luis Potosí in 1985 and 1986). Certainly our evaluation of the two PAN administrations presented below and in the following chapter makes it seem unlikely that the PAN's performance was so poor that is should have been voted out of office in such a dramatic way.

6. One or two appear to have entered with pecuniary advancement in mind, not so much through salaries, but rather with the expectancy of benefitting from contract allocations, bribes, and kickbacks. However, Barrio commented that these individuals left of their own volition, once it become clear to them that such benefits would not materialize, nor would they have been tolerated.

7. Indeed, Barrio only joined the PAN formally when he became its candidate for mayor.

8. See also Ordóñez Barba (1990), who shows that the previous administration of Reyes Estrada, and particularly that of Bermúdez, which followed Barrio's, undertook heavy public-debt contracting in order to cover public works and municipal services.

9. This does not mean that political strongmen do not exist or dominate in local politics. To the extent that political machines exist in Mexico, they have tended to emerge in the labor sindicates, such as those of PEMEX and the teachers' union, which were led by bosses such as "La Quina" and Jonguitud Barrios and whose influence was eventually destroyed by Salinas in 1989.

10. This is a frequent dilemma for opposition governments today, namely whether to seek PRONASOL funding. See Fox and Moguel, this volume.

10

Municipal Autonomy and the Politics of Intergovernmental Finance

Is It Different for the Opposition?

VICTORIA E. RODRÍGUEZ

In this chapter we begin to assess the theory and practice of intergovernmental relations in a changing historical context, marked by the invigoration of constitutional reforms dealing with the municipality and the emergence of opposition government at the local level. Building upon the preceding chapter by Peter Ward, this chapter looks particularly at the political and financial autonomy of the two 1983–86 panista municipalities of Ciudad Juárez and Chihuahua and identifies how the higher levels of government seek to shape and influence local administration. The following chapters by Bailey, Bailón, and Fox and Moguel extend this analysis further, by assessing the experiences of Nuevo León and Oaxaca. All of these essays come together to inform our understanding of how the principles of municipal autonomy operate (or fail to operate) for the governments of the opposition.

The Theory of Municipal Decentralization and Financial Autonomy

Although the autonomy of municipalities is guaranteed by the constitution of 1917, and in particular by the *municipio libre* (free municipality) provisions of Article 115, this autonomy has never been respected by the higher levels of government. At various times there have been half-hearted attempts to enforce these provisions, mostly in response to the demands of local governments, but is was not really until the early 1980s that a turning point was reached. When Miguel de la Madrid ran for the presidency he campaigned heavily for decentralization and genuine autonomy for municipal governments, and shortly after assuming power he proposed a constitutional reform to Article 115 that would make such autonomy a reality. The revised Article 115 became law in 1984, under the banner of what came to be known as the Municipal Reform. In essence

the reform proposed to grant financial autonomy to municipal governments, in the expectation that political autonomy would follow. Of all
the provisions of Article 115 that were amended, the most important is
the one that relates to financial affairs; according to the revised version,
municipalities are entitled to increased sources of revenue (from their
own sources and from intergovernmental revenue transfers), as well as to
decide how to spend their own monies. The drawback, as will be discussed below, is twofold: on the one hand, municipalities are expected to
raise revenue without having the adequate infrastructure to do so (such as
by collecting property taxes and fees for the provision of public services),
and on the other hand, virtually all municipalities have traditionally depended for approximately 80 percent of their budget on transfers from
the higher levels of government.

The reformed Article 115, section IV, states that "municipalities will
have free administration of their finances and revenues." Sources of these
municipal revenues are: taxes, of which the most important are those
relating to property (the *impuesto predial*); federal assistance funds (although these are administered through the state government); and revenues collected for the provision of services (such as water, cleaning, public
lighting, slaughterhouses, and so forth) and referred to as *derechos*. Other
revenues, called *aprovechamientos*, could be generated from fines and
surcharges. Of these, the collection of taxes (which in addition to those
on property includes other minor taxes on public events, gaming, raffles,
and lotteries) has proven to be the most important source of internal
income (*ingresos propios*) for those municipalities that have chosen (or
been allowed) to take advantage of the new provisions of Article 115. In
addition we observe some internal shifts in emphasis, namely away from
derechos and toward aprovechamientos, a change that appears to relate
directly to political breakpoints between PAN and PRI administrations
(Ordóñez Barba 1991:61). It should be noted that municipal income is
not limited to the aforementioned sources, as local governments are free
to seek other revenue-raising alternatives (including, for example, debt
financing).

Based on the Fiscal Coordination Law, or Ley de Coordinación Fiscal,
federal assistance is distributed among the states through two funds: the
General Participation Fund (Fondo General de Participaciones), and the
Municipal Development Fund (Fondo de Fomento Municipal). In accordance with this law, the states must distribute among their municipalities
at least 20 percent of the allocations from the first fund and 100 percent
of the allocations from the second fund. Although there appear to be no

constitutionally established rules that dictate how these funds must be divided among the various municipalities, in effect there exists a formula relating to population size and the fiscal revenue generated by each municipality for the state and federal treasuries. In principle, therefore, the more revenue a municipality generates, the more it should receive back; but in practice the levels of state-municipal financial flows are likely to be subject to manipulation on the part of the state government (Rodríguez 1992; forthcoming).

As is often the case with other areas of public policy, the actual implementation of the principles of municipal autonomy differ significantly from the original legislative intent. Although Article 115 authorizes local governments to assume complete control over their expenses, municipal revenues and administration are in theory to be "supervised" by the state government; that is, records of municipal income and expenditures must be submitted to the local state congress and receive its *visto bueno* (acceptance). Because this evidently denies the autonomy principle, some analysts argue that the provisions of Article 115 fall short of guaranteeing real municipal autonomy. While it would be erroneous to suggest that no autonomy has been gained at the local level, by and large the majority of Mexico's municipal governments, regardless of their party composition, remain highly dependent upon the higher levels of government, both for their operating and (especially) for their development funds. As Fox and Moguel discuss in this volume, the new mechanism for maintaining local governments under control is provided by the national Solidarity program. Thus while the Municipal Reform of 1984 and the sexenio of Miguel de la Madrid provide the backdrop for the two opposition-government experiences analyzed in this chapter, the reader will appreciate from the analyses of Bailey, Bailón, and Fox and Moguel that under President Salinas there has been relatively little movement toward fulfilling the goals implicit in the "free municipality" provisions of the Constitution.

The Practice of Municipal Finance

Financial autonomy is the most critical determinant of municipal autonomy, although the actual exercise of autonomy extends to various areas of governance. Based on the experiences of the 1983–86 panista governments of Francisco Barrio Terrazas and Luis H. Alvarez in Ciudad Juárez and in Chihuahua, respectively, this chapter seeks to address the following questions: first, whether intergovernmental finance during this period served to deny these two cities a level of resources comparable to that which a priísta government might have expected to receive; and second, how successful were these non-PRI governments in generating alternative revenues under the new provisions of Article 115, which allowed them to exercise governmental autonomy in undertaking their urban programs? The research conducted by Peter Ward and myself, described in some detail in the preceding chapter, indicates that the PAN governments did develop alternative sources of income in order to partially fund their urban development agendas and, interestingly, that once the precedent had been set, succeeding PRI governments continued to make extensive use of them. We also uncovered evidence of some financial manipulation on the part of the state government in its conduct with the panista governments, although it was undertaken in a very subtle manner.

The data in table 10.1 comprise state funds allocated to the cities of Chihuahua and Juárez expressed in constant 1976 pesos, excluding the special projects discussed below. As one may observe, the percentage change in the assistance to both cities during this period is virtually identical, suggesting that neither city received preferential treatment relative to the other at any time. Nor does the level of state assistance show any appreciable difference in real terms between the Alvarez-Barrio years and those immediately following. For instance, the Fondo General de Participaciones (the largest and most important category of assistance) increased after 1986 in the following increments: in 1987 by 1 percent, in 1988 by 6 percent, and in 1989 by 4 percent. The statistics for 1990 showed the most dramatic increase: 19 percent. This increase, however, comes a full four years after the 1986 election, making it difficult to sustain any assertion that the increase was due to partisanship.

Perhaps more significant, however, is the fact that there was a 12 percent decrease in state assistance to Chihuahua (and of 11.5 percent to Ciudad Juárez) from 1985 to 1986. While under Governor Ornelas the state government appears to have played more or less fairly with both municipal governments, the substantial decrease in assistance in 1986 coincides with his removal and the interim governorship of PRI hard-liner (and former state treasurer) Saúl González Herrera and points to a financial squeeze on the city for partisan reasons. Yet even here it is impossible to be conclusive; the entire state of Chihuahua suffered a 21 percent loss in revenue from the federal government in 1986, lending support to the contention that the drop in assistance to the cities was the result not of partisanship but of national fiscal austerity.[1] As for the slow but steady increase in state assistance after 1986, it remains unclear whether the

Table 10.1: State and federal allocations to Chihuahua and
Ciudad Juárez 1985–1990 (1976 pesos)

Year	General Participation Fund	Municipal Development Fund	Complementary Fund[a]	Total	Percent Change[b]
1985					
Chihuahua	99,551,000	2,353,000	7,887,000	114,500,000	
Juárez	118,953,000	2,926,000	9,414,000	134,538,000	
1986					
Chihuahua	87,800,000	1,300,000	6,777,000	100,465,000	
Juárez	104,881,000	1,677,000	8,113,000	120,010,000	
1987					
Chihuahua	88,285,000	1,261,000	6,826,000	98,974,000	1
Juárez	105,529,000	1,569,000	8,211,000	118,198,000	1
1988					
Chihuahua	93,866,000	1,295,000	7,245,000	105,615,000	6
Juárez	112,200,000	1,593,000	8,661,000	126,150,000	6
1989					
Chihuahua	97,936,000	1,273,000	7,595,000	110,932,000	4
Juárez	117,645,000	1,568,00	9,056,000	132,451,000	4
1990					
Chihuahua	116,882,000	1,678,000	1,112,000	125,000,000	19
Juárez	139,712,000	2,065,000	1,327,000	149,377,000	18

[a]After 1990, the Complementary Fund was integrated with the General
Participation Fund
[b]Percent increase of total state share received by each city, 1987–90
Source: Budget Office, State of Chihuahua

increase reflects the state's desire to bolster the PRI municipal government or simply reflects Mexico's initial recovery from its economic crisis.
Our interviews elicited contradictory commentaries. The panista treasurer
in Chihuahua argued vehemently that his government received far less
assistance than was the norm, while his counterpart in Ciudad Juárez told
us that they received "ni más ni menos"—neither more nor less funding
than a PRI government might have expected.

   While still allowing for the possibility that partisanship does play a part
in determining the appropriation of state funds to opposition governments, one must necessarily acknowledge that the budgetary evidence
presented in this chapter is open to various interpretations; not least significant, of course, is the fact that the period under study was a time of
severe crisis and budgetary restraint nationally. One must be careful not

to interpret cuts in finance to the two cities as the outcome of partisan-ship, if all cities were being treated more or less the same. Nor is the lack of clear-cut evidence of partisanship in published accounts terribly sur-prising; had alleged partisan financial conduct by the state government been easily documented, it would often have been cited by opposition officials to promote their cause. As this is not the case, it appears that financial obstacles were placed in the path of these municipal govern-ments in much less obvious ways. The information collected from a series of interviews conducted with public officials and politicians of that pe-riod indicates that various techniques were used by the higher levels of priísta government to deny resources to these opposition governments—among them, three are most illustrative and worthy of discussion; slow-ing down the process of transferring funds, denying bank loans, and keeping for itself the construction of the larger public works.

Perhaps the most prevalent of the forms of financial control exercised over both Ciudad Juárez and Chihuahua by the ruling party is the one referred to as *tortuguismo*, a term used for describing the practice of with-holding funds that have already been allocated by slowing down their actual delivery (the word comes from *tortuga*, tortoise). Mayor Alvarez put it most eloquently when he said that although his dealings with Gov-ernor Ornelas had been cordial and mutually respectful, when he requested funds for the municipality, the governor's line was invariably one of "Sí—pero no cuándo" ("yes, you may have the money, but I can't promise when you will get it"). Tortuguismo was often cited by PAN officials as a primary difficulty in dealing with a PRI state government. Although this process would not show up in official state budgets, PRI officials acknowl-edge that it does in fact occur. In 1992 the secretario técnico of Chihua-hua, for example, readily admitted that high-level state bureaucrats intentionally slowed down the delivery of important funds to the city of Chihuahua prior to the municipal elections of 1986. One ought to note here, also, that tortuguismo is not reserved for opposition governments, but rather represents the time-worn fashion in which politics is played out between competing groups within the governmental bureaucracy and/or within the same political party.[2]

Federal financing via the Mexican banking system illustrates another way in which the ruling party was able to deny resources to these opposi-tion governments. According to the Chihuahua city treasurer, the num-ber of much-needed loans to municipalities was curtailed during the 1983–86 period. This was partly due, he explained, to the refusal of panista officials to pay kickbacks for additional loans, which compounded the difficulties of obtaining financing and raised still further the tensions between the two political parties. Of course the majority of banks had been placed in the hands of government and priísta supporters subsequent to the nationalization of the banks in 1982. Although there is no concrete evidence to support this point, one may easily be inclined to conclude that the banking system served to deprive the panista governments of funds that would have ordinarily been made available to a PRI-controlled municipality. The panista government in Cuidad Juárez tried to obtain loans to finance public projects, for example, but the state-influenced banks refused them. Panista leaders further argued that such withholding of funds did not occur during periods of PRI municipal control, and data from an independent study of Ciudad Juárez suggest that the post-Barrio government of Bermúdez raised its public debt in order to continue its public services and public works program. Debt repayment and interest amortization in 1988 reached 10 percent of the total city budget (Ordóñez Barba 1991:76). Thereafter the city finances were in large part kept afloat by the state-authorized sale of the municipality's 10.5-hectare PRONAF (Programa Nacional Fronterizo) site (Ordóñez Barba 1991:76). Permission for such a sale would never have been given to Barrio.

Often omitted from a discussion of state allocations to municipalities are the so-called *proyectos especiales*, precisely because they comprise one-time, special projects. These tend to be directed at particular municipalities and to be heavily subsidized by the state and federal governments. Hospitals, roads, and large-scale housing projects constitute examples of projects normally falling into this category. Indeed a basic task of any governor or municipal president centers around using his or her "pull" at higher levels in order to persuade decision makers to allocate resources to their patch. In many respects this is the other side of the tortuguismo coin—securing resources represents another arena through which politics is played out. PAN officials from the 1983–86 administrations assert that these special projects were fewer in number and smaller in value while they held power. In the case of Ciudad Juárez, it appears that some projects were in fact funded during the first two years of Barrio's administration, while Governor Ornelas occupied the office. However, when Governor Saúl González Herrera replaced Ornelas in 1985, the state government halted this type of assistance. Special funds were reinstituted to Ciudad Juárez after the PRI's 1986 electoral victory.

Withholding of municipal funds designated for non-PRI governments was not apparent from the data perused, but as mentioned above, it was hardly likely to appear in a clear-cut form. As with other aspects of intergovernmental finance in Chihuahua, concrete evidence of a discrepancy between the value of these projects before, during, and after the panista administrations is not available. And even if it were, linking such a discrepancy to a purely partisan motive on the part of the state would be difficult. Moreover, it is generally acknowledged that the extent to which these projects are implemented will vary from year to year, based on a variety of economic factors facing the state government.

The Theory of Municipal Autonomy and
the Provision of Public Services

In accordance with the federal Constitution, the municipalities, with the participation of the state governments when necessary or when determined by law, will be responsible for the provision of the following services: a) water and sewage, b) street lighting, c) street cleaning, d) public market and food supply centers, e) graveyards, f) slaughterhouses, g) streets, parks and gardens, and h) public safety and traffic.[3] This list is not comprehensive, as municipalities are free to assist the federal and state governments in the provision of other services. In theory municipalities may also take on responsibilities in the following areas: a) elementary education, b) fire departments, c) emergency medical attention, d) health, e) disaster prevention, f) pollution protection, g) social communications, and h) the protection of historical, artistic, and cultural patrimony (Rodríguez, forthcoming).

One of the most important problems resulting from this constitutional provision is that it does not guarantee the municipalities exclusive jurisdiction over any service areas. The potential effect of this is dramatic, particularly in those states in which different political parties control the state and the municipal governments and compete with one another to provide the services. While at first glance such competition may appear to offer the basis for better delivery of needed services, it is more likely to be the case that inefficiencies emerge due to unnecessary duplication of responsibilities and to intergovernmental infighting for political advantage.

Given the constitutional vagueness regarding which level of government is responsible for which specific services, municipalities are free to allocate more funds for the provision of certain services, leaving others without sufficient funds. While this allows municipal governments enough autonomy to impose their own policy agenda, the obvious danger is that essential services may be ignored. In addition, the possibility exists that local governments may allocate a significant amount of funds to provide certain services in order to follow their own partisan ideology. The lack of rigor in the Constitution allows both for a more flexible municipal agenda and for stronger ideological motives in creating that agenda. It is against this background that the practice of public administration at the local level in Chihuahua must be addressed.

The Practice of Municipal Administration and Servicing

How did the opposition administrations of Alvarez and Barrio manage to conduct urban governance under a priísta-dominated state, in light of the municipal reform and the new powers and responsibilities conferred on municipalities? The principal objectives of the two mayors were to take control of the areas of municipal autonomy established under Article 115, and to formalize relations with state and federal governments and their respective agencies (Aziz Nassif 1987). These two goals were achieved, to a limited extent, in that both municipalities secured independence and efficiency in certain public services. The salient feature for both the Alvarez and Barrio administrations, however, was a lack of fluid intergovernmental relations, particularly after Saúl González Herrera replaced Oscar Ornelas as governor of Chihuahua in 1985. State-municipio relations deteriorated to such an extent that the panista mayors petitioned the Supreme Court in Mexico City to allow local governments the freedom to control municipal services without harassment from the state (*La Nación* June 1, 1985).

Table 10.2 shows the allocation of responsibilities for services and public works, differentiating between those that are broadly under state or federal control and those that fall under the municipality. As a general rule throughout Mexico, large-scale, expensive projects are the responsibility of higher levels of government, particularly where they are important for production (such as power, water, etc.). In these cases municipalities may have partial responsibility for domestic hookups and/or for the maintenance of domestic supply networks, but the costs of installation of a service and of providing the primary and secondary network of infrastructure invariably fall to federal and/or state commissions. This may be achieved in liaison with a municipal committee, such as the Junta Municipal de Aguas y Saneamiento, but even here the weight of political decision making is heavily in favor of state authorities (Gilbert and Ward 1985). Under the panistas in Chihuahua, the practice of government and intergovern-

Table 10.2: Urban services under Panista control in Chihuahua and
Ciudad Juárez, 1983–1986

Urban Development Responsibilities	Full State and/or Federal Control	Overlap in Function	Full Municipal Control
Services			
Public safety			X
Garbage			X
Slaughterhouse			X
Health		X[a]	
Urban beautification			X
Housing	X		
Land regularization			X
Street nomenclature			X
Human services			X[b]
Works			
Electricity	X		
Water/drainage		X[c]	
Paving		X[c]	
Street repair/street lighting			X

[a]The municipio was responsible for certain health facilities, such as local
rehabilitation centers; otherwise federal and state institutions, or private clinics,
handled health services.
[b]Human services included sports and cultural facilities, community programs,
social centers, etc.
[c]Water/drainage and paving remained gray areas, where the state maintained
significant influence over planning and financial appropriations.
Sources: Interviews and informes from the Barrio and Alvarez administrations.

mental relations were characterized by three different situations: conflict
and tension, where the state directly interfered in municipal affairs or
failed to relinquish municipal services to the ayuntamientos; increased
independence, where the municipalities improved local coordination over
particular services; and autonomy with minimal tension, where municipalities managed public services independently and communicated or dealt
very little with the state.

Conflict and Tension

Both Alvarez and Barrio had to contend with a number of instances
where the state government impeded or refused to grant autonomy over
a variety of municipal functions. In the city of Chihuahua, an example of

this conflict arose when the local government attempted to convert the Legarreta Orchard into a public park. When the Alvarez administration initiated work on the site in 1984, a PRI-affiliated organization, the Comité de Defensa Popular (Popular Defense Committee, CDP), invaded the orchard with the intention of both obstructing further development and antagonizing the PAN. In addition, Governor Ornelas denied Alvarez's request for state police support to remove the CDP, which resulted in an inadequate response by the local government and the death of two municipal police officers. The conflict seriously undermined the credibility of the Alvarez administration, since the state was seen to side openly with the CDP, rather than with the municipal government.

Another area of tension occurred in both cities over the degree of autonomy allowed to the Junta Municipal de Aguas y Saneamiento (Municipal Water and Drainage Board, JMAS). Interviews conducted with PRI and PAN officials involved in public works revealed a general consensus that the JMAS was, for the most part, staffed by municipal authorities but remained dependent on the state government for financial resources. The state traditionally charged the municipality for water fees, while maintaining sole possession of all budgetary records. Upon entering office Alvarez and Barrio demanded that the state open Water Board documents, but they were denied access. By increasing water fees and forcing panista municipios to pay JMAS deficits, the state in effect forced the PAN mayors to implement a highly unpopular policy of raising user fees.[4] As noted already, the provision of water and drainage services imposes heavy financial and technical costs and is a classic area requiring intergovernmental collaboration. Although these federal and state agencies tend to be run primarily according to technical criteria, as Ward elaborated upon in the preceding chapter, the chief of public works in Ciudad Juárez at the time noted that his panista government had experienced difficulty working with both BANOBRAS and SEDUE.

Increased Independence

However, the PAN municipal governments had more success in securing autonomy and formalizing municipio-state relations in several other local functions, such as the *rastro* (slaughterhouse) and public security. Both Alvarez and Barrio made unprecedented advances in achieving local control over the rastro. Slaughterhouse activities in the two cities had traditionally remained in the hands of official organized labor unions, in this case the CTM, which maintained strong corporate ties to the PRI.

After 1983, however, it legally fell under municipal direction. CTM workers were reluctant to diminish their control of the slaughterhouse and threatened to strike. Yet rather than alienate the union workers by rejecting their demands, Alvarez and Barrio drew up new labor contracts and successfully resolved the differences between employees and their administrations. This helped to prove that opposition mayors could, in some instances, negotiate with PRI-affiliated institutions in order to secure autonomy over municipal services.

During past priísta local administrations throughout the state of Chihuahua, the duties of state and municipal public security tended to overlap and had the effect of weakening the autonomy of the local police department. Indeed the governor often expected to appoint municipal chiefs of public security. Not surprisingly, both PAN governments wanted to appoint their own local police chief, since public security had become a major plank of their administrative program. As part of their own moral renovation campaign and their effort to reorganize and improve the departments of municipal security, Alvarez and Barrio broke with the traditional arrangement and placed the local police under full municipal control (Aziz Nassif 1987). This led to uneasy relations with the state government, particularly when interim governor Saúl González Herrera attempted to fire the municipal police chief of Ciudad Juárez prior to the 1986 elections. The chief publicly declared that the governor was stepping beyond his legal bounds and that only Barrio could remove him from office. After a week of unsuccessful threats made against the chief of police and against his staff, the state finally backed down.

Autonomy with Minimal Tension

Functions traditionally overseen by the municipio (garbage collection, street lighting and street nomenclature, urban beautification, human services, land regularization, etc.) continued unhampered by the higher levels of government and their agencies. In some of these municipal responsibilities, the PAN managed to increase the level of service over that achieved by previous PRI administrations. When Saúl González Herrera took over as governor some tensions arose, as the state slowed down funds for local services and became less cooperative with the panista governments. By this time, however, Alvarez and Barrio had already consolidated municipal direction and financing over a majority of local duties (particularly garbage collection, public security, and street lighting), such that there was little the governor could do.

The level of intergovernmental tension was at its lowest during the period when Oscar Ornelas occupied the governor's office. By all accounts, including that of Luis Alvarez himself, Ornelas was a "decent and considerate man," who treated these local governments in a remarkably even-handed way. Perhaps it was precisely his openness that cost him the governorship of Chihuahua, as he was required to step down by President de la Madrid shortly before his period ended. Analyses of the series of events surrounding his downfall suggest that it was primarily due to his willingness to open the political space for the opposition in his state to a degree with which many priístas felt uncomfortable.

The Paradox of Autonomy

While the extent to which interparty conflict led to any significant variation in the level of finances accorded to these two governments of the opposition must remain somewhat speculative and unresolved, there are other areas of municipal financing about which one can be more definitive. One such area is the ways in which each municipality sought to take advantage of the Municipal Reform and to actively develop its internal resources. It is also useful to analyze the way in which the governments under study spent the budgets at their disposal, compared to those that preceded and succeeded them. The paradox here is that while each panista mayor and ayuntamiento was placed under severe financial and political constraint by the state and federal governments, both were able to develop a genuine autonomy *precisely because they were opposition governments.*

This was so for two reasons, one economic and concrete, the other political and more abstract. The former was the reforms to Article 115 of the Constitution; the latter, however, is most interesting and completely unexpected, and thus I shall discuss it first. Often PRI municipal governments are viewed as mere extensions of their priísta state government. Moreover, state capitals tend to be considered as little more than the governor's backyard, and thus the pattern of intergovernmental relations tends to be rather different. In essence state capitals, as dual seats of government (state and municipal), inevitably allow a higher potential for sharp conflicts of interest to exist, as perceived or actual responsibilities overlap. But this was not the case during the Alvarez administration in the state capital of Chihuahua. Precisely because there existed a partisan break between the two levels of government, Alvarez seemed to enjoy greater influence and prominence than would normally accompany a municipal president of the ruling party. Any priísta mayor would be reluctant or unable to challenge the state government, and most certainly not the mayor of a state capital. Here as soon as the priísta gubernatorial candidate is able to do so within the confines of the phasing of elections, he will ensure that one of his own people is put up for election to the mayor's office; assuming that he wins, the latter's role will remain a subservient one. This is not the case where an opposition party wins power and where challenges and clashes between mayor and governor are expected. This discrepancy is illustrated by the fact that opposition mayors are invariably assured of an audience with the governor if they so desire, as Bailey illustrates in the case of the panista mayor of Santa Catarina in Nuevo León. The very fact that municipal autonomy was an issue from 1983 to 1986 surrounded the panista mayors with an aura of importance, thereby increasing the level of autonomy their governments enjoyed.[5] Within the constraints imposed upon them by the administrative structure, opposition mayors could identify their own priorities and mount their own programs, subject only to having the necessary finance as well as the political support and authorization from the cabildo, as Ward explained in the previous chapter. They enjoyed at least *some* measure of political autonomy, whereas often their priísta counterparts did not.

The other source of autonomy alluded to above was due to the Municipal Reform of 1984. Although Article 115 was written into the Mexican Constitution in 1917 and had just recently been reformed, its full provisions had never been invoked by a municipal government until 1984, when Luis Alvarez led a lawsuit against the state. Although a litigated settlement was never reached, the state was obliged to grant the municipalities of Chihuahua certain autonomous rights, the most important of which was the authority to determine and collect property taxes at the local level. In addition to being a sort of moral victory for the opposition, the state's concession gave the panistas access to crucial funds, allowing them to set the more autonomous political agenda discussed in the previous chapter. It also led to a drastic change in the financial autonomy of municipalities.

Over the course of only a few years, the ratio of state to local revenues available to the municipalities changed from around 70 percent *state* funding to over 70 percent *local* funding (ingresos propios). This information, provided by the former Juárez treasurer, has been confirmed by Ordóñez Barba's data, which are reproduced in a revised form in table 10.3. In Ciudad Juárez, specifically, while the proportional increase in state

Table 10.3: Revenue and revenue sources for Ciudad Juárez
1980–1990 (thousands of pesos)

Year	Federal and State Funds	Percentage	Local Funds	Percentage
1980	156,350	59	108,650	41
1981	220,920	58	158,800	42
1982	307,600	62	192,400	38
1983	870,100	70	327,900	30
1984	1,535,888	52	1,417,628	48
1985	2,175,369	41	3,082,233	59
1986	4,837,701	38	7,893,041	62
1987	9,907,260	30	23,116,941	70
1988	21,073,085	25	63,219,256	75
1989	24,999,850	22	88,635,830	78

Source: Gerardo Ordóñez Barba, 1990.

participaciones barely changed in real terms throughout the 1980s, that of ingresos propios rose dramatically, achieving almost a sixfold increase during the decade—an increase initiated by the Barrio regime (Ordóñez Barbo 1990, table 6). Local revenues rose in 1984 by 300 percent in real terms over those of the preceding year. What this means, therefore, is that the rise in real funding available to these two city governments during the 1980s came from an increase in locally generated revenues, not from state appropriations. Significant increases in locally generated revenue of course allowed for greater financial autonomy in both Ciudad Juárez and Chihuahua. Given that is was less easy for priísta administrations to avail themselves of the municipal financial autonomy accorded by Article 115, we believe that this turnaround occurred because a panista government won power.[6] However, once such a turnaround had been established, it was rarely reversed, and successive PRI governments in Juárez and Chihuahua appear to have enjoyed the benefits as well. The PAN began the process of raising the proportion of revenues generated locally, a process that the PRI continued (and intensified), albeit largely by moving away from the panista emphasis upon derechos (service charges, etc.) and concentrating instead on aprovechamientos (fines, surcharges, etc.) (Ordóñez Barba 1990, table 8). In a similar manner, once the PAN had broached the issue of raising the land tax (predial) by making its collection more efficient and by updating the cadastral register upon which the tax was levied, successive administrations maintained the system. The pattern appears to be one of revising the cadaster in the first year of office (thereby achieving a significant real rise in income) and then letting the real value of land taxes decline until after the next election. Needless to say, few governments want to expose themselves to unpopularity in an election year.[7]

Thus one can draw two general conclusions from this examination of intergovernmental finance. First, although the state government in Chihuahua enjoyed important financial leverage over the municipalities, it chose to shape municipal financial autonomy by means of more subtle restraints rather than by blatant manipulation of the official participaciones. While it has been shown that there were cases of direct state intervention in the affairs of the opposition municipal governments, as discussed in the previous chapter, the extent of partisan interference in the realm of intergovernmental finance was less prominent. Second, it can be concluded that in some respects these opposition governments enjoyed a greater degree of freedom or autonomy simply because they were opposition governments. Adding to this freedom was the crucial fact that the implementation of Article 115 allowed municipalities to raise an unprecedented amount of local revenue, thereby facilitating the implementation of their own political agendas. It remains debatable whether the subtle forms of financial manipulation used by the state infringed on the autonomy of the PAN-controlled municipalities in Chihuahua. While such intervention certainly created obstacles for them, it did not seriously detract from their ability to determine and carry out their own policy initiatives. Notwithstanding this debate, there are strong reasons to conclude that opposition municipal governments possess broader autonomous powers than do their priísta counterparts. Therein lies the paradox.

Conclusion

Are municipal autonomy and intergovernmental financial transfers really different for the opposition? The response is the proverbial "yes and no". Yes because there is a considerably lower level of interparty antagonism than one might have anticipated, which inevitably leads to more independence. And no because all lower levels of government are equally unable to fulfill their functions and carry out as many development projects as they would like; regardless of which party they belong to, all municipalities in Mexico are equally short of resources and under the control of the higher levels of government. But there are, nonetheless, some added complications for the opposition. It is evident from the experience of Mayors Barrio and Alvarez that an opposition government indeed faces many difficulties in making transitions within traditional political systems. When the opposition government finds itself surrounded by hostile governments and organizations entrenched within the traditional system, the difficulties multiply. In the early 1980s, Ciudad Juárez and Chihuahua were panista islands in a sea of PRI governments; inevitably both municipalities met a substantial amount of resistance in their attempts to govern. In its role as an opposition government, the PAN had to face the ingrained political attitudes and systems that had developed during the fifty years in which the PRI controlled all levels of government. While they operated with a different focus from that of previous municipal governments, much of the systematic corporatism continued in other cities and particularly at the state level.

In such a context, these opposition governments came to power under expectations of change, and one of the more remarkable changes that occurred was in the pattern of intergovernmental relations. In previous years the PRI had controlled both levels of government, and influence over local administrative responsibilities was much less sharply defined between the state and the municipality. The opposition ayuntamientos of Alvarez and Barrio sought to put their relationship with the state on a more formal basis and to clarify the responsibilities of each. The state was expected to hand over the budget, while the municipality attended to the local duties with which it had become charged under the newly reformed law governing municipal autonomy (Aziz Nassif 1987:185). One assumes that the PAN did not expect this to occur without a fight, but we have seen how in the arena of municipal financing the two governments were not severely prejudiced nor antagonized by the state government. Although the data are ambiguous, my contention is that the state did not hold back major lines of funding, although it is probably fair to conclude that the panista governments were not blessed with special project funding either. Also some uncertainty was engendered through the process of tortuguismo, although as I have pointed out, this is not the preserve of PRI-PAN intergovernmental relations, but rather one that spans the politcal process at large. Although there was an initial hiatus brought about by the lack of funds in the treasury when Alvarez took over, it was promptly resolved. Moreover, as we have seen, the PAN achieved notable successes in its municipal budgeting, mostly through economizing and cutting out waste and through increasing internal revenues by extending and updating various elements of each city's fiscal structure. Once in place, many of these innovations and initiatives appear to have been retained by the PRI governments that succeeded them.

As far as urban administration and the provision of public services are concerned, Alvarez and Barrio were again reasonably successful in demarcating local and state responsiblities. The two mayors were unable to gain full autonomy over large-scale works, especially paving and water and drainage projects, but constitutionally and practically this logically fell beyond their aegis. It was in these areas of overlapping function where the state was able to manipulate and restrict local autonomy to a certain extent. As Alvarez commented in his final public address, the state refused to release BANOBRAS funds for local public utility works, thereby ignoring the juridical premise of Article 115. On the other hand, the PAN did succeed in advancing municipal authority over most public services, such as the rastro and public security. Certainly tensions did mount somewhat when Saúl González Herrera was appointed interim governor, with a mandate to thwart panista progress and to prepare the way for a PRI electoral victory in 1986. Although he did seek to constrain the activities and successes of both municipal governments, the two mayors appear to have been able to govern effectively and to carry out a large proportion of the agenda they had set.

By and large both Barrio and Alvarez exercised a rather remarkable level of autonomy in their municipal governments, but their experiences, unfortunately, cannot be generalized and applied to others. To do so without extending the analysis horizontally (to other municipalities) or temporally (taking more recent cases) would be both premature and unscholarly. These were two notable cases in the early to mid-1980s, led by able (and dominant) leaders, with minimal internal opposition from their cabildos to tie them down. They also had the advantage of being able to enjoy a new political space created by President de la Madrid's reform of Article 115, as well as being an opposition party relatively free of the timeworn practices of party hierarchy and bureaucracy. They could cut through all that and start over.

It is far from clear whether such autonomy would be so forthcoming today. With some exceptions, contemporary opposition governments seem to be much more encumbered by their relations with the other levels of government, on the one hand, and by internal divisions in the cabildo on the other.[8] Both present major obstacles for governance. In addition, the pattern of panista local governmental agendas has become more widely known and predictable, and therefore other tiers of government have become more adept at responding to them. Finally, an important caveat must be entered at this stage: these two experiences were new and in some ways experimental. Perhaps the real challenge and indeed the acid test of whether government styles and behaviors are fundamentally different is to establish some opposition continuity. It is a major achievement to attain a considerable level of autonomy, to turn around municipal finances, and to implement more efficient systems of public administration. It is an even greater achievement to sustain and intensify those processes from one administration to the next. In part that is a challenge with which the PRI has had to live for over sixty years; for the opposition that test has yet to be confronted.

Notes

1. However, Alvarez did comment that Saúl González Herrera had been appointed in order to take a more aggressive line with the panistas and that negotiations with him were more difficult and problematic than they had been with Ornelas.

2. For example, after the earthquake in Mexico City in 1985, the massive funds generated for the reconstruction program were channeled through the Secretaría de Programación y Presupuesto, then headed by Carlos Salinas de Gortari. The sector responsible for the reconstruction was to be SEDUE, but its head had been severely embarrassed by not being able to proceed swiftly enough, because the funds were held up in SPP. President de la Madrid lost patience, sacked him, and replaced him with a salinista from SPP, Manuel Camacho. The latter did an excellent job with the funds now promptly released, and both he and of course Salinas went on to higher things. Tortuguismo may well be, in many cases, the meat of Mexican politics.

3. "Public safety" includes the administration of local prisons.

4. The Chihuahua city treasurer at that time (Humberto Abud Abud) commented that payments on the JMAS debts could potentially bankrupt the municipality (El Heraldo de Chihuahua, March 14, 1985).

5. At the opposition government conference held at UT Austin in April 1992, Guillermo Pizzuto, the immediate past municipal president of San Luis Potosí (a state capital) stated that unlike many PRI municipal presidents in the state, he had no difficulty getting an audience with the governor. As he wryly noted, however, having the door open did not help much in terms of positive outcomes for the city.

6. This inability was due to the traditional dependence of priísta mayors upon the governor and other party higher-ups for future career advancement. For a PRI mayor to press for greater municipal financial autonomy would be to engage in a zero-sum game with the state bureaucracy; the municipality's gain would be at the state's expense, and would therefore have to be forgone.

7. This is a real dilemma for any government and especially for an opposition party coming to power. Any revision in the property tax base must be made in the immediate postelection phase. As Dr. Nava commented at the Austin conference, "Sure I could have raised the *impuesto predial*, but I wouldn't have remained municipal president very long." That Mayors Barrio and Alvarez were able to do so probably reflects the mandate with which they were elected, the speed with which they moved to revise the tax base, and the fact that they dominated their respective cabildos. Elsewhere if local governments are unwilling or unable to raise the real level of taxes levied, then their only option is to make the existing process more efficient, for instance by ensuring that all properties are included in the tax base. Such a "cleansing" may raise the level of taxes collected by up to 20 percent.

8. In the particular case of Baja California, our work suggests that both the Ruffo state government and the four municipalities themselves have actively developed greater autonomy and responsibility for a wide range of activities. That has mostly come about as a result of Governor Ruffo's strong interest in the principle of decentralization and the need to generate resources at the local level.

11

Fiscal Centralism and
Pragmatic Accommodation in Nuevo León

JOHN BAILEY

Given the pronounced centralism in contemporary Mexico, the fate of opposition governments at the state and local level rests in good part on the interaction between the presidency's project to regenerate sustained economic growth along with regime recomposition and the various factors that determine the effectiveness of local oppositions.[1] The argument of this chapter is that the pattern of central-local interaction in the case of Nuevo León after 1985 has promoted a pragmatic accommodation (as opposed to a principled acceptance) of opposition-party mayors. This is because the central government exercises overwhelming control over state and local governments, whether these are in the hands of the PRI or opposition forces. Thus the presidential system can give ground in electoral politics, up to some still-undefined limit, while retaining effective control over governance. Furthermore, the accommodation itself and the program and behavior of the PAN in Nuevo León fit the center's larger purposes. Nuevo León's situation, then, resembles that of Baja California and Chihuahua and differs from that of other states that are marginal to the center's economic reform program, such as Michoacán, Oaxaca, or San Luis Potosí, in which the PRD and/or regional or personalist coalitions figure prominently in local oppositions. In brief, the center needs governability in Nuevo León if growth led by the private sector is to succeed; and governability in that state implies greater pluralism and partisan accommodation.

The larger theoretical question, which my particular discussion will not of course resolve, is whether the pragmatic accommodation that has opened opportunities for oppositions in Nuevo León and other states will evolve toward sustainable democratic practices in which transparent procedural rules will determine who governs. Another possible outcome is a reinvigorated presidentialism reasserting authoritarian control, a modernized form of *dictablanda* or *democradura* (O'Donnell and Schmitter

1986:10–14), in which the presidency decides according to its own calculus of power which electoral outcomes to honor and which to overturn.[2]

My particular perspective on centralism and the case of Nuevo León emphasizes fiscal processes and policies. I shall build on Victoria Rodríguez's discussion of intergovernmental finance (preceding chapter) to show that recent trends in Mexico toward even greater fiscal centralization are products of the economic crisis of the 1980s as well as facilitators of the presidency's project of economic growth and regime recomposition. More simply, the ever-greater concentration of decision-making power in the center provides to some extent the assurances of control that permit a limited opening of political spaces to oppositions at the state and local levels.[3]

I shall integrate the discussion of intergovernmental fiscal relations into the larger political context of the implementation of a new national development project in the second half of the 1980s. My discussion of Nuevo León will show that after 1985, the PRI government worked to reach a pragmatic accommodation with panista mayors. With the election of Sócrates Rizzo (a member of the Salinas inner circle) as state governor in July 1991, the tolerance of the opposition evolved into a sort of tacit "gentleman's agreement" to the effect that the PRI government would administer elections fairly in exchange for the opposition's acceptance of electoral outcomes. In the August federal elections, the PRI swept all ten of Nuevo León's congressional districts, contributing to the party's recapture of undisputed control of the congress. This was President Salinas's prime object, given the need to consolidate reform initiatives. In Nuevo León's local elections of November 1991, the PAN won an unprecedented five (of fifty-one) municipalities.

Salinas: Economic Restructuring and Pragmatic Liberalization

The contemporary situation of opposition municipal governments ought to be viewed in the context of the collapse of a long-standing statist, inward-looking style of governance, marked by centralism and authoritarianism. The Salinas government's project, which combines elements of authoritarianism with economic restructuring and pragmatic political opening, is above all an effort to regenerate sustainable growth. President Carlos Salinas's efforts toward economic restructuring and regime recomposition represent the most recent demonstration of the PRI government's remarkable survival skills.[4] Economic restructuring, which takes priority, means shifting from development led by the state to that led by the private sector. This implies a profound reform of the state, reducing the direct role of government in the economy and promoting efficiency through changes in institutions and regulatory practices.

Two themes are especially important in Salinas's economic project. First, inflation must be reduced to single-digit levels, compatible with the goal of regional economic integration with the United States and Canada. Thus public-sector spending must be contained and the tax base expanded. Second, private-sector investment must be stimulated on a large scale over a long period of time, in order to achieve acceptable growth rates.[5]

An important implication of Salinas's economic project for this discussion is that until structural reforms have brought about sustainable growth, the public sector will continue to be starved for the resources needed to meet the basic requirements of welfare and infrastructure investment. Also the central government will attend to its own financial needs first and foremost, not only to buttress presidentialism, but also to achieve macroeconomic goals. In the meantime state and local governments, long accustomed to a lean diet of revenues, must fend even more for themselves.

Regime recomposition implies a certain compatibility of interests between the PRI and the PAN, while fostering tensions with elements of the old order, primarily most of the labor unions, and the left-populist PRD. Under the banner of "Social Liberalism," the Salinas government seeks more open and positive relations with private entrepreneurs, the Catholic church, and the United States. Rather than the traditional stance of state corporatism and extensive top-down controls over broad spheres of civil society, this government calls for "coresponsibility" and "solidarity" with society. Panista currents have long advocated similar stances. Rather predictably, while the modernization, probusiness rhetoric of *salinismo* resonates well with such former antagonists as the church and some businessmen, it provokes tensions and splits in the PAN, whose leaders see much of their program and support bases being coopted by it.[6] The President's rhetoric and reforms also antagonize members of the old PRI coalition and create problems of legitimating the project in terms of the populist heritage of the Constitution of 1917.

The breadth and thoroughness of Salinas's reform agenda is impressive. Whether essential to its implementation or not, power had been reconcentrated to a remarkable extent. This reconcentration was dramatized in a series of "miraculous acts," such as the commando-style kidnapping and arrest of the leader of the petroleum workers in January 1989 and the imprisonment shortly thereafter of a leading businessman on charges of stock-market manipulation.

Reconcentration is also seen in center-periphery relations, as will be shown with regard to intergovernmental finance.

Recentralization in Fiscal Policy

If we set aside any consideration of credit flows and focus on taxing and spending in recent years, we see that the overall trend has been toward centralization and strengthening the presidency at the expense of state and local governments.[7] This is the case both with respect to which levels of government make the rules (and thereby tend to benefit) and also with respect to how the policies are implemented. I use "recentralization" because I want to show how, following an interesting effort to decentralize (or at least to deconcentrate) aspects of policymaking during President de la Madrid's term, President Salinas's government has recentralized important powers.[8]

Recentralization in Taxation and Revenue Sharing

Rodríguez (forthcoming) shows clearly how the trend in shares of taxation has benefited the central government in recent years. Further, her discussion brings out how the revenue-sharing system in effect since 1980 has made the state governments more dependent on a federalized system, because the states surrendered their independent tax sources in exchange for shares of revenues as determined by a formula. The states in turn are required to pass through to their municipalities a minimum of 20 percent of funds received through revenue sharing. But this is done according to state law (or practice, in the absence of law) and places the municipalities somewhat at the mercy of the (usually) priísta governors, who frequently reward their allies and punish their opponents. Municipalities also receive a much smaller amount directly from the federal government, through the Municipal Development Fund.

Recent debates about revenue sharing in Mexico thus revolve around two themes, one procedural and the other substantive. Revenue sharing was expanded dramatically in 1980, in the form of a legal compact between the central government and the states; in this sense the debate concerns the constitutional prerogatives of the states. As to substance, the question concerns how much of the tax income the central government should keep and how the remainder should be divided among the states.

An important incentive in 1980 to persuade states to forego their constitutional right to tax certain sources was that the state governments were guaranteed more income from the new system. Furthermore, the state governments were to administer the new federal value-added tax (Impuesto al Valor Agregado, IVA), the main source of revenue-sharing funds. State treasury departments collected the IVA and sent the proceeds to the national treasury, which then added revenues from other sources and distributed formula-determined fractions among the states. The states benefited substantially from this arrangement, because they could monitor flows of revenues precisely and thus keep tabs on their federal colleagues. Also state treasuries kept the interest income from short-term deposits of revenues in local banks, which in the high inflation years of the mid-1980s amounted to considerable sums.

Legally, therefore, the states freely entered into a pact with the central government in which state's rights would presumably be preserved. Over time, however, revenue-sharing decision making became governed by a kind of majority-rule principle among the states. One rather predictable implication is that the poorer states wanted the revenue-sharing formula rewritten to strengthen redistribution over derivation (that is, states receive in proportion to their contribution). The central government, for its part, claimed to be dissatisfied with the insufficient rigor with which certain states were administering the IVA. In 1989 the predictable alliance gelled. The administration of the IVA was recentralized and the revenue-sharing formula was rewritten to upgrade population size over economic production. As one might well imagine, the thinly populated, but more efficient and productive states, such as Baja California, Nuevo León, and Sonora, were unhappy with this turn of events. Baja California, with its panista governor, protested vigorously, but to no avail; party discipline helped muffle dissent in the other states. In the case of Nuevo León, its priísta congressional delegation objected, as did the mayor of Monterrey. Governor Jorge Treviño Martínez, however, urged understanding of the central government's financial plight, saying, ". . . you can't get something from someone who doesn't have anything."[9] Nor were the states cheered by the treasury's unilateral decision in 1992 to cut the IVA rate from 15 to 10 percent, in order to bring tax policy into closer alignment with its prospective North American trade partners. The central government covered its revenue shortfall in part by raising gasoline prices; but the solution for state and local governments is not obvious.[10]

Recentralization in Planning and Budgeting

The creation of the Ministry of Planning and Budget (SPP) in 1976 as the centerpiece of a more comprehensive administrative reform constitutes a watershed in center-periphery relations in Mexico. In a relatively brief span, the new agency was able to exercise effective controls over both the central government agencies, including their field offices in the states, and the state and local governments (Bailey 1984; Graham 1990:106–8). Subsequently SPP's coordinating machinery (such as the COPLADE and the CUD) was substantially strengthened by constitutional amendments introduced by President de la Madrid in 1982. These added new provisions or modified existing rules to designate the federal government as the "rector" of national development and to upgrade "democratic planning" to constitutional status. With these reforms de la Madrid introduced a National System of Democratic Planning (SNPD), which had the effect of legalizing the SPP's enhanced powers. In sum, planning provided the tools to extend presidential influence into policymaking within central ministries and, equally significantly, into state and municipal governments.

Throughout his 1982 presidential campaign, de la Madrid emphasized decentralization as a priority goal. One of several steps to implement the goal was the creation in the SPP of the Subsecretariat of Regional Development and the opening of a new budget line, Branch XXVI. At least three ends were sought: first, to consolidate existing regional development programs, such as COPLAMAR and PIDER, into one agency; second, to reinforce federal-state cooperation in planning and budgeting by channeling investment funds through the COPLADE-CUD machinery; and third, to favor somewhat the poorer states. The amounts that flowed through Branch XXVI were comparatively small, but the fact that it was relatively unfettered *investment* spending made it particularly welcome to governors and mayors.[11] And the tendency during 1983–88 was to loosen restrictions on state use of Branch XXVI money. Though there are no independent assessments, the COPLADE structure was probably strengthened as a result. Redistributing money to the poorer states had practical as well as normative rationales. States such as Oaxaca, Chiapas, and Guerrero lacked the planning infrastructure to produce fundable projects at a pace and quality to compete with states such as Nuevo León, Chihuahua, and Jalisco in the regular budgetary process. Branch XXVI was a useful compensatory device.[12]

With President Salinas Branch XXVI was substantially restructured in 1989 as the National Solidarity Program, or PRONASOL. A discussion of the purposes, scope, and complexity of PRONASOL would take us rather far afield.[13] But one administrative effect of PRONASOL has been to replace the various programs of Branch XXVI (such as special coordination or regional employment) with new programs that tend to be subject to greater centralized control (such as municipal aid or "dignified school"). Furthermore, through matching-fund requirements, PRONASOL has had an important effect in shaping state and local spending to meet federal priorities.

In January 1992, midway through President Salinas's term, the SPP was abolished. Most of its planning and budgeting functions were returned to the treasury, but regional development (that is, PRONASOL) was transferred to the Secretariat of Social Development (SEDESOL), a reorganized version of the erstwhile Secretariat of Urban Development and Ecology (SEDUE). Both the administrative restructing and the spending increases budgeted for PRONASOL set the course for recentralization to continue through the Salinas sexenio.[14]

The Logic of Partisan Accommodation in Nuevo León

President de la Madrid's government was laying the foundations of economic restructuring in the mid-1980s, just as political oppositions were reaching their apogee. One of the most violent clashes between the PRI and the PAN took place in Monterrey in July and August of 1985, as a result of the disputed gubernatorial elections of that year. But in the case of this northeastern industrial state, the heavy-handed official fraud and repression of 1985 marked the beginning of a transition toward greater partisan tolerance. Both structural and conjunctural factors account for the tendency.

In demographic and political terms, Nuevo León is something of a city-state, with almost 80 percent of the state's approximately three million residents concentrated in the Monterrey metropolitan region, which consists of the state capital and six adjoining municipalities. The state is among Mexico's wealthiest, ranking at or near the top on measures of income, education, health, housing, and the like (INEGI 1991). The Grupo Monterrey includes the most technologically advanced and export-capable holding companies in the country (Pozas 1990). With access to Texas, some 165 miles to the north, Nuevo León is well positioned for closer economic integration with the United States. And with three notable universities and at least two daily newspapers known for quality and independence (as well as the largest number of television satellite dishes per capita in Mexico), information flows freely.

The point to underline is the structural convergence of the de la Madrid–Salinas modernization project and the geography, society, and economy of Nuevo León. Furthermore, as the modernization project became more clearly defined in the late 1980s and early 1990s, public opinion in the north of Mexico showed increasing support for President Salinas and (to a lesser degree) for the PRI (Bailey 1991). As indicated above, the center's need for governability has implied greater pluralism and partisan accommodation. How has this come about in Nuevo León, and what are some implications for the treatment of opposition mayors, especially with regard to fiscal matters?

State governors enjoy considerable latitude in daily governance, including the treatment of oppositions. Jorge Treviño Martínez, a career administrator in the federal treasury ministry, won the PRI's gubernatorial nomination in Nuevo León in 1985 due to his close friendship with Miguel de la Madrid. Like the president, Treviño was trained in law and did graduate work in public administration, a kind of transitional career pattern from old-style lawyers to "purer" types of *técnicos*. Treviño was hampered by the lack of a personal base in the state, divisions within his own party, opposition by elements of the Monterrey Group, and the violent fraud that marred his election, all of which were magnified by independent media and an unusual degree of international scrutiny. A characterization frequently made of Treviño is that he is "just like de la Madrid," suggesting that the governor was a well-intentioned and thoroughly competent administrator. And a contrast is often drawn with his predecessor, Alfonso Martínez Domínguez, generally regarded as a consummate political operator of the old school. Martínez Domínguez had been selected in 1978 by President José López Portillo, in part to offset the power of former President Luis Echeverría, and in part to deal with urban popular movements in the Monterrey metropolitan area that were complicating governance. Martínez Domínguez grudgingly accepted opposition-party representation in the powerless state legislature, because the reform was an extension of the federal reforms of 1977. But he tolerated no opposition governments in the municipalities.[15]

Treviño, in contrast, adopted an above-the-fray style: good administration is good politics. He refused to cultivate the media or to curry special support with the industrial elite. His independence, feasible given de la Madrid's backing, confounded and irritated the local political elite, who focused on the governor's conspicuous lack of polish in oratory or political etiquette. Treviño's style, however, reinforced administrative autonomy in state government, where Víctor Gómez, treasurer since 1973, had already established a reputation for professionalism and fairness. In electoral matters Treviño insisted on recognizing opposition victories where valid. When in the 1988 elections a left-populist coalition won the small town of Bustamante (population 2,976), and the PAN won the Monterrey suburbs of Santa Catarina and San Pedro Garza García (with populations of 164,000 and 113,000, respectively), Treviño's policy was strict enforcement of state law: opposition municipalities would receive all revenues legally due them.[16]

The case of Bustamante is best understood as result of conflicts within the PRI, leading to schisms and defeat; the town returned to PRI control in 1991. The other two cases are more interesting. With large concentrations of middle- and upper-strata residents, San Pedro is the wealthiest of Monterrey's suburbs. The PAN there has a strong organizational presence, and three different panista mayors have held office, beginning in 1964. The party's success is due to its organizational strength in the area and the electorate's impatience with priísta corruption.[17]

Santa Catarina, a working-class suburb, represented one of the most notorious cases of a long-standing CTM *cacicazgo* (dating from the early 1970s). Descriptions of the union in Monterrey invariably refer to mafiaesque violence, intimidation, and corruption. The election of Teresa García de Sepúlveda as mayor on the panista ticket in 1988 represented not the victory of a party so much as a widespread disgust with union gangsterism. García was forced to govern with little party support and in constant confrontation with a hostile and aggressive union. Governor Treviño complied fully with state and federal laws in allocating resources to the city and in involving Mayor García in the council of mayors established to coordinate policies in the Monterrey metropolitan area. In fact Mayor García stated that she thought Treviño had shown her special consideration and that she noted some irritation from her priísta counterparts on the urban council (interview, Santa Catarina, November 1991). Part of the governor's support might be explained by his own difficulties with the CTM. The battles between the CTM and reform elements in the PRI government at the state level were particularly heated in the last half of Treviño's term.

President Salinas's modernization project shows perhaps its clearest manifestation in Nuevo León. The president proclaims his *norteño* roots in the state; he gave his major campaign speech on economic modernization in San Pedro, Nuevo León. Within months of his nomination, he sent Sócrates Rizzo (longtime member of his core team) to head the state PRI, paving the way for Rizzo's election first as mayor of Monterrey in 1988 and subsequently to the state governorship in 1991. For his part Rizzo as mayor hosted a show-case summit meeting of president Salinas with George Bush to promote the Free Trade Agreement, and as governor he invited leading businessmen to take positions in his cabinet.

With respect to treatment of the opposition, my own interpretation of recent events is that Rizzo made an important advance for the Salinas project by arranging a tacit "gentlemen's agreement" with the PAN before the gubernatorial elections of March 1991. In effect, in exchange for reforms in the electoral law to help assure fairness, the panista candidate was prepared to endorse the outcome. The PAN's willingness to negotiate with the PRI government might have reflected a parallel accommodation between the parties at the federal level. The PRD gubernatorial candidate was much less amenable. The exchange would help the PRI to validate its victories in the eyes of domestic and foreign critics, and it would help the opposition to win fairer rules of competition. Given the context of increased popularity of the PRI, schisms in the PAN, and the minimal support for the PRD, Rizzo's team saw acceptable levels of risk in the agreement. In the August 1991 congressional elections, the PRI won a clean sweep. But in November the PAN won five municipalities, extending its hold on San Pedro and Santa Catarina and adding San Nicolás de los Garza in the Monterrey area.[18] To date there is no evidence of discriminatory treatment by the governor against opposition cities; to the contrary, the most important evidence that opposition mayors have received generally fair treatment is the absence of complaints in a free press.

Along with pragmatic accommodation in Nuevo León has come fiscal crisis and increased dependency on federal government support. In the absence of adequate revenue or federal spending, Governor Treviño created new mechanisms to finance public works, including private investment (such as toll roads), trust funds financed in part through private bank credits (such as FIDEINOR, for development in the northern part of the state), as well as increased state borrowing. Rizzo inherited a substantial state debt, and the first months of his term were devoted to intensive (and ultimately successful) lobbying in Mexico City for additional federal support.[19]

Table 11.1 illustrates aspects of spending implemented (as opposed to approved) by the Nuevo León state government in constant (1980) pesos in 1986–90. We find three interesting messages here. Firstly, expenditures in general behave erratically, suggesting the uncertainty that pervades public finance at the subnational level. Secondly, following substantial increases in 1986–88, total state spending subsequently dropped off rather quickly. Thirdly, subsidies to municipalities more than doubled in 1986–87, but then flattened out through 1990.

Table 11.1: Nuevo León state government expenditure and municipal subsidy, 1986–1990 (millions of 1980 pesos)

| | 1986 | 1987 | 1988 | 1989 | 1990 | Percentage Variation | | | |
						1986/ 87	1987/ 88	1988/ 89	1989/ 90
Municipal subsidy	303	688	718	630	708	117.0%	4.4%	(10.9%)	12.4%
Total Expenditure	6,303	7,563	9,971	8,875	8,140	20.0	31.8	(11.0)	(8.3)

Source: Gobierno del Estado de Nuevo León, Secretaría de Finanzas y Tesorería General

Table 11.2: Distribution of CUD spending in Nuevo León, 1986–1990 (selected items, millions of 1980 pesos)

	1986	1987	1988	1989	1990	Percentage Annual Variation			
						1986/ 87	1987/ 88	1988/ 89	1989/ 90
Obras Transporte	95	184	57	152	222	93.7%	(69.0%)	166.7%	46.1%
Sistema Caminos	131	107	66	213	172	(18.3)	(38.3)	222.7	(19.2)
Municipio Monterrey	71	62	49	163	211	(12.7)	(21.0)	232.7	29.4
Municipio Guadalupe	24	20	17	62	99	(16.7)	(15.0)	264.7	59.7
Municipio San Pedro	12	7	9	48	50	(41.7)	28.6	433.3	4.2
Municipio Escobedo	–	–	–	47	38	–	–	–	(19.1)
Municipio San Nicolás	18	10	6	23	38	(44.4)	(40.0)	283.3	65.2
Total	952	816	556	1,721	1,639	(14.4)	(31.78)	209.5	(4.8)

Source: Nuevo León, Secretaría de Administración y Presupuesto, *CUD: Inversión Total Aprobada por Dependencia Ejecutora* (Mimeo, 1991).

As seen in table 11.2, federal spending in Nuevo León (also in constant 1980 pesos) as channeled through the CUD in 1986–90, also behaved erratically. But interesting changes marked the arrival of the new administration in Los Pinos in Mexico City and in Monterrey's city hall. Whereas state spending dropped by about 11 percent in 1988–89, federal spending nearly tripled. Furthermore, as may be observed in table 11.2, Monterrey's share of CUD spending more than tripled in 1988–89 and rose another 29 percent the following year. While the rising tide of 1988–89 raised all municipalities, San Pedro (under panista administration) benefited most, with spending there increasing by a multiple of five. However, as Fox (1994) correctly points out, we do not know to what extent these funds passed *through* or *around* San Pedro city government.

More to the point is that PRONASOL has come to represent an increasingly vital source of spending in Nuevo León. Governor Rizzo's contacts in the Salinas government have served the state well, in comparison with his counterparts in Baja California and Tamaulipas. Virtually all of Nuevo León's mayors, including those from the PAN, vigorously lobby both Monterrey and Mexico City for shares of PRONASOL spending. In this sense of generalized dependency, then, the center can more easily tolerate oppositions, especially those that tend to support the broader project.

But the tolerance to date must be considered more pragmatic than principled. The positive scenario, often cited in official circles, is that important changes are underway, creating circumstances that will reinforce liberalization. A more critical public, one more prone to demand legal rights, will increasingly insist on procedural fairness. Opposition leaders have become more mature and constructive, attentive to the difficult circumstances of governance as their prospects of reaching power increase. However, for committed democrats there is a negative scenario as well; much rides on the success of President Salinas's economic project. Should the PRI see its popularity in the state dwindle, or if the PAN should adopt more confrontational tactics, or (less plausibly) should the left gather significant support, there is no assurance that accommodation will continue.

Notes

1. The author is grateful for support received from the Fulbright-Hays Program and the Center for U.S. Mexican Studies of the University of California, San Diego. In addition to the editors, Vivienne Bennett and Deborah Odell provided useful comments. The usual disclaimers of responsibility apply. Regime

recomposition, discussed below, refers to efforts by incumbent political elites to transform bases of support for the regime, such as interest groups, party and electoral systems, or ideology, in order to retain power.

2. A particularly useful discussion of possible scenarios for Mexico's political development is Cornelius et al. (1989:36–45). The case of Nuevo León tends to support their scenario of "partial democratization," ". . . which implies a willingness to surrender control of municipal and state governments regularly to the rightist or leftist opposition in their regional strongholds, in the interest of staying in power at the national level" (1989:41). The limited record in Nuevo León, the elections in 1988 and 1991, does not quite justify the notion of willingness to surrender control "regularly."

3. This discussion draws on my work in progress on themes of centralism and political change in Mexico since 1979.

4. President Salinas's strategies can be gleaned from core documents. See Salinas (1988, 1990).

5. "According to the government, only one out of ten people in Mexico comply fully with their fiscal obligations. Of over 21 million people in the workforce, only 2.3 million pay their taxes" (El Financiero, Weekly International Edition, March 30, 1992, p. 5). As to reliance on the private sector, presidential adviser José Córdoba Montoya recently went on record to the effect that Mexico requires US$150 billion new net foreign investment over the next ten years to achieve a 6-percent GDP growth rate, as targeted in Salinas's economic development plan. (El Norte, April 30, 1992, 1-A).

6. The long-simmering feud between neopanistas and the so-called foristas led to a split in the party's national leadership in October 1992.

7. While public credit institutions such as BANOBRAS and NAFINSA remain centralized, the reprivatization of the commercial banking system after 1989 was a step toward decentralization, creating apparently a series of regionally based oligopolies. The argument is developed at greater length in Bailey (1992).

8. I am following Rodríguez's use of centralization, decentralization (or devolution), and deconcentration.

9. Interview, Monterrey, Nuevo León, October 1991; Tijuana, Baja California, April 1992. Quote from Proceso, November 26, 1990, p. 29. Ortega Lomelín (1988) provides excellent background on the evolution of revenue sharing. Detailed discussion of the formula can be found in Ortiz (1991).

10. Some priísta politicians in Nuevo León, in turn, linked part of their 1991 electoral problems to the central government's gasoline price rise.

11. The bulk of federal spending, even more so during the financial crisis of the 1980s, consists of current spending (salaries, rents, supplies, and the like). Investment money goes toward capital creation, in this case small-scale public works.

12. Interview, Mexico City, October and November 1992; Monterrey, November 1991. On decentralization see Rodríguez (1992), Torres (1986). For an official history see SPP (1988).

13. See Dresser (1991), Cornelius et al. (1994), and the chapter by Fox and Moguel in this volume.

14. Palacios (1989) provides an important analysis of the distribution of central government investment in the states.

15. Interviews, Monterrey, September and November 1991; Mexico City, May 1992. On urban movements in Nuevo León, see Bennett (forthcoming). On Martínez Domínguez's style, see Farías (1992:318–22) and a fascinating memoir of the 1979 gubernatorial election by the panista candidate, José Angel Conchello (1980).

16. State law (1985) sets out a clear formula for allocating revenue-sharing funds among the municipios. General and complementary funds: 6 percent in equal shares; 47 percent according to the IVA collected in the previous year; 47 percent according to population. (Gershberg 1990, Annex O).

17. See Livas (1983) for an excellent analysis of the endemic problems of municipal corruption in San Pedro.

18. While the 1991 elections were generally seen as cleaner than previous ones, the losing panista candidate in Monterrey complained bitterly about official fraud. He was unable, however, to mount a sustained popular protest. Official fraud was made to appear both ridiculous and ineffective by the daily *Porvenir,* which placed an informant in a priísta "fraud squad" in the San Pedro mayoral election. Not only did the priísta candidate lose, he was threatened with prosecution by the state's Attorney General!

19. See, for example, "Pedirá Sócrates 10 mil millones más al Pronasol," *Diario de Monterrey,* August 2, 1991, B-1; "Dialoga Rizzo con autoridades de Programación," *El Norte,* August 24, 1991, 3-B; "Urgen recursos para el estado," *El Porvenir,* October 9, 1991, 1-B.

12

Pluralism and Anti-Poverty Policy

Mexico's National Solidarity Program and
Left Opposition Municipal Governments

JONATHAN FOX AND JULIO MOGUEL

President Salinas's high-profile National Solidarity Program (PRONASOL) claims to strengthen municipal governance, making revenue sharing and antipoverty programs more effective through decentralization and publicly accountable service delivery. Critics have charged, however, that PRONASOL is used for electoral manipulation and bypasses opposition municipalities, especially those of the left. Government officials deny that antipoverty policy discriminates, pointing to significant levels of spending in opposition areas. This paper will explore these claims, beginning with an overview of PRONASOL and followed by analyses of Mexico's principal left opposition municipalities in the states of Michoacán and Oaxaca.[1]

Antipoverty policy in Mexico has long been considered an instrument of political control. A wide range of political systems, including many that hold regular elections, oblige poor people to sacrifice their political rights in exchange for access to antipoverty programs. Yet as others before us in this book have noted, President Salinas entered office after a hotly disputed election, declaring that the one-party system was over. As a reformist bent on "modernizing" Mexico's economic and political system, he sought to revive citizen confidence by bypassing both the partisan opposition and the regime's traditional corporatist apparatus. Salinas promised a new relationship between state and society, bringing redistributive spending under the rubric of the National Solidarity Program. The convergence of two different streams of policy reform under the Solidarity umbrella (targeted social policy and efforts to strengthen municipal autonomy) places the municipality at the center of the debate about whether antipoverty policy is actually becoming more pluralistic.

PRONASOL and Social Policy Reform Cycles

The Mexican government launched a series of attempts to reform antipoverty policy beginning in the early 1970s. Each has involved community participation in local public works and the provision of services to some degree. The evolution of these efforts, especially in rural development and urban neighborhood housing and services, has seen some movement away from traditional clientelist politics toward greater room for community participation in the policy process.[2] These policy reforms have been paralleled by the growth of independent representative organizations of low-income people, usually based on producer, consumer, or neighborhood associations. These organizations have often mobilized for increased government accountability in social policy implementation. The government's creation of channels for community participation and oversight involved a growing recognition, albeit slow and very uneven, of autonomous representative groups as legitimate partners in the policy process. Yet this more inclusionary approach to social politics preceded the intensification of electoral competition in Mexico (after 1988), and therefore is not a good "test" of whether antipoverty policy is becoming politically pluralistic as regards elected opposition governments.

While PRONASOL's official discourse of participation and coresponsibility drew from these earlier social programs, four differences are especially notable. First, PRONASOL responded directly to the center-left electoral challenge of 1988. Second, PRONASOL focused on the municipality, not just federal agencies, for service delivery. Third, it concentrated on both the urban and the rural poor, while past programs had dealt with one or the other. Fourth, Solidarity's ideological thrust was much more important, promoting the idea of a new, more balanced partnership between state and society.[3] This cooperation was carried out by reformist state managers who sought interlocutors, or counterparts in society, in their effort to undermine both more rigidly authoritarian colleagues within the regime and their confrontational (*contestatario*) adversaries in the partisan opposition.

PRONASOL and the Municipality

According to Carlos Rojas, PRONASOL coordinator, Solidarity "makes the constitutional reforms to strengthen the free municipality a reality" (Rojas et al. 1991:38). The 1983 amendment of Article 115 of the Mexican

Constitution had given municipalities much more responsibility for service delivery, and town councils were created to decentralize municipal administration. But the reform was partial, since it did not bolster the new capabilities of municipalities with greater sources of revenue (Martínez Assad et al. 1987:312). The decentralization of power to local governments promised to have a contradictory impact, strengthening the provision of public services only insofar as those governments combined both resources and accountability.

The actual degree of accountability and antipoverty targeting of this revenue sharing depended largely on whether the democratic process was allowed to operate in a given locality. Even under democratically elected local governments, moreover, there was no guarantee that Solidarity funding would be clearly targeted to the poorest of the poor.[4] For example, tensions between town centers and outlying villages (*agencias*) are common. Even where public works were built in poor regions, the electoral logic of high-profile bridges, highways, and basketball courts had little to do with poverty alleviation. According to one top policymaker, of PRONASOL's 1991 budget of 5.2 billion pesos, no more than 2 billion should really be counted as targeted antipoverty spending. The rest consisted of untargeted public works.

The municipalities are involved in several different Solidarity programs, including the "Dignified School" renovation program, the Solidarity Children scholarships, on-your-honor Production Supports for campesinos not eligible for bank loans, and Municipal Solidarity Funds (FMS). Nationwide the FMS include about two thousand poor municipalities, in twenty states, for a total expenditure of about 240 million dollars in 1991. Grants are provided for infrastructure and programs to meet basic social and economic needs as well as to create employment opportunites. The community is to be an active participant in the identification, design, implementation, and evaluation of each project. This is to be done through the establishment of municipal councils, the creation of local committees, and coordination with organized social groups. The municipal councils are especially important, since they permit representation of outlying villages (*agencias*) as well as the county seat (*cabecera*). States contribute about one-quarter of the fund and the communities about one-fifth.

Most PRONASOL funding was distributed through state and municipal governments via grants, under the category of "Solidarity for Social Welfare," previously referred to as the Planning and Budget Ministry's Branch XXVI.[5] This federal budget category is officially quite discretionary, in contrast to the technical formulas for most federal revenue sharing. By the late 1980s, these formulas included greater redistribution of revenue from richer to poorer states (Bailey 1992). These revenue-sharing laws also obliged state governments to pass on a greater share of federally allocated tax revenues to the municipalities, yet they left state governments the discretion to allocate funds between more and less favored municipalities (Rodríguez forthcoming). In contrast, Solidarity's federal block grants-in-aid come with strings attached, creating a focal point for serious behind-the-scenes conflicts between salinistas at the federal level and more traditional party-oriented state authorities (priístas), especially those inherited from the previous presidency and not beholden to President Salinas.[6]

PRONASOL and Electoral Politics

It would appear that the underlying rationale for PRONASOL was politically motivated, in that it skillfully targeted disproportionate resources to "recover" contested areas (Molinar and Weldon, 1994).[7] But the targeting of spending to swing districts did not necessarily mean that citizen access to the program's benefits was systematically politically conditioned on traditional forms of subordination. The panorama was varied, but on balance, most of the electorally targeted spending was probably delivered through "semiclientelist" means.[8] In some sense communities were "rewarded" for their political opposition, in that the government competed to win back their support or at least acquiescence, but fraud was still actively used just in case semiclientelism failed.[9] At the same time, selective political violence against the left continued with impunity.[10]

PRONASOL tended to centralize power, promoting a symbolic link between the president and the local community, often bypassing both local authorities and traditional political bosses.[11] At the receiving end, PRONASOL usually required beneficiaries to form Local Solidarity Committees, which in turn could choose from a fixed menu of public works (such as electrification, paved roads, school repair, and so on). Solidarity claimed to have created over a hundred thousand local committees, with an estimated average of 120 people each (Gallegos 1992). They became increasingly important as deliberate counterweights to the official party apparatus, parallel to Salinas's effort to bolster the party's territorial structures and in direct conflict with the traditional corporatist sectors. The president openly encouraged the Local Solidarity Committees to build statewide and possibly national organizations, with what he called the "new mass politics of the Mexican state."[12]

Where opposition political parties managed to both win over the majority of voters and succeed in defending their municipal victories, federal PRONASOL funders appeared not to discriminate; officially PRONASOL worked with almost all opposition municipalities (171 of 173 in 1991).[13] But many opposition mayors frequently protested that the program linked the state and federal government to Local Solidarity Committees, bypassing them completely.[14] The case studies that follow draw out the diverse patterns to be found behind official and opposition claims.

City and Countryside in Michoacán

No one doubted Michoacán's *cardenista* vote in the 1988 federal elections. After all, both father and son had been governors, and Don Lázaro had sunk deep roots in the state when he was president (1934–40). In 1988 the sweep for his son, "The Engineer," for president also carried two of his ranking associates to the senate, one of whom would become candidate for governor four years later. In the municipal elections of December 1989, *cardenismo* again showed its political force in the state; the fraud was exposed and could not prevent the newly formed Party of the Democratic Revolution (PRD) from winning 52 of the 113 municipalities.[15] This sweep accounted for most of the PRD's municipal victories nationwide during the 1989–91 period.

But the situation changed significantly in the 1991 midterm federal elections for the congress and for one-third of the senate. The PRD vote fell to such a degree that many considered it a complete debacle. The PRD won a majority in only 27 districts of the 52 municipalities that it governed in Michoacán, and furthermore its margins of support in 25 of those 27 cases was reduced. It also lost a senate seat (see Bruhn and Yanner, this volume). Many editorialists and political analysts attributed the PRD's defeat in part to its internal conflicts, but above all to the government's steamroller campaign to win the state back. The decisive instrument, according to most analysts, was the National Solidarity Program, which was seen to have politically undermined PRD supporters and mayors. Some analysts further suggested that because of Michoacán's importance as a PRD bastion, the blow to the party was irreversible, ruling out its viability as a contender in the upcoming 1994 presidential race.[16] Subsequent events cast some doubt on these interpretations, since the PRD's effort to render the state sufficiently ungovernable with postelection protests paid off, and President Salinas ended up abandoning his chosen candidate for governor after he had been sworn in and was obliged to appoint yet another temporary compromise priísta.[17]

Analysts who based their projections on the August 1991 congressional race neglected to take into account two factors: first, the relative unimportance of these elections to most voters (compared to presidential, mayoral, or governor's contests) and second, the PRD's critical internal divisions at the time, which were later partially overcome. They were correct to suggest, however, that PRONASOL was key to the government's effort to win back the state. For example, 12 percent of PRONASOL's entire 1992 budget went to the relatively small state of Michoacán, the main base of the center-left PRD, timed to fall just before the heated gubernatorial elections. One-fourth of the twenty-five hundred PRONASOL promoters nationally were deployed for the Michoacán governor's race (Cantú 1992). In addition to PRONASOL, an independent estimate of the governor's election campaign expenses topped US$30 million dollars, over $70 per vote officially cast for the PRI (Chávez 1992).

Clearly Michoacán's impressive quantity of PRONASOL resources was driven more by electoral competition than by objective considerations of the degree of absolute poverty in the state.[18] But if antipoverty resources were "politicized" to this degree, how did they affect PRD municipal governance? The pattern was not uniform; two layers of patterns can be found. Statewise the PRD mayors divided into two camps: those less committed to the national leadership and more willing to bargain for local benefits; and those who took a more militant stance in support of the party's national emphasis on clean elections. Since the PRD in Michoacán was largely composed of former priístas, divisions over whether and how to negotiate with the government were not surprising. Even among the municipalities where the PRD was strong, however, different patterns of relations with PRONASOL emerged.

The clearest pattern of PRONASOL's politicization of relations with PRD mayors combined boycott with the organization of parallel authorities by state and federal authorities in the form of the Local Solidarity Committees. This pattern was most notable in the state capital of Morelia, by far the state's largest urban center and therefore high priority for the PRI's planned electoral comeback. Morelia's mayor, Samuel Maldonado, accused the federal government of "invading" functions that belong to the municipality; the federal government announced and carried out public works projects without local consultation (Cantú 1992).[19]

In terms of Solidarity's operation at the local level, one president of a Local Solidarity Committee in Morelia, Alberto Avalos Ceja of the Colonia

Primo Tapia, said that "the system imposed the program. We have received support from the state and federal government; on the other hand, the PRD city government has been unable to help us." He said that the committee is not ideological, "but we all know where Solidarity comes from." Other local Solidarity leaders were more direct: "if folks are grateful, they'll know who to vote for." As Juan Ciro Martínez, advisor of the Solidarity Committee of Ampliación Primo Tapia put it, "It's all political. PRI folks came here . . . and said that we had to affiliate with the party to solve our problems. Since we didn't accept, there's been no response to our requests." He further explained that a PRI candidate for the state legislature was one of those involved; "he came and he said that for each ten requests that the PRI received, they would take care of nine; while for the other parties, only one in ten requests would be met" (Cantú 1992).

In this effort to weaken PRD municipalities, most Solidarity funds passed only nominally through town treasuries; they often came with predefined projects and lists of required recipients attached.[20] This pattern was most notable in the larger, more electorally important municipalities, but it was also found in some smaller rural towns. According to Jesús Romero, mayor of Ziracuaretiro, Solidarity "was the black part for us; the town hall had to regularly confront the program officials because from the very beginning they went ahead without the municipal authorities. Projects proposed by the citizenry were ignored and there was no planning of any kind, limiting Solidarity to the solution of a few social needs. I'd say that it put us into conflicts with townspeople, at the same time as we were used." On the one hand, he felt his community was being divided, and when the resources did come, their use was out of his control. The mayor of Parangaricutiro reported a similar experience: "The program was *viciado;* it jumped over the municipality. The government agencies involved dealt directly with the producers." According to the mayor of Mújica, "PRONASOL violates the Constitution because it undermines the municipality and reduces it to the role of delivery boy."[21]

In contrast to this pattern, José Luis Esquivel Zalpa, mayor of Paracho in the heart of the pro-Cardenista Purépecha highlands, reported that "a long talk" with Carlos Rojas had led to his community getting 1000 million pesos for the restoration of an old boarding school, to turn it into a crafts and cultural center. He then took advantage of one of President Salinas's many visits to the state to bargain for the paving of a key road; "if the president was going to come, we had to charge him a toll . . . but the only thing we won, that we rescued [out of PRONASOL] was that we [were the ones who] formed the Solidarity Committees rather than the government agencies; only that way were we able to get the most out of the projects."[22] In Paracho the PRD was able to make the local committees work for them instead of against them, implying that political negotiation styles and skills may have affected PRONASOL implementation. There were some cracks in the system after all.

Many PRD municipalities were bypassed and undermined by PRONASOL, but not all, and not even all of those who remained firmly within the PRD camp. The larger PRD municipalities tended to be undermined, with PRONASOL appearing to take advantage of internal division with the PRD itself. But among the many small, rural municipalities, the pattern was much more diverse. Furthermore, a systematic comparison with priísta municipalities in the state would be required to come to firmer conclusions, since some progovernment mayors also complained that they were bypassed by federal authorities coming in and setting up their own Solidarity Committees. One rural PRD mayor reported that the priísta mayor of a neighboring municipality said that "he envied us, because at least we were able to protest, and he doesn't even have that right."[23] This is the "paradox of autonomy" to which Rodríguez refers in her chapter in this volume.

Juchitán, Oaxaca

Juchitán is another key case for analyzing the degree of pluralism in PRONASOL–opposition municipality relations. While not as politically and economically important as Morelia, it is the second largest city in Oaxaca (120,000 inhabitants) and occupies a strategic position in the Isthmus of Tehuantepec. Juchitán is especially notable for its role as Mexico's first significant municipality won by the left opposition, from 1981 to 1983 (when the state government removed it by force).[24]

After almost two decades of regional electoral and social mobilization, the Coalición de Obreros, Campesinos, y Estudiantes del Istmo (COCEI) won official recognition of its 1989 municipal election victory as an affiliate of the PRD. However, in contrast to Morelia and many of the other PRD municipalities in Michoacán, Juchitán was not boycotted or bypassed by PRONASOL. The COCEI administration actually benefited greatly from PRONASOL resources, according to mayor and longtime COCEI militant Hector Sánchez (Sánchez 1991). Why is there such striking variation? It would appear that the Juchitán experience is a case in which one of PRONASOL's main structural problems, its high degree of centralized discretionality, was turned to the opposition's advantage.[25] The COCEI had long been bitterly opposed by Oaxaca's governor and by the local ruling party. If revenue sharing and PRONASOL block grants had been allocated only through the state government, as was the case in many states and most of Oaxaca, then the COCEI would have been frozen out. Instead the COCEI was able to bargain directly with federal PRONASOL authorities, bypassing its adversaries in the state government.

In contrast to the rest of the PRD, the COCEI mayoralty negotiated directly with PRONASOL from the beginning. With a huge backlog of unmet local needs, the municipal administration did not share the national party's strategic decision to reject the Salinas government as illegitimate (because of fraud in the 1988 presidential elections). The PRD's position was that since Cárdenas had actually won the election, to deal or "concert" with the government was to implicitly legitimate the president's victory. Thus the strong implication was that any social movements or elements of the party that did bargain with PRONASOL were in effect breaking ranks.

Certainly it seems likely that at least at the outset (1989–91), Salinas's team may have intended to open relations with the COCEI and with other pragmatic groups from the social left both inside and outside the PRD, as part of an effort to drive a wedge between the more confrontational national PRD leadership and some of its local allies. One important goal was to be able to win political points by signing and publicizing official *concertación* agreements between PRONASOL and social movements, even those on the left. It is not coincidental that President Salinas, in exchange for the first concertación agreement with the COCEI, required that they sign it together in a massive public event welcoming him to Juchitán. Nor was it coincidental that elements of the PRD bitterly criticized the COCEI as a result.[26] By 1991, however, the PRD's position had moderated, recognizing that their sympathizers should both claim their right to development funds as citizens and taxpayers and still vote their conscience. Even once this point of conflict abated, the COCEI municipality continued to receive PRONASOL funds, in part because of its own administrative and bargaining skills, and it began to cover a long list of local infrastructure, service, and productive needs. The COCEI administration presented itself as a "government for all" (Sánchez 1991).

In contrast to several of the Michoacán cases discussed above, where the Local Solidarity Committees became bypass mechanisms for creating pro-PRI counterweights, the COCEI was not weakened by divide-and-rule tactics. The COCEI experience was more like that of Paracho, where the opposition appropriated the local Solidarity Committees. Juchitán's 150 officially reported Solidarity Committees were actually based on the COCEI's long-standing structures and process of community action. Nonetheless Juchitán's administration did have some problems with Solidarity, including a notable 1991 budget cut that blocked the continuation of several projects then under way.[27] One cannot assume, however, that such problems were necessarily political, because the COCEI maintained its PRD affiliation.[28] Such complaints are also heard from some priísta municipalities and are due, above all, to the "structural weaknesses" of PRONASOL: its discretionality, little citizen participation in determining project budgets or contents, serious problems in resource delivery, abrupt cuts, and turf battles with state governments.[29]

Was the federal government using PRONASOL to try to coopt the COCEI? To deal with the question, one must take into account the COCEI's history. The federal government's decision to reject the partisan entreaties of Oaxaca's state government and to channel significant resources to the opposition municipality involved several factors. First, federal authorities were convinced that the COCEI had sunk such deep roots in Juchitán that it was a lost cause from the point of view of the official party. Moreover, the COCEI had demonstrated a greater capacity for representation and governance than had local PRI elites, having managed to survive and flourish under the most hostile political conditions for two decades. The second factor was the uniqueness of the COCEI's alliance with the PRD. The COCEI had emerged from Mexico's locally based, nonpartisan "social left," in spite of its various electoral alliances with national left parties.[30] In this context the COCEI's high degree of autonomy vis-à-vis the national PRD leadership allowed it to pursue its own negotiation strategy with PRONASOL.

Conclusions

The federal government used PRONASOL to undermine some, but not all, PRD municipalities; some in fact gained access. PRONASOL boycotted and bypassed the left opposition in many cases, both as part of a multifaceted campaign against the flagship municipality of Morelia, as well as through the simpler mechanism of creating pro-PRI counterweights in Ziracuaretiro, Parangaricutiro, and Mújica. In other cases, some PRD municipalities in Michoacán less committed to the national leadership accepted PRONASOL's divide-and-rule efforts, effectively drawing them away from the opposition and, in two cases, returning them to the PRI. Other PRD municipalities, such as Paracho (Michoacán) and Juchitán (Oaxaca), strengthened their capacity for governance with PRONASOL resources, while remaining identified with the opposition. On different scales, in both municipalities the opposition was able to "appropriate" the Local Solidarity Committees in ways that resonate with the official discourse of participatory development and coresponsibility. The range of relationships between PRONASOL and opposition municipalities was therefore not determined by the government's two-track strategy alone (boycott or attempted cooptation) but rather depended as well on the strategies and bargaining capacity of the opposition social and political actors themselves.

The Juchitán authorities were able to draw upon their long-standing political autonomy in order to maximize their bargaining power for PRONASOL resources. The COCEI's symbolic power as a militant pillar of the opposition made it an especially attractive partner for the Salinas government in its search for interlocutors. At the same time, the COCEI's area of influence was regionally circumscribed and, while accounting for most of the PRD votes in the state, did not threaten to spill over into other regions and thereby threaten PRI control of the governorship. PRONASOL support for the COCEI administration may have irritated the state government, but it did not weaken it in other regions.

In Michoacán, in contrast, the PRD did pose a statewide threat. To strengthen opposition municipal governance capacity therefore did conflict with the government's broader goal of keeping the PRD out of state office. Thus it would be difficult to argue that the PRD in Morelia missed an opportunity to negotiate a less conflictive relationship, such as that in Juchitán. Morelia was the party's *línea de fuerza* for the state, and by extension, key to its claim to national status on a par with the National Action Party (which already governed several state capitals). For PRONASOL to have supported pro-PRD local Solidarity Committees and projects in Morelia would have conflicted with the regime's central political strategy of rolling back the PRD in its own stronghold. In conclusion, PRONASOL's relations with left opposition municipalities did tend to be politicized in an effort to divide them from the PRD national leadership, but some room for maneuvering remained, depending on the state electoral context and local bargaining strategies.

Notes

1. For overviews of municipal politics and the independent left, see López Monjardín (1986, 1991) and Fox and Hernández (1992).

2. These policies included the PIDER rural development program in the mid-1970s and the FONHAPO urban housing and CONASUPO-COPLAMAR rural food store programs in the early 1980s, as well as the housing programs that followed the 1985 Mexico City earthquake. For further discussion see Fox (1992, 1994) and Ward (1986, 1993).

3. Solidarity combines various ideological strands. From the center right, it draws from the traditional Christian Democratic beliefs in nonantagonistic community participation in the provision of public goods, as distinct from the Mexican state's traditional populist recognition of the legitimacy of class organization and conflict. It draws from the Mexican social left, which since the early 1970s has called on the state to abandon its support for authoritarian corporatist organizations and to cede power to autonomous social movements. Some currents in the Mexican social left share with Solidarity the idea that group involvement in the direct provision of material benefits is more important than participation in civic or partisan debates about broader national policy issues. See Moguel (1994).

4. For example, regardless of the validity of the voting process in and of itself, municipal authorities generally underrepresent indigenous citizens (except for Oaxaca), who account for 15 percent of Mexico's population. In recognition of this problem, Solidarity supports a major new development program which is jointly administered by the National Indigenous Institute and the Regional Solidarity Funds (FRS). The FRS program aims to turn local socioeconomic investment decision making and revolving loan funds over to autonomous regional councils of elected indigenous social and economic organizations. In contrast to most nonmunicipal PRONASOL programs, where the state creates its own interlocutors, the FRS claim to attempt to bolster existing representative organizations. Research in Oaxaca, where one-fifth of the FRS operate, shows that they have been relatively pluralistic. Out of twenty regional funds, only three clearly excluded organizations that should be included according to the program's own criteria (Fox 1994). Many autonomous and opposition-identified producer organizations participate, including, for example, many members of the autonomous Coordinadora Estatal de Productores de Café de Oaxaca (CEPCO), which represents almost half of the smallholders in the state (on CEPCO, see Aranda and Moguel 1992). In the process diverse indigenous organizations developed new pluralistic *instancias* of resource-allocation decision making at the regional level, introducing genuine, if not always balanced, power sharing among contending organizations of civil society for the first time. On PRONASOL's mixed relations with coffee smallholders and its other major effort to support indigenous producers, see Hernández and Celis (1993).

5. According to the official data, this category accounted for 90 percent of PRONASOL spending in 1989 and 80 percent in 1990 and usually required cofinancing from state and local governments. Officially "in this way, Solidarity has articulated with traditional social policy, but added an important modification in the institutional behavior, attitudes, and thinking" (González Tiburcio 1991:9).

6. According to one credible report, a top PRONASOL official confided that as of October 1991, just before the president defined PRONASOL as the "political base" of his government, twenty governors "did not accept PRONASOL and differed with its strategies and principles." The commentator observed that "we are speaking of two-thirds of the country's governors, most toward the end of their terms, who owe their careers and their posts to the old political system and the party that sustained it" (Fernández 1991).

7. PRONASOL's geographical choices in its Regional Development programs are especially revealing, since they explicitly target areas that were hotly contested in the 1988 presidential race (La Laguna, eastern Michoacán, the Isthmus of Tehuantepec, the state of Mexico, the Tierra Caliente area of Guerrero, and the Oaxaca coastal region). PRONASOL defined itself as a "programa de gobierno," to highlight its ostensibly nonpartisan character, later describing itself as "political, because of its link to the people, but not partisan" (cited in *La Jornada*, July 28, 1992).

8. Under traditional clientelism, authoritarian controls required political subordination in exchange for material benefits. Semiclientelism is defined here as a system that also attempts to extract obedience for benefits but lacks strong enforcement mechanisms. Clientelism depends on both carrots and sticks, while semiclientelism shifts the mix toward the carrots, because it has less recourse to sticks. For elaboration see Fox (1994).

9. For example, PRONASOL milk outlets distributed election propaganda in Michoacán, and at the moment of checking the requisite "consumer card," the program beneficiary was invited to attend campaign events; "we were never obliged, but they did invite us. . ." (Cantú 1992). In general, however, Solidarity programs did not have the capacity to sanction noncompliance at the individual level, so it would not be considered traditional political clientelism as defined above. Some election observers critical of the program tended to ignore the subtle variations in PRONASOL's capacity to effectively condition access to votes, assuming that any citizen who received benefits with propaganda would simply follow orders (see Convergencia 1992). The key variable is whether the ballot is actually secret; in Michoacán secrecy was violated in one-fifth of the precincts observed. In these semiclientelist transactions, voters may have the option of voting their conscience, but it must also be remembered that this shift from sticks to carrots takes place in the context of the generally flawed electoral system. For example, over a hundred thousand likely opposition voters were reportedly "shaved" from the registration rolls in Michoacán, especially in urban PRD strongholds (Bardacke 1992).

10. See America's Watch (1990, 1991). The PRD reported that 145 of its members have been killed as a result of political violence since 1988 (*La Jornada*, July 29, 1992). Over 70 percent were killed in the states of Guerrero, Michoacán, Oaxaca, and Puebla. Approximately 30 percent of the cases were directly linked to antifraud protests, 50 percent occurred during the tense aftermath, and 20 percent were social activists killed by local bosses (PRD Human Rights Commission 1992:viii).

11. For analyses of PRONASOL in the national political context, see Dresser (1991, 1992) and Cornelius et al. (1994).

12. In this context, as the president once told a long-time friend, a renowned radical leader of the urban popular movement: "You were my teacher: everywhere I go I leave a base of support." At a meeting of five hundred representatives of five thousand urban Solidarity Committees, the president called for the creation of the Coordinadora Nacional de Colonias Populares, appearing to bypass the PRI's own efforts to modernize its old corporatist organization for the urban poor. Participants even chanted "Salinas, again!" breaking the official taboo against calling for the reelection of the president (cited in Lomas 1991). This gathering was an extreme example of salinismo in action, as distinct from priísmo.

13. Where democracy did not prevail at the municipal level, however, and citizens' groups persisted in pressing charges of fraud, they were perceived as contesting the government's legitimacy and tended to be excluded from Solidarity funds. Note for example the case of Atoyac, the last municipal conflict in Guerrero's controversial 1989 elections to be resolved. While civic and opposition movements failed to win new, cleaner elections, they participated in negotiations that led to the naming of a consensus priísta for mayor, instead of the governor's much more contested ally. Even with a PRI mayor, Atoyac was treated as enemy territory; the governor froze the municipality out of Solidarity funds, using them instead to bypass and undermine the principal independent social organization in the area, the nonpartisan Coalition of Ejidos of the Costa Grande of Guerrero. The growing number of consensus mayors and governors who come from the PRI but result from compromises after antifraud campaigns constitute an important political gray area in Mexico. In the Atoyac case, the compromise mayor was overthrown by force in 1991, when the governor's state police commander arrived at the town hall proclaiming, "aquí traigo mil hombres para dialogar . . ." (cited in Nava 1991).

14. Official denials of partisan use of Solidarity municipal funds fail to clarify the issue, since they simply affirm that the government is being fair without actually providing detailed responses to the charges (see Gallegos 1992).

15. On municipal election fraud in 1989, see Tribunal (1989).

16. For an overview of the PRD's performance in the 1991 elections, see Moguel (1991b).

17. According to The New York Times, "Government officials said that even after Mr. Salinas had made a strong show of his support for the new Governor, the leftist party's protest rallies and takeovers of government buildings across the state created a stark choice between political chaos and the use of force . . . (A) senior official said "massive repression could have had very serious political consequences." Salinas announced his concession on the eve of traveling to Texas to initial the final text of the North American Free Trade Agreement (Golden 1992b).

18. Cited in Golden (1992a). According to one of Mexico's more reliable official studies of the geographical distribution of poverty, Michoacán was thirteenth from the bottom (COPLAMAR 1982:31). While this study predates the economic crisis of the 1980s, it is unlikely that the 12 poorer states moved up in the list after that time.

19. Maldonado mentioned the examples of bridges Michoacán 1 and 2, which cost 1,000 million pesos each, in contrast to a similar bridge built by the municipality, which cost 500 million pesos (Cantú 1992). The Solidarity "bypass

operation" against the Morelia city government was reinforced by the so-called "garbage war," which was launched by progovernment (pro-PRI) city workers and by disruptive protests by priísta street vendors.

20. Only one of Solidarity's many different programs, the Municipal Funds, tended to strengthen municipal autonomy generally, but Michoacán's governor did not permit this program to operate in his state. One high level federal Solidarity official speculated that the Municipal Funds' monies could have made electoral manipulation more difficult than other lines of Solidarity funding, and the governor preferred more discretionality.

21. Julio Moguel is quoting these mayors from the Primer Acercamiento al Balance de Tres Años de Gestión Popular en la Zona Purépecha, held in Ziracuaretiro, October 24, 1992. The meeting was attended by fifteen PRD mayors, mainly from the indigenous Purépecha region, sponsored by the Convergencia Campesina, an autonomous regional peasant organization.

22. Ibid.

23. Ibid.

24. For background on Juchitán politics, see Moguel et al. (1989) and Rubin (1987, 1990).

25. For critiques of PRONASOL discretionality, see Moguel (1991a) and Dresser (1991).

26. The "model" for the president's public agreement signing with left social movements was first tried out in March 1989 with the Popular Defense Committee of Durango (CDP), which had sided with Cárdenas in 1988. The CDP later broke with the PRD, forming the national Labor Party, built around other groups from the social left. Analysts still debate whether this split was predetermined or was caused more by the mutual recriminations surrounding the CDP's dealings with PRONASOL. See Haber (1989, 1992a, 1992b).

27. As Héctor Sánchez said in a major official ceremony, "we are concerned about the way in which our budgets for projects already committed are cut; even more if we take into account that some past commitments have not been met . . . Recently, we have had to suspend the continuation of some projects already begun, since Oaxaca's (state) Secretary of Planning has argued that in 1990 Juchitán received more and other municipalities less" (1991:116–17).

28. Even if the COCEI had left the PRD, it would still have been the state government's number one political adversary, because it represents the largest autonomous counterweight in Oaxaca. Moreover, if the PRD and the COCEI ever do part ways, it will probably be due more to their own political differences than to government manipulation. For example, the PRD-COCEI alliance was severely strained after the national party leadership named a former priísta adversary of the COCEI as the PRD 1992 candidate for governor of Oaxaca.

29. Conflicts between local committees and political elites entrenched in state governments are widespread across the spectrum. As one leader of a Local Solidarity Committee said in an evaluation workshop, "It is incredible that even now there are states where the Program budget is still being allocated with patrimonial criteria . . ." Notably this statement was reported in one of Solidarity's mass outreach publications (*Gaceta de Solidaridad* June 15, 1992).

30. In spite of the Mexican independent left's many branches since the 1960s,

most groups can be understood as part of either the social left or the party left. The party left was organized around national party structures, such as the Mexican Communist party, the Revolutionary Workers party, and the Socialist Unified Party of Mexico. The social left was organized in national networks of locally based mass organizations, such as neighborhood groups, trade unions, and peasant movements. Most of the social left rejected electoral participation until the cardenista movement of 1988, with the notable exception of the COCEI. See Moguel (1987). Until recently, Mexican electoral law required local and regional opposition groups such as the COCEI to ally with registered parties to get on the ballot.

13

Municipios, Opposition Mayorships, and Public Expenditure in Oaxaca

MOISÉS JAIME BAILÓN

The southern Mexico state of Oaxaca, despite possessing extensive agricultural, mining, forestry, and fishery resources, continues to be one of the most backward states of the republic in matters of social welfare, employment, and income level.[1] Sixteen of the nearly sixty indigenous groups found in the country coexist in the interior of this state, as well as 570 of the country's 2,392 municipalities and more than 20 percent of lands of communal origin.

These characteristics are not new. Unlike any other Mexican region, Oaxaca developed through a long process of struggle, confrontation, and conflict that has led to the relationships of power being constructed by permanent negotiations between the political elites that have managed the region and *campesino* (peasant) organizations comprising multiple communities that have enjoyed a large degree of local political autonomy throughout the centuries, even as they have constituted the basis for the different prevailing forms of exploitation and surplus extraction.

In this chapter I will describe the development of the local party system in the elections for municipal authorities in the last decades, and I will also analyze some of the relationships that have been established between the state and federal governments and the municipal councils (ayuntamientos) controlled by parties other than the PRI in the beginning of the 1990s.

"Communitary" Municipal Structures

The normal struggle of electoral politics does not exist in all of the 570 municipios of Oaxaca. In most of them (more than 450), the processes of designating local authorities take place outside of the formal political system. Thus there is a traditional system of elections in the state that results from the particular form in which the communities are organized. Since colonial times, in contrast with the northern zones of Mexico, where indigenous peoples were largely exterminated, in Oaxaca their communities managed to survive. Indeed they recovered socially, repopulated themselves, and began to consolidate aspects of local political organization that allowed a level of autonomous administration. As a result of a complex system of internal organization, and notwithstanding the poverty and the need for services from which many communities suffer, the indigenous peoples have maintained that autonomy. This explains in part why almost 24 percent of the nation's municipios are concentrated in this state.

In most of the Oaxacan municipios, the organization of the process of selecting a new municipal government and mayor is undertaken by the population, with no external interference. Through communitary assemblies in which the citizens deliberate, the people elect the new municipal authority by taking into account public responsibilities that the proposed individuals have previously carried out. The highest position in the community is that of mayor, arrived at only after scaling a long ladder that begins with responsibilities taken on since childhood, such as the care and sweeping of the church and running errands, or later to be appointed to the *topil,* the municipal police. Municipal public offices are generally obligatory and have no financial compensation. This system of public responsibilities applies not only to positions of authority but also to other development activities, such as the construction of a road, a school, or a potable-water system. In such cases the citizens are under obligation to provide days of voluntary labor. This institution is known in Oaxaca as the *tequio.*

Once the community has selected the new authorities through its system of assembly, they are registered in the offices of the PRI. When the official election day comes around (established under the local electoral code), the communities simply reiterate what they had agreed upon through their own procedures. This majority group of municipios, however, does not represent any idyllic community structure. Although they enjoy political autonomy, at the same time they have to confront an environment in which poverty, isolation, and lack of services are prevalent. In addition, in some cases the process of communitary designation of local leaders is distorted by an authoritarian cacique (political boss). Furthermore, not all citizens have the same power and influence in decision making, since those who predominate are the elders, who have undertaken more posts or given more effort to the development works the community has undertaken. However, the community system of municipal governance generally appears to express the feelings of the people.

By respecting this community election system, the official party (the PRI) usually wins the support of the people and reaffirms a historical compromise; the party accepts the popular decision and in exchange obtains the priísta allegiance of the community, as well as its endorsement in the legislative, gubernatorial, and presidential elections.

Municipalities in Bipartisan Struggle

Part of the origin of the opposition to the official party may have arisen from those cases in which communitary decisions were not in fact recognized and accepted by the delegates of the PRI. This provided a basis for opposition parties to proliferate in a number of municipios, especially those in which there was a wider social differentiation among the population, more diverse economic activities, and several sectoral organizations of the official party (medium-sized worker and campesino groups, often in competition with one another). There are fewer than 150 municipalities that possess these characteristics, but it is here that competition and the presence of parties other than the PRI has tended to be concentrated.

For several decades the discontent that has emerged in some municipios concerning the manner in which the PRI structured its electoral slate (*planilla*) has generated two broad responses. The first one is for those individuals in disagreement to seek to support an opposition candidate. Or alternatively, aware that any municipio won by the opposition is unlikely to receive financial support from the government, they form an independent slate not linked formally to any political party. When these groups of citizens ally themselves with an opposition party, they appear to express a greater rejection of the PRI and position themselves farther away than the independent groups or slates. The latter usually continue to turn to the PRI or to some of its delegates and enjoy a greater degree of priísta support, notwithstanding the fact that they rejected the PRI's choice of candidates. To a great extent, the formation of nuclei of opposition party activists in the municipios is due to the discontent arising precisely from the PRI's selection of candidates and the negative outcomes of many of the PRI's municipal administrations. Subsequently, through co-optation, the opposition is often brought back into the fold, to become PRI activists once again.

In past decades opposition to the PRI's designations was focused largely within the party itself. Opposition parties existed (usually the PAN, the PPS, and the PARM) only in a very few municipios. However, during the past twenty years the state of Oaxaca has undergone an important transition. In the 1970s the regional system of dominance began to be questioned by popular movements that demanded urban and rural land, higher wages, and the democratization of their institutions of government and representation. Part of that social mobilization began to express itself through electoral mobilizations to gain control of some municipal governments. Increasingly the opposition parties have gained a presence in the state, and those of the left have gone from persecution and isolation to become the main competitors to the PRI in the struggle for control of the municipalities. In 1974, for example, independent slates and opposition parties demanded that their electoral victories be respected in some eleven municipalities (including Juchitán). The number of opposition slates presented in the 1977 elections grew dramatically, and in that year they were successful in thirteen municipalities, where their triumphs were recognized, and indirectly in a further six, which were considered so conflictive that compromise arrangements of administrative juntas were established. The same pattern continued through the early to mid-1980s, with the opposition winning between thirteen and seventeen municipalities. But elections were hotly contested and conflict was frequent, often leading to the anullment of results and the imposition of administrative juntas.

Into the 1990s

By 1989 Oaxaca was entering the most pluralistic period in its municipal political history. The opposition was active in more than a hundred municipalities and had gained victory in no less than thirty-three cases. The PRD became the second force in the state and won Juchitán for the second time, two municipios on the isthmus, seven in the *mixteca* region, four in the valleys, and one each on the southern coast and in the sierra, for a total of sixteen municipios (Comisión Estatal Electoral, Oaxaca 1990).[2] The PARM had come to govern four municipios in the mixteca and one in the Papaloapan, in addition to the district capitals of Sola de Vega in the south and Pochutla on the coast (Comisión Estatal Electoral, Oaxaca 1990).[3] The PAN controlled the city of Huajuapan, four other municipios in the mixteca, and another in Miahuatlán (Río Hondo).[4] The

PFCRN controlled two municipios on the coast and one in the mixteca, while the PPS governed Santo Domingo Zanatepec for the third time in the decade (Comisión Estatal Electoral, Oaxaca 1990).[5]

Faced with the difficulty of resolving a conflict of forces vying for power and having practically the same political clientele, a Junta de Administración Municipal was established in Magdalena Ocotlán, a municipio that had been conflictive throughout the period. In two cases the conflicts have continued. In Tlacolula, where the PRI was said to have won, the Frente Unico Democrático de Tlacolula (FUDT) (an opposition movement that had governed the municipio during the previous term and which competes under the registration of the PRD) rejected the results and refused to give up control of the municipal palace. Thus the "elected" mayor was obliged to operate out of a private home. A similar situation prevailed in Xoxocotlán.

Proportional representation exists in 138 of the state's municipalities, indicating that the opposition obtained at least a minority level of votes in them. In 105 of these cases the PRI's mayors dominate, while opposition mayors govern in the remainder (the PRD in 16, the PARM in 7, the PAN in 6, the PFCRN in 3, and the PPS in 1). In the remaining 432 municipios, the PRI continues to be the only force and the dominating party, due to the alliance it continues to maintain with the indigenous communities, a pact that depends heavily upon the respect that the state and regional management of the PRI accord the internal life of the communities.

Current Dimensions of Opposition Government in Oaxaca

In numerical terms the opposition is the dominant party in 5.7 percent of Oaxacan municipios, with a total population of 254,146 (8 percent of the total state population; INEGI 1991). The population of each municipio governed by the opposition can be found in table 13.1. As can be observed in that table, the PRD is the second political force in the state, followed by the PARM, the PAN, the PFCRN, and the PPS, measured in each case by both the number of municipios governed and the population involved. However, in the 1991 elections for federal deputies and senator, the PAN displaced the PARM from third place, to become the third political force in the state (CEPES 1991).[6]

If we analyze the presence of parties other than the PRI by region, we find that in the mixteca in 1992 there were seventeen opposition

Table 13.1: Oaxacan municipios governed by opposition parties

	Population	Municipal Appropriations, 1989 (millions of pesos)	Public Investment, 1991 (millions of pesos)
PRD Municipios			
San Pedro Jicayán Jam.	8,602	52.836	452.682
San Fco. Tlapalcingo Sil.	1,414	24.441	248.847
San Marcos Arteaga Huaj.	2,230	42.353	953.383
San Vicente Coatlán Ej.	3,286	24.441	314.413
Santiago Yucuyachi Sil.	1,409	28.395	1,309.67
Ixpantepec Nieves Sil.	2,184	27.676	318.179
Calihuala Sil.	1,205	27.916	209.211
Teotongo Tepos.	1,296	39.777	765.169
Sta. Ma. Mixtequilla Teh.	3,631	27.916	5,229.43
Coatecas Altas Ej.	3,920	34.985	101.965
Santa Ma. Texcatitlán Cuic.	1,093	24.441	882.9
San Jacinto Amilpas Ctro.	2,434	24.441	3,285.104
Santa Ma. Xadani Juch.	4,955	50.919	1,599.387
Silacayoapán Sil.	11,025	244.716	4,150.273
Zaachila Zaa.	11,945	244.713	1,101.035
Juchitán Juch.	66,525	2,447.126	28,328.04
Subtotal	127,154	3,367.092	49,249.69
PARM Municipios			
Santo Domingo Tonalá Huaj.	6,601	50.68	936.702
San Jorge Nuchitá Huaj.	3,649	24.441	1,126.846
Santiago del Rio Sil.	1,154	24.441	173.422
San Lorenzo Victoria Sil.	1,519	24.441	354.412
Sta. Ma. Jacatepec Tux.	8,127	34.985	567.29
Sola de Vega Sola	11,171	244.715	7,858.385
Pochutla Poch.	25,621	391.542	4,222.442
Subtotal	57,842	795.245	15,239.49
PAN Municipios			
San Mateo Rio Hondo Miah.	3,844	28.635	262.459
San Juan Ihualtepec Sil.	1,095	24.441	83.168
San Juan Bta. Suchixtepec Huaj.	538	24.441	173.117
Asunción Cuyotepeji Huaj.	817	24.441	274.2
Santiago Ayuquililla Huaj.	2,405	29.833	444.598
Huajuapan de León Huaj.	38,992	391.544	33,101.30
Subtotal	47,691	523.335	34,338.84
PFCRN Municipios			
San Nicolás Hidalgo Sil.	1,076	24.441	75.697
Sto. Dgo. de Morelos Poch.	5,654	45.049	368.128
San Andrés Huaxpaltepec Jam.	4,991	34.266	502.339
Subtotal	11,721	103.756	946.164

Table 13.1, continued

	Population	Municipal Appropriations, 1989 (millions of pesos)	Public Investment, 1991 (millions of pesos)
PPS Municipios			
Sto. Domingo Zanatepec Juch.	9,738	64.338	2,223.195
Subtotal	9,738	64.338	2,223.195
Grand Total	254,146	4,853.766	101,997.4

Sources: Comisión Estatal Electoral Oaxaca (1990), INEGI (1990b), Gobierno del Estado de Oaxaca (1991)

Notes: The population data were taken from the Eleventh Population Census of March 1990. The municipal appropriations mentioned are those of 1989. Public investment corresponds to the budget that state and federal government agencies allocated during 1991 to those municipios governed by the opposition. Therefore, the public investment came from the normal federal and state programs and from those designated by the Convenio Unico de Desarrolo and the National Solidarity Program to be managed directly by the municipal authorities.

All of the cases described involve municipal authorities in power from January of 1990 to December of 1993. Not included in the groups of opposition governments are the cases of Magdalena Ocotlán, which is managed by an administrative junta, nor Tlacolula and Xoxo, where elections were won by the PRI but political problems have continued as a result of the social movements of the opposition.

Most of these municipios were not governed by the opposition in 1985, which is why the comparison between the two years is necessary, in order to observe financial behavior under opposition governments since 1990.

municipios (among them the important city of Huajuapan and the district capital of Silacayoapan). Seven of these municipios were managed by the PRD, five by the PAN, four by the PARM, and one by the PFCRN. The opposition governed four municipios in each of the regions of the isthmus, the valleys, and the coast. In the first region, three were controlled by the PRD and one by the PPS (one of them being the city of Juchitán). In the central valleys, four municipios were in the hands of the PRD, including the city of Zaachila. On the coast the PFCRN governed in two municipios, the PRD in one, and the PARM in the city of Pochutla. In the southern sierra, the opposition controlled two municipios, one of which was the district capital of Sola de Vega. In the mountain valley region the PRD governed one municipio, as did the PARM in Tuxtepec.

In summary, the opposition governed in six cities that were district capitals. Juchitán on the isthmus, Zaachila in the valleys, and Silacayoapan in the mixteca were controlled by the PRD; Sola de Vega in the southern sierra and Pochutla on the coast were held by the PARM; and Huajuapan in the mixteca was governed by the PAN. In the state congress, the PRI controlled the eighteen majority deputyships, while the PRD was allocated two deputies through proportional representation, and the following parties one each: PAN, PPS, PARM and FCRN.

Public Expenditure and the Municipalities

It is often argued that opposition mayorships suffer major problems in their administration, principally because the priísta state government blocks their progress and provides them with very limited resources. However, even though this might be true in some cases, in reality the data for resources assigned to opposition municipalities in Oaxaca seem to show contrary evidence (see also Fox and Moguel, this volume).

The presence of the federal government has been very important in the consolidation of emergent pluralist political participation in Oaxaca. At the beginning of the 1980s, when the COCEI (a campesino and student political movement) governed in Juchitán in alliance with the PCM, it was federal support for political reform that enabled recognition of the victory of the opposition and permitted its stability for more than two years, even though there were frequent confrontations between the municipal government of Juchitán and the state government of Oaxaca. Moreover, there was intense class conflict between the COCEI (which invaded urban and rural lands, generated strikes, and attacked entrepreneurs) and the local congress, which would eventually lead to the refusal to recognize the municipal government of Juchitán. However, from those years onward the presence of the opposition gradually gained greater importance and began to win more respect and recognition (especially in urban zones), although not without coming into occasional conflict with the state government and with the official party.

One of the indicators of this opposition and conflict is the attempt of the government to block municipios governed by the opposition through influencing the level of resources assigned to them. Below I propose to analyze two of these elements: municipal appropriations (*participaciones municipales*) and public investment.

Municipal Appropriations

Municipal appropriations are those resources the federal government grants to the state government based on its contribution to the nation's total fiscal income, as well as on other variables, such as the level of the state's underdevelopment, the size of the population, the existence of oil deposits, etc. Of the total appropriations received in Oaxaca, 20 percent are channeled directly to the municipios (see Rodríguez and Bailey, this volume, for details on the rules regarding municipal financing).

Although the data are not reproduced in full here, I have analyzed the levels of municipal funding assigned in 1985 and 1989 to the municipios governed by the opposition in 1989–92, as well as to the rest of the municipios, governed by the PRI. In 1985 total municipal appropriations amounted to 6.3 billion pesos. Of that total, the thirty-three municipios the opposition governed received approximately 510.5 million pesos, 8 percent of the total, while the rest of the municipios received the remaining 91 percent. By 1989 overall appropriations had increased to 59 billion pesos, split again in the same proportions as in 1985, a pattern that was repeated in 1990. We see, then, that regarding funding there was no alteration of municipal assignations when the municipios in question were in the hands of the opposition in 1989. This derives in part from the very limited level of resources assigned, so that they are generally very scarce for all of the municipios in the state, with the exceptions of Oaxaca de Juárez, Tuxtepec, Juchitán, Huajuapan, and Loma Bonita, all of which received an important share of the funding due to their size and economic importance.

If we wish to examine the allocation of resources by party to those municipalities governed by the opposition, then we find that there were no alterations in the amounts given to each opposition group in the two years (table 13.2). However, the municipios governed by the PRD benefitted the most, although this reflects the economic importance and higher population of those particular municipios. In both 1985 and 1989, the municipios governed by the PRD received more than 69 percent of the total appropriations received by opposition municipalities, followed by the PARM and the PAN.

Public Investment

Although I have not found substantial alterations in the state's government response to those thirty-three municipios once they began to be

Table 13.2: Oaxacan opposition municipal appropriations

Party	Municipal Appropriations, 1985 (millions of pesos)	Percentages, 1985	Municipal Appropriations, 1989 (millions of pesos)	Percentages, 1989
PRD	354.1085	69.3	3,367.092	69.3
PARM	83.6395	16.3	795.245	16.3
PAN	55.0477	10.7	523.33	10.7
PFCRN	10.9117	2.1	103.756	2.1
PPS	6.7683	1.3	64.338	1.3
State Totals	510.4760	1.00	4,853.766	1.00

Sources and note: See table 13.1.

governed by the opposition, the situation is somewhat different regarding public investment. The public investment considered here (that of 1991) is made up of the allocations received by the state government through the CUD (Convenio Unico de Desarrollo). This comprises investment through the federal agencies and programs in the state, through state gubernatorial investment, and through loans and grants from international organizations, credits, and contributions received from the target beneficiary groups themselves. In sum, this public investment is the total resources that various governmental and financial sources provide in order to finance the works of social infrastructure, support, and production in Oaxaca.

Tables 13.3 and 13.4 are useful for examining public investment in the municipios, depending upon whether they are governed by the opposition or by the PRI. In tables 13.1 and 13.3 we can see that the investment assigned to municipios led by the opposition was 101,997 million pesos, as opposed to 813,915 million for the remaining areas. Thus while opposition municipios contain only 8 percent of the population, they receive 11 percent of the investment (table 13.4). This becomes even clearer if we analyze public investment and appropriations per capita (table 13.3). While municipal appropriations per capita in both groups represent the same value (19,000 pesos), in the case of public investment opposition municipios receive an average of 401,000 pesos per capita, whereas those governed by the PRI receive 294,000 pesos. This is a significant difference.

Table 13.3: Oaxacan municipios and public funding

Government	Municipios	Population	Municipal Appropriations (millions of pesos)	Public Investment (millions of pesos)	Municipal Appropriations Per Capita (thousands of pesos)	Public Investment Per Capita (thousands of pesos)
Opposition	33	254,146	4,853.766	101,997.4	19.098	401.333
PRI	537	2,767,476	54,146.23	813,915.6	19.565	294.100
State Totals	570	3,021,612	59,000.0	915,913.0	19.526	303.120

Sources and note: See table 13.1.

Table 13.4: Oaxacan municipios and public funding—percentages

Government	Municipios (%)	Population (%)	Municipal Appropriations (%)	Public Investment (%)
Opposition	5.7	8.4	8.2	11.1
PRI	94.2	91.5	91.7	88.8
Total	100	100	100	100

Sources and note: See table 13.1.

These tables suggest that in states such as Oaxaca, which are priísta administration strongholds, opposition-party power is directly related to the ability to negotiate and exert pressure. PRI municipalities tend to be more loyal to the state government, but they receive less compared with the opposition, which gains greater investment resources through mobilization and pressure.

Table 13.5 illustrates the outcome of negotiations between the opposition and the government, carried out in order to obtain investment resources for 1991. The PAN appears to be the party with the highest success, as measured in resources per capita, with 720,000 pesos, followed by the PRD with 387,000 pesos per capita, and the PARM with 263,000. The PAN's level of funding seems to be the result of special investments that were made that year in the city of Huajuapan de León, thereby apparently placing the PAN in the highest position, which in reality probably corresponds to the PRD.

Conclusion

In spite of the limited nature of the electoral reforms that have been put into effect in Mexico in the last few decades, in the case of Oaxaca they have translated into new conditions, which have contributed to the modernization of its political system. In the first place, the majority of Oaxacan municipalities continue to be governed by the PRI under the compromise arrangement it holds with traditional systems of community representation. Second, the permanent presence of competing opposition parties that sometimes win is growing, especially among those municipios that have larger populations and more diversified social structures and

Table 13.5: Oaxacan opposition municipios and public funding, by party

Government	Municipios	Population	Municipal Appropriations (millions of pesos)	Public Investment (millions of pesos)	Municipal Appropriations Per Capita (thousands of pesos)	Public Investment Per Capita (thousands of pesos)
PRD	16	127,154	3,367.092	49,249.69	26.480	387.323
PARM	7	57,842	795.245	15,239.50	13.748	263.467
PAN	6	47,691	523.335	34,338.84	10.973	720.027
PFCRN	3	11,721	103.756	946.164	8.852	80.723
PPS	1	9,738	64.338	2,223.195	6.606	228.300
Total	33	254,146	4,853.766	101,997.4	19.098	401.333

Sources and note: See table 13.1.

economic activities. Third, there is no apparent decrease in the central or state government's assignment of municipal funds to opposition municipios, since the figures indicate that the percentages assigned to them continue to be the same as in previous years. Fourth, contrary to expectations, opposition parties manage to develop the capacity to negotiate with governmental administrations in a way that contributes to genuine political pluralism in Mexico. This often translates into public investment quotas even higher than the populational percentages they represent. In contrast, and within the same parameters, PRI municipalities appear to receive fewer investment resources from a government headed by their own party.

These findings suggest a more positive interpretation of the relationships between the opposition and governmental structures. Times have changed and so have the configurations of political power. We should take these new conditions into account in future analyses.

Notes

1. The author wishes to thank the Universidad Autónoma "Benito Juárez" of Oaxaca, together with the following institutions, for their support and funding assistance, which have made the present work possible: the Instituto de Investigaciones Humanísticas; the Fulbright Commission; the Center for U.S.-Mexican Studies at the University of California, San Diego; and the Consejo Nacional de Ciencia y Tecnología, Mexico City.

2. The municipios governed by the PRD were the following: Juchitán, Santa María Xadani and Santa María Mixtequilla in the region of the isthmus of Tehuantepec; San Francisco Tlapalcingo, San Marcos Arteaga, Santiago Yucuyachi, Ixpantepec Nieves, Calihuala, Teotongo, and the district capital of Silacayoapan in the mixteca; the city of Zaachila, San Jacinto Amilpas, Coatecas Altas (again) and San Vicente Coatlán (again) in the central valleys of the state; San Pedro Jicayán on the coast and Santa María Texcatitlán in the mountain valleys (Comisión Estatal Electoral, Oaxaca, 1990).

3. The municipios governed by the PARM were the cities of San Miguel Villa Sola de Vega in the southern sierra and San Pedro Pochutla on the coast, in addition to the following: Santo Domingo Tonalá, San Jorge Nuchitá, Santiago del Río and San Lorenzo Victoria in the mixteca, and Santa María Jacatepec in Tuxtepec (Comisión Estatal Electoral, Oaxaca 1990).

4. The municipios governed by the PAN were those of the city of Huajuapan de León (for the second time in the decade), the municipios of San Juan Ihualtepec, San Juan Bautista Suchixtepec, Asunción Coyutepeji and Santiago Ayuquililla (again) in the mixteca, and San Mateo Río Hondo in the southern sierra (Comisión Estatal Electoral, Oaxaca 1990).

5. The municipios governed by the PFCRN were those of San Andrés Huaxpaltepec, which it has controlled for most of the decade (previously as the PST), and Santo Domingo de Morelos (both on the coast) and San Nicolás Hidalgo Silacayoapan in the mixteca (Comisión Estatal Electoral, Oaxaca 1990).

6. In the elections of August of 1991, out of a total of 647,225 votes cast, the PRI won 466,208 (72 percent), the PRD 60,380 (more than 8 percent), the PAN 34,973 (more than 5 percent), the PARM 23,136 (4 percent), and the rest went to the other parties (CEPES 1991).

Part Four

Opposition Governments:
Perspectives for the Future

14

Conclusion

Regents From the Opposition

Victoria E. Rodríguez and Peter M. Ward

If the subtitle of the Austin conference (Past Experiences and Future Opportunities) signaled our intentions, the title of this chapter anticipates our conclusions; we will return to the theme of "regents" in a moment. Our intention is to speculate upon the true nature and status of opposition government experiences as we have seen them in our research and in the various preceding contributions. We must emphasize, however, that this is our personal view, and it does not necessarily reflect either the deliberations that came out of the Austin conference nor should they be attributed to any of the individual contributors. We wish to develop our appraisal around five broad points.

The Need for Further Research

It is almost de rigueur for any academic treatise to conclude that more research is required; rarely can this call have had greater veracity. As we noted in the introductory overview, while there has been a considerable amount of work on opposition parties, systematic studies of non-PRI governments are nonexistent. Indeed even studies dealing with the exercise of governmental power by the official party at the state and municipal levels are few and far between. With the single exception of Fagen and Tuohy's now classic study on Jalapa, researchers have failed to examine in detail how local and state governments operate on a daily basis. Only at the federal level has there been any serious attempt to analyze the politics and outcomes of public administration in Mexico.

In addition to learning more about non-PRI governments, we should, perhaps, as Peter Smith urged at the Austin conference, analyze how the PRI exercises government at the lower levels, as a control. That would help us understand the ways and extent to which opposition governments are different in degree or in kind. It would also illuminate the important ways in which the PRI has changed its modus operandi of exercising government—now often adopting some of the more positive elements of opposition administrations. As far as non-PRI government experiences are concerned, we need a wider range of studies that embrace the principal opposition parties at the state and municipal levels, which will help us to understand the regional variations that exist. Not least we need to know more about why opposition governments have emerged in regions such as Yucatán, Michoacán, Guanajuato ("the cradle of Mexican independence") and, of course, in the north. Clearly there is no single reason that can account for all of these cases, as they are widely different among themselves. Thus if factors such as a free press can help explain the opposition's success in the north and in Yucatán, this is certainly not the case in Guanajuato, Michoacán, or particularly, in San Luis Potosí. Here one must look to the role of human agency: the leadership of Dr. Nava in San Luis; the weight of the Cárdenas tradition in Michoacán; the wish of the Salinas government to "experiment" with greater political openness in contexts such as Guanajuato and Baja California.

These regional differences aside, we need to know more about how the PRD and the PAN, respectively, respond to exercising government. Are their agendas radically different? We have observed in this volume how they invoke different responses from the center, and we may expect, therefore, that their relative success will vary markedly. Most studies thus far have focused upon larger city administrations, and we need to know how the size of a municipality may impinge upon the structures and exercise of governance. In short, we need studies of governments as governments, whether they are PRI or opposition.

Why Regents of the Opposition?

The concept of regency describes the temporary reign of an individual serving until the true heir comes of age or is able to take up his or her duties. Interpreted literally the concept would appear to have little relevance to Mexico. But in a broader interpretation, we believe that it does offer insight into the way in which opposition parties have come to power and, perhaps, the role that they are being invited to play in the emergence of a more pluralist political system. For example, we have witnessed that the emergence of these governments has been at the behest of the federal executive, initially through a process of *apertura política* that gave the opposition a presence within congress and to a lesser extent at the municipal level. Latterly state and municipal governments have won power either directly or indirectly, as a result of Salinas' willingness to recognize their victories. Even in the cases of Baja California and Chihuahua, which were won outright by the PAN, it seems likely that there were careful negotiations prior to the elections, in order to ensure that the electoral process would be conducted smoothly and that the results would be respected. Elsewhere the victories have been achieved indirectly (the most important being the governorship of Guanajuato), through presidential fiat. Thus the manner in which the opposition gains power and the constraints under which it is obliged to govern broadly resemble those of a regent. Indeed the concept of regency not only applies to the opposition but to many priísta governors as well. We have witnessed how governors who are elected by popular mandate may be removed by presidential will—'I will you into power, I will you out of it': *dedazo* in reverse. In the first four years of his administration, Salinas removed no less than sixteen state executives, either in order to promote or demote them. These, too, are regents serving at the president's behest until the true ruler arrives.

In another sense the idea of regency can be applied in Mexico in that a regent serves for a limited duration only and in the place of the true ruler. This certainly appears to have been the case in the earlier experiments of the de la Madrid administration. Non-PRI governments were only allowed to serve one term. We are less certain that this time limitation applies in the 1990s, since in many cities there has been a continuity of consecutive opposition governments (Ensenada, for example, has been governed uninterruptedly by the opposition since 1983). In many respects these governments have superceded their status as regents and become rulers in their own right, as the political system itself has matured and become more of a republic than a monarchy.

From Party to Government

In November of 1991, Abel Vicencio Tovar, a senior panista and congressional representative, commented to us that "it is one thing to win an election; to govern is an entirely different matter." He commented further that even then his party had not seriously begun to consider how it should advise and train its party faithful for the exercise of government. In fact all parties (the PRI included) come to municipal power relatively ill prepared. Parties in Mexico do not have a clearly enunciated ideology that readily transforms into a government agenda. Nor do parties run for office on the basis of a proposed platform of specific actions that they propose to undertake if elected. Rather, the discourse is based upon broad pronouncements of intent that have little specific relevance or meaning. For example, when Sócrates Rizzo ran for the municipal presidency of Monterrey, one of his principal platform issues was regulation of the city's *cantinas*, hardly a substantive policy agenda for a city of the size and importance of Monterrey. This is typical and in part a product of the relatively limited responsibilities charged to municipal governments. But it also reflects the relative immaturity of the Mexican political system, whereby parties become clearly identified with significantly different policy agendas and approaches to government. This is a feature that we expect will change in the future, as the pluralist party structure consolidates.

Invariably the personnel coming to power in representation of the successful parties lack experience or background in urban governance. In the case of non-PRI parties, we have seen how public officials have had to be recruited from the private sector and how this, in turn, shaped their performance while in office. This problem is accentuated by the shortness of terms and by the constitutional no reelection clause. Although junior personnel may show some continuity in office, the rule in the past has been for all senior officers to change with the election of a new municipal president. For the PAN, the recent continuity in many city governments that they have held now for two consecutive periods provides some opportunity for them to learn from experience and to be better equipped to govern the second time around. However, as yet there is little research that will allow us to evaluate how successfully they have learned their lessons. Governor Barrio certainly learned much both from his experience as municipal president in Ciudad Juárez and from the way he conducted his gubernatorial campaigns in 1986 and 1992. The same applies to Governors Ruffo and Medina Plascencia, who certainly learned from their experiences as municipal presidents of Ensenada and of León, respectively. But apart from Dr. Nava in San Luis, we have no knowledge of any municipal president who has returned to serve in the same capacity at a later stage.

This lack of experience applies also the PRI, even though it has enjoyed the preserve on power for over half a century. The system whereby mayoral candidates are selected rarely has much to do with local knowledge and urban expertise, but rather relates to the old system of rewards and patronage exercised through the party and through state governors. The rationality was one of maintaining quiescence among the local population and serving as one's political overlords demanded. However, it is our impression that all parties are increasing their expectancy that the elected officials demonstrate greater technical competence and managerial efficiency in their conduct of urban affairs. Although it seems unlikely that in the short term the three-year period of municipal government will be extended (even though there has been much discussion to this effect), this would be a logical trend, given the greater technocratization in Mexico's public administration and the need for greater policy continuity.

One major area where non-PRI governments have been at a disadvantage is in their lack of corporate, sectoral, or constituency links with civic society. The PRI, of course, has always been able to work through its corporate sectors and through its institutionalized organizational structure. Other parties have had to start from scratch, and although elected by a local electorate dissatisfied for whatever reasons with preceding PRI governments, they have had only partial success in developing and consolidating local partisan organizational structures. Ultimately this may be their undoing, as was proven in Chihuahua in the 1986 election. In Baja California, too, the PRI's ability to retain its corporatist basis of support has allowed it to remain as a viable political force that must be contended with at election time, as the 1992 elections demonstrated.

Intergovernmental Relations with the Opposition

The intensification of *presidencialismo* over electoral decisions extends to the pattern of intergovernmental relations. As we have seen in the case of Nuevo León, a new recentralization of power is under way via control of state and local finances from the center. Through Solidarity, too, new mechanisms of control have been instituted that further intensify the centralization of decision making and the allocation of resources. In both cases it is the state government that has ultimately lost out.

Conversely, the data we have analyzed in detail in this volume indicate that panista governments are not castigated by the withholding of funds that rightfully belong to them. But both PRD and PAN municipal governments have suffered insofar as discretionary lines of funding for more elaborate special projects and programs (dams, highways, housing projects, and so forth) are concerned. However, this has created the need for these same governments to take greater control and become far more creative in the internal generation of revenues. As they have done so, we have observed the apparent paradox of opposition governments exercising greater municipal autonomy and power than their PRI counterparts. This decentralization of power and responsibility was first envisaged in the municipal reform of 1984 but was only seriously enacted once opposition governments took office. Interestingly, where PRI administrations have subsequently won back control at the local level, they too have enjoyed greater political space and, consequently, autonomy from the governments above.

Although the case of Baja California Norte has not been analyzed in detail in this volume, our recent research on intergovernmental relations in that state indicate a clear tendency toward a genuine decentralization of responsibilities, funding, and decision-making authority from the state to the local level (Rodríguez and Ward 1994). Whether this reflects Ruffo's personal desire to give greater authority to municipalities such as those he once governed himself or is an outcome of the inadequate resources that he is receiving from the federal level remains uncertain. Certainly the municipalities themselves have demonstrated greater confidence and competence in managing their own affairs. Both panista and priísta municipal governments have become so self-assured that in several occasions they have bypassed the state level and gone directly to Mexico City in search of resources and support. By and large there appears to be a consensus in Baja California that decentralization is actually occurring; whether this is by default or by design, however, is not yet clear.

Opposition Governments and Democratization: Is the Glass Half Full or Half Empty?

For the pessimist, the glass here is definitely half empty. The process of creating a plurality has been largely stage-managed from the center—specifically by the president himself. The grass roots remain only nominally involved in the selection of candidates and in determining electoral outcomes. In this view, the conduct of elections and the institutions responsible remain under the direction and control of the government and of the PRI, and notwithstanding improvements in the electoral system in general, considerable uncertainty continues to abound in every election due to a variety of electoral irregularities. Elections have become marred by unrest and disturbances often provoked by the opposition parties seeking to secure the overturn of what may often be a legitimate result. In short, the widely held view that final results are negotiated among all competing parties undermines the credibility of the democratization process. Nor is the playing field level insofar as access to media and other campaign resources are concerned. The latter are apportioned according to the percentage of votes secured in the previous election, which therefore unquestionably intensifies the advantage of the PRI in most districts. Also, the media tend overwhelmingly to favor the PRI in their coverage.

For the optimist, on the other hand (and we consider ourselves among this group) the glass is filling up, although it is not yet quite half full. Nor do we expect the level to rise much farther in the remainder of the Salinas administration. Granted there have been dramatic improvements. The very existence of the opposition governments we have described is itself a major advance. So too the real possibility that they may be reelected is a reflection of the greater maturity that the political system has achieved. No longer are local populations so intimidated by authoritarian leaders (whether these are elected or not), and the substantial improvements in respect for human rights, although still far from perfect, have encouraged local citizens to exercise their rights of protest and mobilization. However, notwithstanding the greater participation of the Mexican people, the grass roots remain largely marginalized. As Dr. Nava underscored at the Austin conference, a true democracy must be demanded from below, not imposed from above.

Thus we recognize the very real achievements that have been secured by the Mexican political system in a relatively short period of time. We agree with President Salinas when he says that much still remains to be done, but that the accomplishments thus far should not be disdained or dismissed because they are not absolute. But writing in early 1993, we suspect that not many more significant strides will be taken in the duration of the Salinas presidency. With barely two years left, President Salinas must direct his efforts to consolidate what he has achieved thus far, rather than embarking upon new ventures. He has indicated that he is not prepared to intervene in overturning any more election results, nor will he tolerate postelection disturbances designed to undermine electoral legitimacy and credibility. A conciliatory approach may have been the watchword for the first four years (at least as far as the PAN was concerned), but that is no longer necessarily the case. Nor can the PRI live with many more reversals mandated from on high; they seriously erode its credibility in local elections, as the case of Guanajuato so clearly demonstrated.

Internally, though, the PRI is a very different organization from that of the mid-1980s. There has been some experimentation with the idea of candidate selection through primaries, and although it is still ephemeral, there is a greater willingness and preparedness within the PRI to select candidates who command respect at the local level. The caliber of those selected and ultimately elected to office is also much higher than ever before. Positions in government are no longer considered short-term sinecures and payoffs for services rendered; neither is there the certainty of the past that once selected, one is elected. Carrying out the duties of public office has now become a professional responsibility to be efficiently and effectively fulfilled.

In part, of course, the PRI has learned its lesson the hard way—by evaluating the past experiences of opposition governments. Further reform of the political system, such that it allows for possible defeat of the official party, will not occur until the next sexenio and perhaps not even then. In part the preparedness of the PRI and of the new executive to rectify continuing anomalies within the electoral system will be shaped by the 1994 election results themselves. Only then will we be in a position to assess with greater confidence the future opportunities of opposition governments in Mexico.

Bibliography

Adler Hellman, J. [1978] 1988. *Mexico in Crisis*. New York: Holmes & Meier Publishers, Inc.

Aguilar Camín, H. 1989. *Después del milagro*. México: Cal y Arena.

Alemán, R., and M. Cuéllar. 1992. "El caso de Michoacán hace indispensable una profunda reforma electoral en el país." *La Jornada*, July 31, pp. 1, 14.

Americas Watch. 1990. "Human Rights in Mexico: A Policy of Impunity." New York: Human Rights Watch.

Americas Watch. 1991. "Unceasing Abuses: Human Rights in Mexico One Year after the Introduction of Reform." *Americas Watch* (September)

Ames, B. (1970. "Bases of Support for Mexico's Dominant Party." *American Political Science Review* 64:153–67.

Aranda, J., and J. Moguel. 1992. "La Coordindadora Estatal de Productores de Café de Oaxaca." In J. Moguel, C. Botey, and L. Hernández, eds., *Autonomía y nuevos sujetos del desarrollo rural*, pp. 167–93. México, D.F.: Siglo XXI/CEHAM.

Arreola, A. 1985. "Elecciones municipales." In P. González Casanova, coord., *Las elecciones en México; evolución y perspectivas*, pp. 329–348. Mexico: Siglo XXI/UNAM.

Avalos, Bernardo and J. Alfaro. 1993. Cuadros de Coyuntura. *Nexos*, Cuadernos, (182)(February):10–11.

Avila García, P. 1991. "Estudio preliminar sobre el deterioro socioambiental en la ciudad de Morelia: El caso del agua." In Gustavo López Castro, ed., *Urbanización y desarrollo en Michoacán*, pp. 233–59. Zamora: El Colegio de Michoacán.

Aziz Nassif, A. 1987a. Prácticas electorales y democracia en Chihuahua. Cuadernos de la Casa Chata, no. 151. México, D.F.: Centro de Investigación y Estudios Superiores de Antropología.

———. 1987b. "Electoral Practices and Democracy in Chihuahua, 1985." In *Electoral Patterns and Perspectives in Mexico*. A. Alvarado, ed. San Diego: Center for U.S.-Mexican Studies, University of California, Monograph Series No. 22 pp. 181–206.

———. 1991. "San Luis Potosí: Memorias y olvidos." *Cuaderno de Nexos* 36:16–17.

———. 1992. "San Luis Potosí: La repetición de un agravio." *Eslabones* 3:6–19.
Baca Olamendi, L., and I.H. Cisneros Ramírez. 1988. "La cultura política en la derecha social mexicana." *Revista A* 9:23–24. México D.F.: UAM-A.
Bailey, J. 1984. "Public Budgeting in Mexico, 1970–1984." *Public Budgeting and Finance* 4(1)(Spring): 76–90.
———. 1987. "Can the PRI Be Reformed? Decentralizing Candidate Selection." In J. Gentleman, ed., *Mexican Politics in Transition*, pp. 63–92. Boulder: Westview Press.
———. 1988. *Governing Mexico: The Statecraft of Crisis Management*. New York: St. Martin's Press.
———. 1991. "Public Opinion and Regional Aspects of Liberalization in Mexico, 1987–90." Paper presented at the meeting of the Latin American Studies Association, Washington, D.C., April, 1991.
———. 1992. "Fiscal Recentralization in Mexico, 1979–1991." Paper presented at the meeting of the Latin American Studies Association. Los Angeles. September.
———. 1994. "Fiscal Recentralization in Mexico, 1979–1991." In W. Cornelius, A. Craig, and J. Fox, eds., *Transforming State-Society Relations in Mexico: The National Solidarity Strategy*. La Jolla: Center for U.S.-Mexican Studies, UCSD.
Bailón, M.J. 1984. "Elecciones locales en Oaxaca 1980." *Nueva antropología* 25:67–98.
———. 1990. "Los problemas de Morro Mazatán: La lucha por el control de una agencia municipal en el estado de Oaxaca." *Estudios sociológicos* 7(22)(January-April):67–86.
———. 1992. "Conflictos municipales, una historia no tan nueva: Elecciones locales en Oaxaca 1920–1970." Paper presented at the meeting of the Latin American Studies Association, Los Angeles, September, 1992.
Barberán, J., et al. 1988. *Radiografía del fraude: análisis de los datos oficiales del 6 de julio*. México, D.F.: Nuestro Tiempo.
Bardacke, T. 1992. "The Lion Learns New Tricks." *El financiero internacional*, July 20, p. 12.
Barrio, F. 1992. "Mensaje de Francisco Barrio." Speech delivered at conference on Opposition Government in Mexico: Past Experiences, Future Opportunities, The University of Texas at Austin, April 3.
Bartra, Roger, E. Boege, P. Calvo, J. Gutiérrez, V.R. Martínez Vázquez, and L. Paré. 1975. *Caciquismo y poder político en el México rural*. México, D.F.: Siglo XXI.
Bartra, R. 1989. "Changes in Political Culture: The Crisis of Nationalism." In W. Cornelius, J. Gentleman, P. Smith, eds., *Mexico's Alternative Political Futures*. San Diego: Center for U.S.-Mexican Studies, UCSD.
Basáñez, M. 1990. *El pulso de los sexenios: 20 años de crisis en Mexico*. México, D.F.: Siglo XXI.
Béjar Navarro, R., and H.M. Capello. 1988. *La conciencia nacional en la frontera norte*. México, D.F.: UNAM-CRIM.
Beltrán del Río, P. 1990a. "Solidaridad, oxígeno para el PRI, en el rescate de votos." *Proceso* (718)(August 6):8–11.

———. 1990b. "El memorandum de Pichardo, prueba de que el Pronasol es para servir al PRI." *Proceso,* (718)(August 6):8–11.

———. 1993a. "Sin visos de solución los conflictos poselectorales en Puebla y Michoacán. *Proceso,* (846)(January 18):29–30.

———. 1993b. "Causa conmoción política la renuncia de Beatriz Paredes." *Proceso,* (849)(February 6):13–15.

Beltrán del Río, P., and F. Castellanos. 1992. "El caso michoacano puede darse por cerrado: Cristóbal Arias." *Proceso,* (832)(October 12):16–21.

Bennett, V. 1995. *The Politics of Water: Urban Protest, Gender, and Power in Monterrey, Mexico.* Pittsburgh: University of Pittsburgh Press.

Bezdek, R. 1973. "Electoral Oppositions in Mexico: Emergence, Suppression, and Impact on Political Processes." Unpublished Ph.D. dissertation. Columbus: Ohio State University.

———. 1984. "Electoral Opposition in San Luis Potosí: The Case of Nava." Epilogue in K. Johnson, *Mexican Democracy: A Critical View,* pp. 242–63. New York: Praeger.

———. 1989. "The 1988 Mexican Elections: Challenges to PRI." Paper presented at the meeting of the Western Social Science Association, Albuquerque, New Mexico, April 26–29.

Booth, J. and Seligson, M. 1984. "The Political Culture of Authoritarianism in Mexico: A Reexamination." *Latin American Research Review* 19:106–24.

Borjas Benavente, A. 1992. "El tratamiento periodístico de la información del movimiento político denominado navismo: 1958–1963." Unpublished bachelor's thesis. Mexico City: Universidad Iberoamericana.

Calvillo, T. 1986. *El navismo o los motivos de la dignidad.* San Luis Potosí: Formas Impresas Kaiser.

———. 1992. "Parcialidad del periodismo potosino," *Este país* (13)(April).

Camp, R. 1980. *Mexico's Leaders: Their Education and Recruitment.* Tucson, Arizona: University of Arizona Press.

———. 1987. "Opposition in Mexico: A Comparison of Leadership." In J. Gentleman, ed., *Mexican Politics in Transition,* pp. 235–260. Boulder: Westview Press.

———. 1991a. "Religion and Politics, the Laity in Mexico." Paper presented at the meeting of the American Political Science Association, Washington, D.C., August 27–31.

———. 1991b. "Mexico's 1988 Elections, A Turning Point for Its Political Development and Foreign Relations?" In E. W. Butler, and J. A. Bustamante, eds., *Sucesión Presidencial: The 1988 Mexican Presidential Election,* pp. 95–114. Boulder: Westview Press.

Campbell, W., and R. Lau. 1990. "Chihuahua: La otra Iglesia." *Cuadernos del norte* (9)(April-May):13–16.

Cantú, J. 1992. "Solidaridad, además de electorero, se manejó en Michoacán coercitivamente." *Proceso* (819)(July 13):14–15.

Castañeda, J. 1991. "El fraude moderno." *Proceso* (773)(August 26):34,36.

Castaneda, J. and R. Pastor. 1989. *Límites en la amistad; México y Estados Unidos.* México, D.F.: Joaquín Mortiz/Planeta.

Centro de Estudios Políticos, Económicos y Sociales. 1991. "Balance global de la jornada electoral federal para el estado de Oaxaca." Oaxaca: CEPES.

Chávez, E. 1992. "Michoacán: cada voto del PRI costó 239,188 pesos; cada voto del PRD costó 6,916 pesos." *Proceso* (821)(July 27):22–7.

Coleman, K. and C. Davis. 1988. *Politics and Culture in Mexico*. Ann Arbor: Center for Political Studies.

Comisión Estatal Electoral, Oaxaca. 1990. *Resultados de las elecciones ordinarias y extraordinarias para concejales municipales*. 3 vols., Oaxaca: Comisión Estatal Electoral.

Conchello, J.A. 1980. *El trigo y la cizana*. México, D.F.: Editorial Grijalbo.

Convergencia de Organismos Civiles por la Democracia. 1992. "Informe de observación electoral." *Perfil de la Jornada*, August 16.

COPLAMAR. 1982. *Necesidades esenciales en Méxcio: Geografía de la marginación*. México, D.F.: Siglo XXI/COPLAMAR.

Cornelius, W.A. 1973. "Contemporary Mexico: a structural analysis of urban caciquismo.: In *Caciques: Oligarchical Politics and the System of Caciquismo*. Robert Kern, ed., Albuquerque, N.M.: University of New Mexico Press, pp. 135–91.

———. 1975. *Politics and the Migrant Poor in Mexico City*. Stanford: Stanford University Press.

———. 1986. "Political Liberalization and the 1985 elections in Mexico." In *Elections and Democratization in Latin America, 1980–1985*. P. Drake and E. Silva, eds. San Diego: Joint publication of the Center for Iberian and Latin American Studies, the Center for U.S.-Mexican Studies, and the Institute of the Americas, University of California, pp. 115–42.

———. 1987. "Political Liberalization in an Authoritarian Regime: Mexico, 1976–1985." In J. Gentleman, ed., *Mexican Politics in Transition*, pp. 15–39. Boulder: Westview Press.

Cornelius, W.A. and A. Craig. 1991. *The Mexican Political System in Transition*. La Jolla: Center for U.S.-Mexican Studies, UCSD.

———. 1992. "Politics in Mexico." In G. Almond, and G. Powell, Jr., eds., *Comparative Politics Today: A World View*, pp. 463–519. New York: Harper Collins Publishers.

Cornelius, W., A. Craig, and J. Fox, eds. 1994. *Transforming State-Society Relations in Mexico: The National Solidarity Strategy*. La Jolla: Center for U.S.-Mexican Studies, UCSD.

Cornelius, W.A., J. Gentleman, and P. Smith. 1989. "Overview: The Dynamics of Political Change in Mexico," in W.A. Cornelius, J. Gentleman and P. Smith, eds., *Mexico's Alternative Political Futures*, pp. 1–55. La Jolla: Center for U.S.-Mexican Studies, University of California, San Diego (Monograph Series, 30).

Crespo, J.A. 1992. "Un autoritarismo diferente." *Este país* (12)(March)

———. 1991. "La evolución del sistema de partidos en Mexico." *Foro Internacional* 31(4):599–622.

Dahl, R.A. 1989. *Democracy and its Critics*. New Haven: Yale University Press.

Díaz Montes, F. 1989. "Elecciones municipales, conflicto y negociación: Oaxaca 1986." *Cuadernos de investigación*. Occasional papers series. Oaxaca:

Instituto de Investigaciones Sociológicas, Universidad Autónoma "Benito Juárez" de Oaxaca.

Díaz Montes, F. and J. L. Ornelas López. 1989. "Problemática municipal de Oaxaca." *Cuadernos de Investigación.* Occasional papers series. Oaxaca: Instituto de Investigaciones Sociológicas, Universidad Autónoma "Benito Juárez" de Oaxaca.

Domínguez, J. and J. A. McCann. 1991. "Whither the PRI? Explaining Voter Defection from Mexico's Ruling Party in the 1988 Presidential Elections." Paper presented at the meeting of the Western Political Science Association, Reno, Nevada, April, 1991.

Dresser, D. 1991. "Neopopulist Solutions to Neoliberal Problems. Mexico's National Solidarity Program." Current Issues Brief No. 3. La Jolla: UCSD, Center for U.S.-Mexican Studies.

———. 1992. "Pronasol: los dilemas de la gobernabilidad." *El cotidiano* (49)(July-August)

Dye, T.R. 1990. *Who's Running America?,* 5th ed. Englewood Cliffs: Prentice-Hall.

Escobar, A. and B. Roberts, 1991. "Urban Stratification, the Middle Classes, and Economic Change in Mexico," in M. González de la Rocha and A. Escobar Latapí, eds. *Social Responses to Mexico's Economic Crisis of the 1980s.* La Jolla: Center for U.S.-Mexican Studies. pp. 91–114.

Estrada M.A. 1963. *La grieta en el yugo.* s.l.: s.n.

Fagen, R. R. and W. S. Tuohy. 1972. *Politics and Privilege in a Mexican City.* Stanford: Stanford University Press.

Farías, L. M. 1992. *Así lo recuerdo: testimonio político.* México, D.F.: Fondo de Cultura Económica.

Fernández, J. 1991. "El PRI ante su propia transición." *Uno más uno,* November 7, pp. 1, 7.

Foweraker, J. and A. Craig, eds., 1990. *Popular Movements and Political Change in Mexico.* Boulder: Lynne Rienner Publishers.

Fox, J. 1993. *The Politics of Food in Mexico, State Power and Social Mobilization.* Ithaca: Cornell University Press.

———. 1994. "The Difficult Transition from Clientelism to Citizenship: The Politics of Access to the Solidarity's Indigenous Programs." In W. Cornelius, A. Craig, and J. Fox, eds., *Transforming State-Society Relations in Mexico: The National Solidarity Strategy.* La Jolla: Center for U.S.-Mexican Studies, UCSD.

Fox, J. and L. Hernández. 1992. "Mexico's Difficult Democracy: Grassroots Movements, NGOs and Local Government." *Alternatives* 17(2)(Spring): 165–208.

Frente Cívico Potosino. 1991. Análisis y balance de las elecciones: San Luis Potosí, 1991. s.l.: s.n.

Gallegos, E. 1992. "Refuta Carlos Rojas el uso partidista del Pronasol: Michoacán, "el mejor ejemplo." *La jornada,* September, 5, p. 17.

García, B. 1988. *Desarrollo económico y absorción de fuerza de trabajo en México 1950–1980.* México, D.F.: El Colegio de México.

Garza Ramírez, E. 1985. *Nuevo León 1985: Un ensayo sobre las condiciones y perspectivas de la transición del poder público.* Monterrey: Universidad Autónoma de Nuevo León.

Gershberg, A. I. 1990. "Decentralization and Public Finance in Mexico: An Overview of the System and its Recent Evolution." Draft report submitted to the Urban Institute.

Gibson, E. 1991. "Conservative Parties and Democratic Politics: Core Constituencies, Coalition-Building, and the Latin American Electoral Right." Paper presented at the meeting of the Latin American Studies Association, Washington, D.C. April, 1991.

Gilbert, A. and P. Ward. 1985. *Housing, the State and the Poor: Policy and Practice in Three Latin American Cities.* Cambridge: Cambridge University Press.

Gobierno del Estado de Oaxaca. 1991. *Oaxaca, V informe de gobierno (anexo programático presupuestal).* Oaxaca. Gobierno del Estado.

Golden, T. 1992a. "Point of Attack for Mexico's Retooled Party Machine: The Leftist Stronghold." *The New York Times,* July 12, p. L3.

———. 1992b. "Mexico Politician Out, Blow for Chief." *The New York Times,* October 7, p. A3.

Gómez, A. and J. Moguel. 1992. "Economía y política en las nuevas luchas rurales: La experiencia de Convergencia Campesina de Michoacán." *La jornada del campo* (6)(September 29).

Gómez Tagle, S. 1987. "Los adjetivos de la democracia en el caso de las elecciones de Chihuahua, 1986." *Revista argumentos.* Universidad Autónoma Metropolitana-Xochimilco. (June)

González Casanova, P. 1970. *Democracy in Mexico.* New York: Oxford University Press.

González Tiburcio, E. 1991. "PRONASOL: Hacia la nueva síntesis." *Cuadernos de Nexos* (No. 40) (October):pp. x–xii.

Graham, L. S. 1990. *The State and Policy Outcomes in Latin America.* New York: Praeger.

Granados Chapa, M. 1992. *¡Nava Sí, Zapata No!* Mexico: Grijalbo.

Grindle, Merilee. 1977. *Bureaucrats, Politicians and Peasants in Mexico: A Case Study in Public Policy.* Berkeley: University of California Press.

Guadarrama, G. 1987. "Entrepreneurs and Politics: Businessmen in Electoral Contest in Sonora and Nuevo León, July 1985." In A. Alvarado Mendoza, ed., *Electoral Patterns and Perspectives in Mexico,* pp. 81–110. La Jolla: Center for U.S.-Mexican Studies.

Guerrero, J. 1989. *Las elecciones del 88.* México, D.F.: Ediciones Quinto Sol.

Guillén López, T. 1987a. "Political Parties and Political Attitudes in Chihuahua." In Arturo Alvarado, ed., *Electoral Patterns and Perspectives in Mexico.* San Diego: Center for U.S.-Mexican Studies, University of California, Monograph Series No. 22, pp. 225–52.

———. 1987b. "Crisis y conducta política." *El cotidiano* 1(4):36–41.

———. 1992. "Baja California, una década de cambio político." In Tonatiuh Guillén López, ed., *Frontera Norte: una década de política electoral,* pp. 139–85. El Colegio de la Frontera Norte-El Colegio de Mexico.

———. 1993a, *Baja California, 1989–1992. Balance de la transición democrática.* México, D.F.: COLEF-F. Ebert.

———. 1993b. "Baja California." In S. Gómez Tagle, ed., *Las elecciones de 1991. La recuperación oficial*, pp. 69–92. Mexico: La Jornada-G.V. Editores.

Haber, P. 1989. "Cárdenas, Salinas and Urban Popular Movements in Mexico: The Case of the CDP de Durango." Paper presented at the meeting of the Latin American Studies Association, Washington, DC, April 1991.

———. 1992a. "Collective Dissent in Mexico: The Political Outcome of Contemporary Urban Popular Movements." Unpublished Ph.D. dissertation. New York: Columbia University.

———. 1992b. "The Art and Implications of Political Restructuring in Mexico: The Case of Urban Popular Movements." Paper presented at the National Autonomous University of Mexico City, June, 1992.

Hansen, R. 1974. *The Politics of Mexican Development*. 2nd ed. Baltimore, Maryland: Johns Hopkins University Press.

Hernández, L. and F. Celis. 1992. "PRONASOL y la cafeticultura." *El cotidiano* (49)(July-August):78–87.

Iglitzin, L., and R. Ross, eds. 1986. *Women in the World*. Santa Barbara: ABC Clio.

INEGI (Instituto Nacional de Estadística, Geografía, e Informática). 1990a. *Michoacán: Resultados definitivos, tabulados básicos, XI Censo General, 1990*. Mexico: INEGI.

INEGI-Gobierno del Estado de Oaxaca. 1990b. *Anuario estadístico del estado de Oaxaca*. Aguascalientes: INEGI.

INEGI. 1991a. *Estados Unidos Mexicanos. Perfil demográfico, XI censo general de población y vivienda, 1990*. Mexico: INEGI.

———. 1991b. *Resultados preeliminares del XI Censo de población y vivienda: Oaxaca*. Aguascalientes: INEGI.

Instituto Nacional de Solidaridad. 1992. "Espacio de convergencia de fuerzas populares." *Gaceta de solidaridad* 3(53)(June 15)

Instituto Nacional Indigenista. 1990. *Programa Nacional de Desarrollo de los Pueblos Indígenas, 1991–1994*. México, D.F.: Instituto Nacional Indigenista.

Jaquette, J.S. 1984. "Female Political Participation in Latin America: Raising Feminist Issues." Paper presented at the meeting of the American Political Science Association, Washington, D.C. August 29–September 2.

Kirkwood, J. 1985. "Feministas y política." *Nueva sociedad* (Venezuela), (78):82–91.

Klesner, J. 1991. "Challenges for Mexico's Opposition in the Coming Sexenio." In Butler and Bustamante, *Sucesión Presidencial: The 1988 Mexican Presidential Elections*. Boulder: Westview Press.

Krauze, E. 1986. *Por una democracia sin adjetivos*. Mexico: Editorial Joaquín Mortiz.

Lau, R. 1989. "Las elecciones en Chihuahua 1983–1986." *Cuadernos del norte* (1):53–70.

———. 1990. "Crisis y distinción electoral 1980–1990." *Noesis* 4(January-June):53–70.

Levy, D. and G. Székely. 1987. *Mexico: Paradoxes of Stability and Change*. Boulder: Westview Press.

Linowitz, S. 1988/89. "Latin America: The President's Agenda." *Foreign Affairs* (67):45–62.

Livas, J. 1983. *Corrupción y burocracia municipal: la resistencia al cambio.* Monterrey: Editorial Plata.

Loaeza, S. 1989. *El llamado de las urnas.* Mexico: Cal y Arena.

Lomas, E. 1991a. "La democracia ya no es de las cúpulas, afirma Salinas." *La Jornada,* September 13, p. 17.

———. 1991b. "Salinas: nueva relación Estado-sociedad civil." *La Jornada,* September 15, pp. 1, 12.

López Monjardín, A. 1986. *La lucha por los ayuntamientos.* México, D.F.: Siglo XXI/UNAM.

———. 1991. "Movimientos políticos, movimientos sociales." In V. Gabriel Muro, and M. Canto Chac, eds., *El estudio de los movimientos sociales,* pp. 21–36. Morelia: Colegio de Michoacán/UAM-Xochimilco.

Mabry, D. 1973. *Mexico's Acción Nacional, A Catholic Alternative to Revolution.* Syracuse: Syracuse University Press.

Macridis, R. and S. Burg. 1991. *Introduction to Comparative Politics: Regimes and Change.* New York: HarperCollins Publishers.

Malloy, James M., ed. 1977. *Authoritarianism and Corporatism in Latin America.* Pittsburgh: University of Pittsburgh Press.

Márquez, E. 1987. "Political Anachronisms: The Navista Movement and Political Process in San Luis Potosí, 1958–85." In A. Alvarado Mendoza, ed., *Patterns and Perspectives in Mexico,* pp. 111–25. San Diego: Center for U.S.-Mexican Studies, UCSD.

Martínez, Assad, C. Ziccardi, and A. Ziccardi. 1987. "El municipio entre la sociedad y el Estado." *Mexican Studies/Estudios Mexicanos* 3(2)(Summer):287–18.

Martínez Assad, C. 1985. "Nava: de la rebelión de los coheteros al juicio político." In C. Martínez Assad, ed., *Munciipios en Conflicto,* pp. 55–74. México, D.F.: Instituto de Investigaciones Sociales, UNAM.

Martínez Vázquez, V. R. and A. Arellanes. 1985. "Negociación y conflicto en Oaxaca." In C. Martínez Assad, ed., *Municipios en conflict,* pp. 203–37. México, D.F.: Instituto de Investigaciones Sociales, UNAM.

Massolo, A. 1983. "Las mujeres en los movimientos sociales urbanos de la ciudad de México." *Iztapalapa* (9)(June-December):152–67.

Meisel, J. H. 1962. *The Myth of the Ruling Class: Gaetano Mosca and the "Elite."* Ann Arbor: University of Michigan Press.

Mendoza Rivera, I. 1958. "El dramático final de Gonzalo N. Santos." *Mañana,* August 23.

Meyer, L. 1992. *La segunda muerte de la Revolución Mexicana.* 3rd ed. Mexico: Cal y Arena.

Middlebrook, Kevin. 1986. "Political Liberalization in an Authoritarian Regime: The Case of Mexico.: In P. Drake and E. Silva, eds., *Elections and Democratization in Latin America, 1980–1985.* San Diego: Joint publication of the Center for Iberian and Latin American Studies, the Centre for U.S.-Mexican Studies, and the Institute of the Americas, University of California, pp. 73–104.

Mizrahi, Y. 1992. "Rebels Without a Cause? The Politics of Entrepreneurs in Chihuahua." Paper presented at the meeting of the Latin American Studies Association, Los Angeles, California, September, 1992.

——. 1994. "The New Conservative Opposition: The Political Organization of Entrepreneurs in Chihuahua." Unpublished Ph.D. dissertation. Berkeley: University of California.

Moguel, J. 1987. *Los caminos de la izquierda*. México, D.F.: Juan Pablos.

——. 1991a. "El Programa Nacional de Solidaridad, ¿para quién?" *Cuadernos desarrollo de base* (2):277–98.

——. 1991b. "El PRD y el difícil camino hacia la democracia." *El cotidiano* 8(44)(November-December):20–6.

——. 1992. "Cinco críticas solidarias a un programa de gobierno." *El cotidiano* (49)(July-August):41–8.

Moguel, J. et al. 1989. *Juchitán, lucha y poesía*. México, D.F.: Editorial Extemporáneos.

Molinar Horcasitas, J. 1987. "The 1985 Federal Elections in Mexico: The product of a System." In A. Alvarado, ed., *Electoral patterns and Perspectives in Mexico*. La Jolla: Center for U.S.-Mexican Studies, University of California, Monograph Series No. 22, pp. 17–32.

——. 1989. "The Future of the Electoral System". In *Mexico's Alternative Political Futures*. W. Cornelius, J. Gentleman, and P. Smith, eds., La Jolla: Center for U.S.-Mexican Studies, University of California, Monograph Series No. 30, pp. 265–90.

——. 1991a. "La legitimidad perdida". *Nexos* (164)(August):7–10.

——. 1991b. *El tiempo de la legitimidad. Elecciones, autoriarismo y democracia en Mexico*. México, D.F.: Cal y Arena.

Molinar Horcasitas, J. and J. Weldon. 1994. "Electoral Determinants and Effects of Pronasol." In W. Cornelius, A. Craig, and J. Fox, eds., *Transforming State-Society Relations in Mexico: The National Solidarity Strategy*. La Jolla: Center for U.S.-Mexican Studies, UCSD.

Montaño, J. 1976. *Los pobres de la ciudad de México en los asentamientos espontáneos*. México, D.F.: Siglo XXI.

Montejano y Aguiñaga, R. 1987. "Gobernadores y comandantes militares del Estado de San Luis Potosí: 1824–1988." *Cuadrante* 11(3):223–62.

Nava, M. 1991. "Violento desalojo de la Presidencia Municipal de Atoyac, Guerrero; 18 Perredistas detenidos." *El Financiero*, June 19, p. 29.

Navarette, I.M. de. 1970. "La distribución del ingreso en México: tendencias y perspectivas." In *El perfil de México en 1980*, Vol. 1. D. Ibarra, et al., eds. Mexico, D.F.: Siglo XXI, pp. 15–71.

Newell, R. and L. Rubio. 1984. *Mexico's Dilemma: The Political Origins of Economic Crisis*. Boulder: Westview Press.

Nuncio, A. 1986. *El PAN: Alternativa de poder o instrumento de la oligarquía empresarial*. México, D.F.: Nueva Imagen.

O'Donnell, G. and P. Schmitter. 1986. *Transitions from Authoritarian Rule: Tentative Conclusions about Uncertain Democracies*. Baltimore: The Johns Hopkins University Press.

O'Donnell, G. and P. Schmitter. 1988. *Transiciones desde un gobierno autoritario:*

Conclusiones tentativas sobre las democracias inciertas. Buenos Aires: Paidós.

Ordóñez Barba, G. M. 1990. "Participación política y administración municipal: El caso de Ciudad Juárez (1980–1988)." Unpublished Master's Thesis. Tijuana: El Colegio de la Frontera Norte, Maestría en Desarrollo Regional.

Ortega Lomelín, R. 1988. *El nuevo federalismo: La descentralización.* México, D.F.: Editorial Porrúa.

Ortiz, M. 1991. "Comentarios al nuevo sistema de participaciones federales a estados y municipios." *Revista Indetec* (April-May):11–16.

Padgett, L. [1966] 1976. *The Mexican Political System.* Boston: Houghton Mifflin.

Palacios, J. J. 1989. *La política regional en Mexico, 1970–1982.* Universidad de Guadalajara.

Palma, E. 1988. "Notas sobre el neopanismo y la cultura política norteña." *Revista A* 11(23–24):pp. 93–105.

Partido de la Revolución Democrática, Human Rights Commission. 1992. *The Political Violence in Mexico: A Human Rights Affair.* Mexico City: Human Rights Commission Parliamentary Group.

Partido de la Revolución Democrática, Secretaría de Defensa del Voto. 1992. *Tablas comparativas.* México, D.F.: PRD.

Pazos, L. 1986. *Democracia a la mexicana.* México, D.F.: Editorial Diana.

Pozas, M. 1990. "Estrategias empresariales ante la apertura externa." In B. González-Arechiga, and J. C. Ramírez, eds., *Subcontratación y empresas transnacionales.* México, D.F.: Colegio de la Frontera Norte and F. Ebert.

Przeworski, A., and J. Sprague. 1986. *Paper Stones.* Chicago: University of Chicago Press.

Purcell, S. K. and J. Purcell. 1980. "State and Society in Mexico: Must a Stable Polity Be Institutionalized?" *World Politics.* Vol. 32, pp. 194–227.

Putnam, R. D. 1976. *The Comparative Studies of Political Elites.* Englewood Cliffs: Prentice-Hall.

Ramírez Saiz, J. M. 1986. *El movimiento popular en México.* México, D.F.: Siglo XXI.

Rangel, S. 1989. *Forjando mi destino: apuntes de mi vida.* México, D.F.:

Rascón M. and P. Ruiz. 1986. "Chihuahua: La disputa por la dependencia" *Cuadernos Políticos* No. 47. Mexico: ERA.

Reyna, J. L. (date). "Redefining the Authoritarian Regime." In J. S. Reyna, and R. Weinert, eds., *Authoritarianism in Mexico,* pp. 155–72. Philadelphia: ISHI.

Reynolds, C. W. 1978. "Why Mexico's Stabilizing Development Was Actually Destabilizing (With Some Implications for the Future)." *World Development,* 6:1005–18.

Riva Palacio, R. 1992. "Neme Castillo y la prensa." *Este país* (12)(March)

Rivera Godínez, C., ed. 1991. *Siete puntos sobre el Padrón Electoral de San Luis Potosí, 1991.* México, D.F.: Praxis, A.C.

Rodríguez, V. E. 1992. "Mexico's Decentralization in the 1980s: Promises, Promises, Promises. . . ." In A. Morris, and S. Lowder, S., eds., *Decentralization in Latin America,* pp. 127–43. New York: Praeger.

———. Forthcoming. *Decentralization in Mexico: The Façade of Power.* Boulder: Westview Press.

Rodríguez, V. E. and P. M. Ward. 1991. "Opposition Politics, Power, and Public Administration in Urban Mexico." *Bulletin of Latin American Research* 10(1):23–36.

———. 1992. *Policymaking, Politics and Urban Governance in Chihuahua: The Experience of Recent Panista Governments.* Austin: Lyndon B. Johnson School of Public Affairs, The University of Texas at Austin.

———. 1994. *Political Change in Baja California: Democracy in the Making?* La Jolla: Center for U.S.-Mexican Studies.

Rojas, C., et al. 1991. *Solidaridad a debate.* México, D.F.: El Nacional.

Rubin, J. W. 1987. "State Policies, Leftist Oppositions and Municipal Elections: The Case of Juchitán." In Alvarado, A., ed., *Electoral Patterns and Perspectives in Mexico,* pp. 127–160. La Jolla: Center for U.S.-Mexican Studies, UCSD.

Rubin, J. W. 1990. "Popular Mobilization and the Myth of State Corporatism." In J. Foweraker, and A. Craig, eds., *Popular Movements and Political Change in Mexico,* pp. 247–270. Boulder: Lynne Rienner.

Salas-Porras, A. S. 1991. *Los grupos empresariales en Chihuahua (1920–1990).* México, D.F.: Centro de Investigación y Docencia Económicas, Documento de Trabajo.

Salinas de Gortari, C. 1988. *El reto.* México, D.F.: Editorial Diana.

———. 1989. "Mexico-United States: A New Era of Cooperation and Friendship." Address by the President of Mexico to the Joint Session of the Congress of the United States of America, October 4, 1989.

———. 1990. "Reformando al estado." *Nexos* 148(April):27–32.

San Pedro: 3 años de resultados. 1991. San Pedro Garza García, Nuevo León.

Sánchez Gutiérrez, A., ed. 1992. *Las elecciones de Salinas. Un balance crítico a 1991.* México, D.F.: Plaza y Valdes-FLACSO.

Sánchez, H. 1991. "Aires de cambio en Juchitán." In C. Rojas, et al., eds., *Solidaridad a debate,* pp. 107–118. México, D.F.: El Nacional.

Sánchez Susarrey, J. 1991. "México: ¿Perestroika sin Glasnost?" *Vuelta* (176)(July):47–51.

Santos, G. 1984. *Memorias: Gonzalo N. Santos.* México, D.F.: Grijalbo.

Scott, D. C. 1992. "Mexico's Public-Works Program Bolsters President as It Aids the Poor." *The Christian Science Monitor,* September 16.

Scott, R. 1964. *Mexican Government in Transition.* Urbana: University of Illinois Press.

Searing, D. 1969. "The Comparative Study of Elite Socialization." *Comparative Political Studies,* Vol. 4, No. 4(January 1969):471–500.

Secretaría de Programación y Presupuesto. 1988. *Mexico: desarrollo regional y descentralización de la vida nacional—experiencias de cambio estructural, 1983–1988.* México, D.F.: SPP.

Skidmore, T. and P. Smith. 1989. *Modern Latin America,* 2nd ed. New York: Oxford University Press.

Smith, P. 1979. *Labyrinths of Power: Political Recruitment in Twentieth Century Mexico.* Princeton, N.J.: Princeton University Press.

Staudt, K. and C. Aguilar. 1992. "Political Parties, Women Activists' Agendas and Household Relations: Elections on Mexico's Northern Frontier." *Mexican Studies/Estudios Mexicanos* 8(1):87–106.

Stevens, E. 1974. *Protest and Response in Mexico.* Cambridge: MIT Press.

Stevens, E. P. 1987. "The Opposition in Mexico: Always a Bridesmaid Never Yet the Bride." In J. Gentleman, ed., *Mexican Politics in Transition,* pp. 217–34. Boulder: Westview Press.

Stoner, K. L., ed. 1988. *Latinas of the Americas: A Sourcebook.* New York: Garland Press.

Story, D. 1986. *The Mexican Ruling Party: Stability and Authority.* New York: Praeger.

Tarrés, M.L. 1988. "Más allá de lo público y lo privado: Reflexión sobre la participación social y política de las mujeres de la clase media en Ciudad Satétite" In O. Oliveira, ed., *Trabajo, Poder y Sexualidad.* Mexico: El Colegio de Mexico.

Teichman, J. 1988. *Policymaking in Mexico: Boom to Crisis.* Boston, Mass.: Allen & Unwin.

Tello, C. 1978. *La política económica en México, 1970–1976.* México, D.F.: Siglo XXI.

Torres, B., ed., 1986. *Descentralización y Democracia en México.* México, D.F.: El Colegio de México.

Tribunal Independiente de Ciudadanos. 1989. *Fraude en Michoacán, continuidad de una política electoral.* México, D.F.: Grupo Parlamentario Indepediente.

Tuñón Pablos, E. 1991. "Informe de la visita preelectoral a Ciudad Juárez y Chihuahua". Typescript. México, D.F.: UNAM.

Ureña, J. 1991. "Clase política." *La Jornada,* August 18, p. 6.

Valdez, L. 1989. "Tres tipologías de los setenta: el sistema de partidos en Mexico, sus cambios recientes." *Sociológica* (Universidad Autónoma Metropolitana, Azapotzalco) 11:9–26.

Vargas, A. 1977. "Coup at Excélsior." *Columbia Journalism Review* 15(3)45–48.

Ward, P. 1986. *Welfare Politics in Mexico: Papering Over the Cracks.* London: Allen & Unwin.

———. 1993. "Social Policy and Political Opening in Mexico." *Journal of Latin American Research* 25:613–28.

Weintraub, S. 1990. *A Marriage of Convenience, Relations between Mexico and the United States.* New York: Oxford University Press.

Wilkie, J. 1971. "New Hypotheses for Statistical Research in Recent Mexican History." *Latin American Research Review* 2:3–17.

Yanner, K. 1992. "Democratization in Mexico, 1988–1991: The Surge and Decline of Support for the Neocardenistas." Unpublished Ph.D. dissertation. St. Louis: Washington University.

Contributors

John Bailey holds a Ph.D. in political science from the University of Wisconsin, Madison, and is currently Professor of Government at Georgetown University. Since 1979 he has published numerous articles and book chapters on Mexico's bureaucracy and policy-making (with emphasis on the Ministry of Programming and Budget), the presidency, the PRI and electoral politics, and issues related to political liberalization and to U.S.-Mexican relations. In 1988 he published *Governing Mexico: The Statecraft of Crisis Management*, and most recently, "Centralism and Political Change in Mexico: The Case of National Solidarity," in Wayne Cornelius et al., eds., *Transforming State-Society Relations in Mexico: The National Solidarity Strategy*. Professor Bailey has served as a consultant to various U.S. and international organizations; since 1980 he has chaired the Advanced Area Seminar on Mexico at the U.S. Department of State's Foreign Service Institute.

Moisés J. Bailón is Researcher at the Instituto de Investigaciones Humanísticas, Universidad Autónoma "Benito Juárez" de Oaxaca. Since 1993 he has served as Contralor General for the state government of Oaxaca.

Robert Bezdek is professor of political science at Texas A&M—Corpus Christi. He received his Ph.D. from Ohio State University in 1973, and since that time has worked and published extensively on opposition politics in Yucatán and in San Luis Potosí. A close friend of the Nava family since the 1970s, he is currently working on a book manuscript about the late Dr. Salvador Nava Martínez.

Kathleen Bruhn received her doctorate in Political Science from Stanford University in 1993. Her research focuses upon the emergence and development of *Neocardenismo* in Mexico. In 1992–93 she was a research fellow at the Center for U.S.–Mexican Studies at the University of California, San Diego. Currently she is assistant professor in the Department of Political Science at the University of California, Santa Barbara.

RODERIC AI CAMP joined the Political Science department of Tulane University in 1991. Professor Camp has served as a visiting professor at the Colegio de México, the Foreign Service Institute, and the University of Arizona, and was a research fellow at the Woodrow Wilson Center for International Scholars, Smithsonian Institution. His special interests include Mexican politics, political recruitment, and civil-military relations. In an academic career that has spanned over twenty years, he has written a multitude of articles and book chapters, and over a dozen books. His most recent publications include *Politics in Mexico, Generals in the Palacio: The Military in Modern Mexico, Entrepreneurs and Politics in Twentieth Century Mexico,* and *The Successor,* a political thriller.

JOSÉ ANTONIO CRESPO is researcher at the Centro de Investigación y Docencia Económica (CIDE) in Mexico City, and has held teaching positions at the Universidad Autónoma Metropolitiana-Iztapalapa, the Instituto Tecnológico Autónomo de México, and the Universidad Iberoamericana. He is author of numerous articles on Mexican politics and contributes regularly as a political commentator to Mexico's journals and press. Currently he is working on a book manuscript comparing democratic structures in Mexico, India, and Japan.

JONATHAN FOX is Associate Professor of Political Science at the Massachusetts Institute of Technology. He received his doctorate from Princeton University. He is author of *The Politics of Food in Mexico: State Power and Social Mobilization,* co-editor (with Wayne Cornelius and Ann Craig) of *Transforming State-Society Relations in Mexico: The National Solidarity Strategy,* and publishes regularly in a variety of journals and magazines. Professor Fox serves as a consultant for international organizations, and maintains close working relationships with a variety of non-governmental organizations in Mexico, especially those related to agrarian production.

TONATIUH GUILLÉN LÓPEZ holds a doctorate from the Colegio de México and is currently a researcher and Director of the Departamento de

Administración Pública at the Colegio de la Frontera, Tijuana. He has conducted widespread research on various aspects of Mexico's changing political culture and opposition government in the border states, most notably Chihuahua and Baja California. He is author of several books, the most recent of which is *Baja California 1989–92: Balance de la Transición Democrática.*

YEMILE MIZRAHI received her doctoral degree in 1994 from the Department of Political Science at the University of California, Berkeley. She has worked extensively on *Panista* politics in Mexico, particularly in the state of Chihuahua. The role played by entrepreneurs in the PAN in Chihuahua is the subject of her doctoral dissertation and of several articles she has recently published. She is a researcher at the Centro de Investigación y Docencia Económicas (CIDE) in Mexico City.

JULIO MOGUEL is Professor of Economics at the National Autonomous University of Mexico. He is author or co-author of numerous books, the most recent of which is *Autonomía y los nuevos sujetos del desarrollo rural.*

VICTORIA E. RODRÍGUEZ is an Assistant Professor at the Lyndon B. Johnson School of Public Affairs, The University of Texas at Austin. She is currently co-directing with Peter M. Ward a major research project on opposition governments in Mexico. Together they have written two volumes on the subject (*Policymaking, Politics and Urban Governance in Chihuahua: The Experience of Recent Panista Governments* and *Political Change in Baja California: Democracy in the Making?*). She is the author of the forthcoming *Decentralization in Mexico: The Facade of Power* and of several articles dealing with Mexican politics and public administration. Her principal research interests revolve around the broader topic of political and administrative decentralization in Mexico, particularly intergovernmental relations and municipal politics. She is currently serving as a consultant for the World Bank on a project on decentralization and regional development in Mexico.

LILIA VENEGAS AGUILERA is a doctoral candidate and researcher at the Instituto Nacional de Antropología e Historia in Mexico City. Her current research deals with the role that women of the popular sector play in Mexican politics. About this subject she has recently co-authored *Testimonios de participación popular femenina en la defensa del voto, Ciudad Juárez, Chihuahua, 1982–1986.*

PETER M. WARD is Professor of Sociology and Public Affairs and Director of the Mexican Center of the Institute of Latin American Studies at The University of Texas at Austin. Prior to coming to the U.S. in 1991, he held senior positions at the Universities of London and of Cambridge, England. In addition to numerous articles and book chapters on public policy in Mexico and Latin America, he is co-author of *Housing, the State and the Poor: Policy and Practice in Latin American Cities*, and author of *Welfare Politics in Mexico: Papering Over the Cracks* and *Mexico City: The Production and Reproduction of an Urban Environment*. All these books have been translated into Spanish. He is currently completing a study on residential land values and land development policy in Mexico, a part of which is *Methodology for Housing and Land Market Analysis* (1994, with Gareth Jones). His principal research interests are housing, planning, urban development, and the politics of public administration in Mexico. At various times he has served as advisor to the Mexican government.

KEITH YANNER is Assistant Professor of Political Science at Central College in Pella, Iowa. He recently received his Ph.D. from Washington University in St. Louis, and has worked extensively on elections and politics in Michoacán, the subject of his doctoral dissertation.

Index

About the Book and Editors

Opposition Government in Mexico
EDITED BY VICTORIA E. RODRÍGUEZ AND PETER M. WARD

The political system in Mexico is changing to a more open and democratic one. The transformation is evident in the genuine multiparty competition in elections, which since the mid-1980s has resulted in opposition parties winning office at the municipal and state levels. Once in power, these opposition parties have sought to deliver on their campaign promises while also dealing with the old regime, especially in seeking to establish effective relations with the ruling PRI (Partido Revolucionario Institucional).

The fourteen original essays in this book, by scholars working in both Mexico and the United States, are ground-breaking case studies of opposition governments of both the right and the left. Addressed are the transition from opposition party to party in government, the bases of support for the opposition, and the day-to-day public administration and governance under the opposition. The experiences of these governments suggest that in spite of limited electoral reforms in Mexico, modernization of the political system is underway. This new pluralism is most evident in the larger municipalities.

"Opens up a new line of research in Mexican politics that is crucial to our understanding of the contemporary political process."—Professor Judith Gentleman, author of *Mexican Politics in Transition*

Victoria E. Rodríguez and Peter M. Ward are on the faculty of the University of Texas at Austin. Each has published widely on politics in modern Mexico.